D1457556

LABOR UNDER SIEGE

LABOR
UNDER
SIEGE

BIG BOB MCELLRATH AND THE ILWU'S
FIGHT FOR ORGANIZED LABOR IN
AN ANTI-UNION ERA

Harvey Schwartz with Ronald E. Magden

UNIVERSITY OF WASHINGTON PRESS
Seattle

Labor under Siege was made possible in part by a grant from the University of Washington Libraries and the Libraries Excellence Fund.

Composed in Adobe Caslon Pro, typeface designed by Carol Twombly

26   25   24   23   22   5   4   3   2   1

Printed and bound in the United States of America

UNIVERSITY OF WASHINGTON PRESS
uwapress.uw.edu

Library of Congress Cataloging-in-Publication Data
Names: Schwartz, Harvey, 1939– author. | Magden, Ronald, author.
Title: Labor under siege : Big Bob McEllrath and the ILWU's fight for organized
    labor in an anti-union era / Harvey Schwartz, with Ronald E. Magden.
Description: Seattle : University of Washington Press, [2022] | Includes
    bibliographical references and index.
Identifiers: LCCN 2021052492 (print) | LCCN 2021052493 (ebook) |
    ISBN 9780295750323 (hardcover) | ISBN 9780295750330 (paperback) |
    ISBN 9780295750347 (ebook)
Subjects: LCSH: McEllrath, Robert. | International Longshore and Warehouse
    Union—History. | Labor unions—United States—Officials and employees—
    Biography. | Labor movement—United States—History.
Classification: LCC HD8073.M393 A3 2022 (print) | LCC HD8073.M393 (ebook) |
    DDC 331.88/33092 [B]—dc23/eng/20220207
LC record available at https://lccn.loc.gov/2021052492
LC ebook record available at https://lccn.loc.gov/2021052493

♾ This paper meets the requirements of ANSI/NISO Z39.48-1992 (Permanence of Paper).

*To the ILWU faithful, especially all who helped us over the years,
and to the memory of Ron Magden*

CONTENTS

INTRODUCTION

Bridges probably talked for forty minutes. They gave him a standing
ovation. I mean the guy was good. At that time there was never one
thought in my brain that I would ever be standing in his shoes.

ROBERT MCELLRATH

When Bob McEllrath heard Harry Bridges speak in Portland, Oregon, in
1971, he was a twenty-year-old longshoreman. Bridges was then the longtime president of the West Coast International Longshore and Warehouse
Union (ILWU). Known widely for his left-wing politics, Bridges was
also the visionary founder of the union and the hero of the great Pacific
Coast maritime strike of 1934.

Thirty-five years later McEllrath was himself president of the ILWU.
He held that post between 2006 and 2018 after serving in several other
key ILWU positions. At six foot four, with an athletic background and a
direct and engaging speaking style, "Big Bob"—his waterfront handle—
was a charismatic leader who, like Bridges, enjoyed great popularity with
the membership.

Labor under Siege is an oral history of McEllrath's life and union service as told by him, people close to him, members of his traditionally
diverse organization, and some of his marine trades allies overseas. It is

also a history of the ILWU in the late twentieth and early twenty-first centuries. Through oral history interviews, it explores how one of America's most storied and progressive unions survived in an era when the US labor movement was under attack and seemingly in decline everywhere. In the widest sense, this book exemplifies the challenges faced by organized labor in the United States during recent decades.

By the time McEllrath took office, the number of ILWU longshore workers who had been on the Pacific Coast waterfront in the 1940s and 1950s under the guidance of Bridges had declined. The "container revolution" of the 1960s and 1970s saw labor-intensive "break-bulk" freight handling replaced by the use of huge metal cargo boxes lifted on and off ships by giant cranes. Productivity increased dramatically while the numbers of dockworkers fell.[1] There had been 26,695 fully qualified ILWU Longshore Division members on the Pacific Coast in 1948.[2] The number was often half that from the late 1960s on, sometimes nearing 20,000 but never again approaching the high enrollment of the early post–World War II years.

The union persevered. But between the time McEllrath took office on the International level in the 1990s and his retirement on January 1, 2019, it confronted grave threats from corporate employers, government officials, law enforcement agents, legal challenges, and even other unions. In McEllrath's era the union did not always achieve unqualified success in a strike or a lockout. Sometimes its efforts to meet the threat of issues like advancing automation achieved useful but limited gains. Sometimes problems external to the ILWU, like the direction of American labor law, were beyond McEllrath's or the union's control.

Still, under McEllrath's leadership the ILWU retained much of its earlier cohesion and vibrancy, especially in its core dockside jurisdiction. This oral history offers a unique, close-up view of how decisions were taken and policy carried out to ensure the ILWU's sustainability during a challenging time for labor. The historical account should inform all working people, whether unionized or not, and should engage anyone interested in the current status of American labor.

The precipitous decline of the American labor movement during the late twentieth and the first two decades of the twenty-first century began with the ascendency of Ronald Reagan to the presidency of the United

States. Nine months after his November 1980 election, Reagan fired eleven thousand members of the Professional Air Traffic Controllers Organization (PATCO) when they struck for better wages and a shorter workweek. The Republican president even imposed a lifetime ban on rehiring the PATCO strikers. In October 1981, the Federal Labor Relations Authority decertified PATCO. The union ceased to exist.[3]

The long-term repercussions of PATCO's defeat were devastating for American unions. Before the 1981 strike, American labor negotiations had focused on the size of unionized workers' raises and the extent of improvements to their benefit packages. But Reagan's PATCO example emboldened employers to attack organized labor with mounting vigor. Corporate leaders began demanding drastic concessions even in negotiations with well-established unions. Firing workers who went on strike became far more prevalent. Employers increasingly fought organizing drives by engaging professional union-breaking consultants who promised a "union-free environment."[4]

For decades before 1980 there had been three hundred strikes a year in the United States, many for union recognition. By 2006, that number had dropped to thirty. "Union density," the percentage of workers in American unions, was 20.1 in 1983. In 2019 that figure was down to 10.3 percent. Private sector union density was even lower. Only the more robust public sector unions kept overall union density as high as 10 percent. During the same period, 1983 to 2019, union wages, adjusted for inflation, remained flat.[5]

Bob McEllrath, who came from a longshore family, won his first responsible posts in the ILWU the same year Reagan was elected president. On August 13, 1980, Bob was selected to serve on the executive board of his local, ILWU longshore Local 4 of Vancouver, Washington. Then, on November 12, he ran successfully for Local 4 alternate dispatcher. He was just twenty-nine at the time. Dispatcher is an important position in an ILWU longshore local. Whoever holds that position is pledged to distribute waterfront jobs equitably among the local's members. Clearly, Bob's fellow workers trusted him. Three years later Bob became the primary Local 4 dispatcher. He held that office for a decade before leaving Vancouver for San Francisco to take an important ILWU job of coastwide significance.[6]

Coming of age during the Reagan era had an impact on Bob. He knew that the union movement in the United States was under siege. An athlete and a man of action, he nevertheless learned in office to calculate carefully and to preserve his organization while sailing in troubled waters. In waterfront parlance, he learned to "watch the game." Sometimes, when faced with dire threats, he felt compelled to accept compromises to ensure that the union would "live to fight another day," as one interviewee aptly put it. The results could be mixed. This book recounts how that game plan played out over time in different situations.

In facing difficult challenges, adjusting, and persevering, the ILWU resembles many other American unions of the late twentieth and early twenty-first centuries. McEllrath's and the union's approach to survival may sound familiar to many observers of recent American unionism. But there are also ways in which the progressive ILWU is unique in the history of American labor. It is the one union that survived intact after the Congress of Industrial Organizations (CIO) purged it and ten other left-wing unions in 1949–50 during the early Cold War red scare. Although the United Electrical, Radio, and Machine Workers of America (UE) also survived the purge, its membership and power were drastically reduced by raiding from other organizations.[7]

Since the ILWU's beginning on the West Coast in 1934 under Bridges, the union has stood for internal democracy, clean governance, social justice, militancy, and international solidarity.[8] It has long boasted a diverse membership in the majority of its California, Oregon, Washington, Hawaii, Alaska, and Canada locals. That diversity is evident in those interviewed for this book: among the forty-one interviewees are ILWU men and women of African American, Asian American, Latino, and Northern European descent who also represent the major geographical areas of the union's jurisdiction.

From the 1930s on, the ILWU has officially championed equal access to membership and jobs for Blacks and other workers of color. African Americans entered San Francisco's longshore local in 1934. During 1945–46, shortly after the end of World War II, hundreds of Black workers got jobs in San Francisco and Oakland through the ILWU warehouse local. Many were military veterans unable to find employment elsewhere. Since

1969 more than half of the Northern California ILWU longshore local's members have been African American.[9]

The ILWU practices much local autonomy. Consequently, a few ILWU locals have resisted inclusiveness at various times. Despite such local opposition, however, the ILWU's overall record has been superior to that of countless other unions, including many in the skilled construction trades.[10] In Hawaii, since the mid-1940s, the ILWU has represented thousands of workers of Japanese, Filipino, Chinese, and Native Hawaiian backgrounds. Since its early days, too, significant numbers of Mexican Americans in Los Angeles have been members of the union's longshore and warehouse locals. And from 1934 onward, thousands of women have been ILWU members through the union's warehouse and agricultural locals on the US mainland and in Hawaii.[11]

As part of its stance against discrimination and racism, the ILWU opposed fascism in the mid-1930s, and, during the decades of decolonization following World War II, it consistently protested American overseas wars against developing countries, such as Vietnam, Iraq, and Afghanistan, that had formerly been subject to Western domination. In recent years, the union has also repeatedly censured abuses of human and labor rights by corporations forcibly embracing globalization and privatization.

Speaking to the ILWU International Convention in 1957, Bridges summarized the union's worldview in a now often-cited statement: "We stand, as we always stood, with the working people of our own country and the working people of the world. We intend to go forward, and we can always be sure of one thing: There will be a place for us somewhere, somehow, as long as we recognize and see to it that the working people must always struggle on, fight for everything they have, and everything they hope to get, for dignity, equality, democracy, to oppose war and to bring to the whole world a better life."[12]

Notably, over time the ILWU's worldview, with its distinctly progressive stamp, has differed from that of a number of other unions. Regardless, like them, the ILWU has had to survive in an environment increasingly hostile to organized labor. One major concern the ILWU shares with all US collective bargaining organizations is the challenge that American labor law has presented since shortly after World War II. Workers had gained protections with the passage of the 1935 National Labor Relations Act (NLRA), or Wagner Act, as part of President Franklin D. Roosevelt's New Deal. These included the right for workers to organize and bargain collectively through representatives of their own choosing. The act created a National Labor Relations Board (NLRB) with the power to certify unions and to prosecute employers who violated the law.[13]

But in 1947, two years after World War II ended, a newly elected conservative Republican Congress undermined the original intent of the NLRA when it amended the act. Although the original New Deal legislation helped enable labor's rise during the Great Depression of the 1930s, these postwar changes in the legislation laid the foundation for the decline of the labor movement long before Ronald Reagan became president.

Known as the Taft-Hartley Act, the new amendment defined "unfair labor practices" that unions could be charged with, including sympathy strikes, mass or aggressive picketing, and secondary boycotts against non-primary businesses. Unions had used secondary boycotts and other solidarity actions as successful organizing tools during the great unionization drives of the 1930s. The "closed shop," in which all employees had to be union members, became illegal. States could now enact "right to work" laws that banned union shops, which required nonunion employees to become union members within a certain period of time.

Under Taft-Hartley the president of the United States was empowered to suspend a strike by initiating an eighty-day "cooling-off" period. In most cases, stopping a strike for several weeks works to the disadvantage of unionists. The new act also protected employer "free speech." Now employers could intimidate organizing workers in captive audiences or in one-on-one meetings. Taft-Hartley provided for decertification of a union through an NLRB process, too. Enacted at the dawn of the Cold War, the 1947 edict even contained an anticommunist clause, although it was later declared unconstitutional.[14]

The ILWU itself suffered from the passage of the Taft-Hartley Act. In 1948 the West Coast waterfront employers charged that the union's control over waterfront hiring was in violation of the new legislation. In 1934 the longshoremen had won the right to have a union member installed as dispatcher in joint-run hiring halls. This amounted to a successful union bid to end employers' corrupt and discriminatory hiring practices. The importance of saving control over dispatching was a major factor in the union's strike in 1948. That year the employers also repeatedly referenced Taft-Hartley in red-baiting Harry Bridges for his left-wing political views. President Harry Truman criticized the act as an abuse of labor rights, but it was enacted over his veto. Still, in 1948 Truman temporarily suspended the beginning of the longshore strike by using the eighty-day cooling-off option. ILWU longshoremen protested by boycotting an NLRB vote on the employers' last offer before the eighty days began. The union still won the strike, although it took a major effort.[15]

Almost immediately after the Taft-Hartley Act was passed, the ILWU was sued by the Juneau Spruce Company of Alaska for engaging in a newly illegal secondary boycott. The case worked its way through the courts between 1947 and 1952. At one point the Juneau Spruce case reached the US Supreme Court. When it was finally settled in 1955 it cost the union $250,000.[16] Adjusted for inflation, that would amount to more than $2,500,000 in 2021. The ILWU was also punished during Richard Nixon's presidency when the Taft-Hartley Act was invoked again, this time to stop the union's coastwide 1971–72 longshore strike for eighty days. This probably weakened the union's position during the dispute, which dragged on for one hundred and thirty-four days. President George W. Bush called upon the Taft-Hartley Act to stop an employers' coastwide waterfront lockout in 2002. That year the Bush administration was planning to expand its war in the Middle East. It wanted the docks cleared for military cargo. Regardless, by 2002 the resort to Taft-Hartley by an American president for any reason gave ILWU people cause for serious concern.

Not surprisingly, most laborites called Taft-Hartley a "slave labor act" as soon as it was enacted. Bob, too, came to view the amended NLRA as more of a hindrance than an aid. In early 2012, when the ILWU was trying to secure a contract in Longview, Washington, with the multinational conglomerate Export Grain Terminal Development (EGT), he warned about the possibility of an injunction against the union, citing "the Taft-Hartley Act that criminalizes worker solidarity." The union, he said, had to "cut a narrow path" to dodge being charged with breaking the law's ban on sympathy strikes.[17] A year later, during an oral history interview,

Bob declared, "We need to teach people what the laws are doing to us as is happening today." Bob held these views along with countless other American labor leaders. The story of how he handled Taft-Hartley and other serious challenges while in office is of great importance to everyone concerned with both the recent history and the future prospects of the American labor movement.

∞

The idea for this book grew out of a three-day series of oral history interviews done with Bob in 2013, five years before he retired. During his previous years in office, the union had already survived several serious crises. Obviously, Bob was an important figure in the union's history. Only Harry Bridges and Jimmy Herman had served longer as ILWU International presidents. By 2013 the union had a well-established ILWU Oral History Collection, with more than three hundred interviews of officers and rank-and-file members going back to the 1970s.[18] It was no surprise when several ILWU members urged that Bob be recorded about his long career. Once Bob agreed to participate in the project, he asked Ronald E. Magden and me to conduct recording sessions with him.

Ron and I had each worked on history projects with the ILWU for many years. Ron's knowledge about waterfront unionism in the Pacific Northwest was unsurpassed. He lived in Tacoma, Washington, where he taught history at Tacoma Community College. Ron had written two books dealing with the Tacoma waterfront and one about the participation of Seattle longshore workers in union struggles between the 1880s and the great West Coast maritime strike of 1934. I had published an account of the union's organizing drive inland from the Northern California waterfront following the 1934 strike, as well as a general oral history of the ILWU. Full citations to these books are located in the Further Reading section of this publication.

When the early interviews with Bob were completed, Bob accepted the proposal that Ron and I write an oral history of his life and his years in ILWU office. Between 2013 and 2018, we interviewed thirty-eight people to accommodate varying perspectives and to reconcile conflicting accounts.

I interviewed three more people in 2019. We also consulted traditional written sources to authenticate and supplement the recorded testimonies. A list of all those interviewed for the project is provided in the back of this book. Whether quoted extensively, briefly, or not at all, everyone listed contributed significantly to our understanding, to this final written product, and ultimately to the ILWU Oral History Collection.

Most of our recording sessions were full-life interviews, the accepted standard for oral history. Interviews with unionists customarily proceed from stories about family background and early youth through education; military service, if any; work experiences; union and political activity; and reflections upon retirement. Gaining the trust of interviewees can be an issue in oral history, but our long association with the ILWU secured the confidence of our narrators. We consistently approached interviewees with an attitude that for us the interview was a learning experience. Put another way, we applied the insight of Italian master oral historian Alessandro Portelli that "one of the things that makes oral sources different is that they are the achievement of a shared labor between the narrators and the researcher."[19]

Thirty-one of the recordings for this project are stored in digital format as part of the ILWU Oral History Collection housed in the archives at the union's Harry R. Bridges Building, the ILWU International headquarters in San Francisco. All were transcribed through the help of the ILWU archivist, librarian, and director of educational services, Robin Walker, and the good offices of the union. Ten of the oral histories quoted here were recorded separately by Ron and me as part of a different oral history project sponsored by the ILWU Pacific Coast Pensioners' Association (PCPA). These interviews are housed in the Labor Archives of Washington at the University of Washington in Seattle. Conor Casey, the head of the Labor Archives of Washington, provided technical assistance and sometimes asked insightful questions during PCPA recording sessions. All of the PCPA interviews used here were transcribed through Casey's agency. The list of interviewees in the back of the book identifies those interviews recorded as part of the PCPA project.

Using oral history transcripts for publication inherently requires decisions about the extent of editing allowed. Verbatim transcripts of recordings are generally too rough for unedited use. For smooth text flow and direct impact, we have eliminated our questions. On occasion, when it seemed necessary to clarify references or provide continuity to a testimony, we have added a name or a date, substituted a noun for a pronoun, or inserted a small transitional detail. Still, we always tried to preserve the manner of speaking and tone of our interviewees, since these provide oral history with its most valued qualities—authenticity and credibility. With this in mind, we have followed another lead from Portelli, who wrote that he consistently "retained the speakers' choice of vocabulary, grammar, syntax, and construction."[20]

In some places we have reordered statements by a person or combined a narrator's multiple descriptions of an event for clarification or for better chronological progression. We also eliminated distracting asides and dead-end or irrelevant utterances. But in making these editorial decisions, we always worked to retain an interviewee's meaning by following the guidelines of experienced advocates for oral history methodology like Donald Ritchie, who wrote, "Editing and rearranging interviews for clarification and cutting away tangential material are appropriate as long as the original meaning is retained."[21] These are the established standards we have sought to uphold.

Sadly, Ron Magden passed away on December 31, 2018. It has been left to me to complete this project. I hope I have done so in a way that honors his distinguished career and legacy.

HARVEY SCHWARTZ
El Cerrito, California

1

"Assholes and Elbows"

Local 4 Dispatcher, 1980–1993

> One day I wound up working right beside my dad in the hold of a ship. We were humping sacks and throwing boxes. Here's my father raised me and he's probably in his forties then and I'm making the same amount of money he is. So I said to myself, "Well, if he can raise a family and buy a house on this job, I should be able to do the same thing." And I just never looked back.
>
> BOB MCELLRATH

Most of this book deals with Bob's rise to union leadership and with the ILWU's survival of multiple challenges. But this chapter looks at McEllrath's early years, the experiences that helped shape his character, the people who influenced his life, and his preparation for a far bigger role in the ILWU than seemed likely given his small-port origins. Most ILWU International officers come from major ports like Los Angeles/Long Beach. Bob did not.

Robert Michael McEllrath was born on February 5, 1951, in Vancouver, Washington, a small Columbia River town in the Pacific Northwest, ten miles from Portland. In 1969, when he was eighteen, Bob followed his father in going longshoring at the Port of Vancouver. Founded in 1912, the Vancouver port handled logs, lumber, bulk grain, gigantic paper rolls, and heavy sacks of products like flour and tapioca. This was labor-intensive, hand-done work.[1]

Over time the longshoremen who did that work organized themselves for collective bargaining. By the early 1930s, they were affiliated with the East Coast–based International Longshoremen's Association as Local 38-67, Pacific Coast District, ILA. When the great 1934 West Coast maritime strike erupted over long-held grievances such as corrupt hiring practices and abusive and unsafe job conditions, the local's seventy members voted unanimously to join. Three years later they moved to the newly formed Pacific Coast ILWU as Local 4.[2] This is the local Bob and his father belonged to.

In this chapter Bob recalls his youth, cargo handling on the waterfront, technological changes he witnessed, the 1971–72 West Coast longshore strike, race relations in Local 4, and his early union activity. We also hear from Tom Wallenborn, Bob's high school basketball coach; Mike Johnson, Bob's work partner on the Vancouver waterfront; Sally McEllrath, Bob's wife and a key source of his fortitude; George O'Neil, a member of ILWU longshore Local 8 in Portland, Oregon, who worked closely with Bob; and Don Birrer, a Local 4 member of long standing.

BOB MCELLRATH

My whole youth was in Vancouver, not in town but in the outskirts, the rural area out in the country.[3] Growing up, we raised ducks, chickens, pigeons, rabbits, all that type of thing. I had two brothers and a sister and I lost a sister. Since we lived out in the rural area, I could go down in the back pastures and walk the woods. I loved the woods, loved to fish and hunt. When I was eight or nine years old my father gave me my first gun, a single-break action .410 shotgun.

I had a beagle and I'd hunt rabbits. My dad would say, "Here you go, you got five shells. I want to see the shells when you come back to see how many rabbits you got and how many times you shot." My dog would chase the rabbits. I'd go out there all afternoon and hunt rabbits and come back with two, three, or four. Then my dad would show me how to hang them and skin them and my mom would fry them up. I started hunting like that and then I would go deer hunting. I don't think I've missed a season since I was eleven or twelve.

It was relayed to us that my grandpa came out from "the Old Country" to America with a brother. They said that we're Irish and Scotch. The history has it that we were kicked out of Ireland and sent over to Scotland. Then from Scotland they came this way. Anyway, I was told we were from Ireland. I said, "Geez, you got to be pretty bad to get kicked out of Ireland."

As a kid I loved sports. I was seven, eight, nine years old and I wanted to be a fighter. My dad had a speed bag and a heavy bag for me. I used to go out there and punch those things. I'd have to get rags and wrap my knuckles because they'd get bloody. I didn't have a pair of those leather gloves we used later. In school, the teacher would ask, "What would you like to be when you grow up?" I said, "I'd like to be the heavyweight champion of the world." So my first real love of a sport was boxing.

When I was a freshman in high school I played football. My position was defensive end. A bunch of us got into a scrum where bodies are hitting and flying. My leg wound up on a guy's back. Another guy fell and snapped my leg like a twig. The bone didn't come out, but it was right there. I screamed, "I broke my leg!" At first they said, "You sprained your ankle." But I picked up my leg and it hung straight down. I was in a cast for three months. The leg shriveled down to nothing.

I got out of the cast at the end of football season. I was planning on playing on the freshman basketball team. Hobbling around, I could no more run than the man in the moon. The coaches kept telling me, "Quit limping, quit limping. Your leg's fine, don't favor it." I wasn't on the team but I turned out for basketball every night. When the coach was coaching I'd sit and listen. When they ran drills I'd run with them off to the side. They'd be done by the time I got down the gym floor and back. I was there every day, never missed a practice.

Last game of the season the coach took a vote whether to suit me up. The guys said, "Yeah, suit him up." They got way ahead. The coach said,

"Okay, go in." I went in there with all my buddies. They threw me the ball. I must have shot that ball from every angle. That was a pretty big thing for the team to do that for me. The following year I trained, got faster, lifted weights. I did a lot of running and jumping. I wore weights on my legs and all kinds of things.

As a sophomore I played football and basketball again. They had me at center in football because I didn't have to be as quick as a defensive end. When I was a junior I got fast. We went to state basketball tournaments, made all league. Playing, I'd tell my guys, "You ain't tired, come on, man, we're going to kick these guys' asses." I was always pumping them up, getting them ready to go. As a junior I was awarded most improved athlete. When I was a senior they gave me the most-inspirational trophy.

Tom Wallenborn taught and coached in the Evergreen School District for thirty years. He coached Bob's ninth-grade and junior- and senior-year high school basketball teams. Wallenborn was interviewed in 2013. His comments attest to the budding leadership ability that would serve Bob well over time.

TOM WALLENBORN

When we organized that ninth-grade basketball team, Bob worked hard and always brought a lot of spirit to practice. I knew he could develop. He was happy just to be part of the team. Then, during his junior year, the Evergreen High School basketball coach's job opened up. I applied and got it. Bob was on the varsity. For a kid who had barely made the ninth-grade team to being the sixth man on a state tournament roster was a mighty improvement. He never gave up and he was contributing mightily.

There is a photo of one of our Centralia High School games. Bob and a Centralia fellow went up for a rebound. They're both at the height of their jump. They collided. The Centralia fellow fell away. Bob came down with the ball, smiling. He wasn't showboating, just a happy "don't mess with me" look. I will have that moment in my mind forever. What a tough kid! The core to his character is enthusiasm, a supreme love of the game. Nobody worked harder. He wanted to be as good as he could be and he got there.

In Bob's senior year we had a very good team. We had a good post combination. Bob volunteered to play outside and learn to be a good shooter.[4] He said he'd do it and he did. He led us to the conference championship and fourth place in the state tournament. The basketball team and the Lettermen's Club voted him the most-inspirational player. I knew almost from the start that Bob had leadership capabilities. If I had to pick a team out of all the kids I've taught, he'd be one of those because of his attitude, work ethic, and enthusiasm. He loved to compete. That was bred in him.

Bob talks about his wife, Sally, one of the great influences on his life.

BOB MCELLRATH

During high school, me and Sally Hitchcock had our son, Pete, who is now [2013] president of the ILWU foremen's local in Portland. In 1968 things were totally different. I couldn't play sports and Sally had to leave school. Then the school board gave me an exception to play. But Sally was put in a home for pregnant girls. When she had the baby, the doctors came in and said, "We're taking it." Sally wouldn't let it go. She said, "You're not taking my baby!" I was there. I said to myself, "There's a woman that's strong in her convictions. She's telling everybody, 'I'm standing here. I ain't giving it up and I ain't signing no paperwork.'" I thought, "There's a strong woman." She was sixteen years old and I was seventeen. I learned something from that woman. It was the first time I'd ever seen anything like that.

BOB MCELLRATH

When I got out of high school we got married and we're married today [2013], forty-four, forty-five years. I wound up working at the Crown Zellerbach Paper Mill in Camas, Washington, for a month or two, whatever it was, not very long. Then my dad, who was on the Vancouver waterfront, said, "They're giving casual cards out." So I went down and got a casual card. I dropped the mill job and went to work on the docks. It was 1969. I was still only eighteen. I was one of the youngest guys on the waterfront.

TOM WALLENBORN

Kenneth McEllrath kept Bob in line, taught him how to hunt and fish. He came to the ball games and demonstrated a proud spirit of his son's success. There was great love between the two of them. A lot of what Bob is today [2013] is because of his strong relationships. His wife, Sally, is his rock. They were in the same grade in school. She is one of the people behind him being a success.

CHAPTER I

BOB MCELLRATH

My father was pretty strong. He was hands-on, but he was always the leader. During World War II, he served with Darby's Rangers.[5] He got hit with a grenade. It blew his kidney out.[6] The army brought him out to the VA Hospital in Vancouver. He made a life there. Most all the family was back in Illinois, but they came out to Washington because my dad was there. When the doctors were taking care of my dad he met my mother, Rosemary Catherine Seymour. She went by Rose. My parents got married and stayed at Vancouver. My mother worked for Portco Packaging. They made plastic bags. My dad drove a truck for almost twenty years. He was a Teamster and he delivered to the docks.

Bob recalled how his father got onto the Vancouver waterfront. His reference to freedom highlights one of the long-standing benefits of work on the West Coast under the ILWU longshore hiring-hall system—the freedom to skip work for any reason without penalty. This does not hurt the employers, who call the hall for workers as needed.

BOB MCELLRATH

While working, my dad got to know a lot of ILWU longshore Local 4 guys. They said, "Hey, they got applications going." So he put an application in. This was in the mid-sixties. They were still pretty closed. You had to know somebody or be a relative. My dad didn't have no relations there, but he got on. He liked longshoring better than truck driving 'cause he could come home at nights. A lot of times he'd be up early in the morning driving a truck, get home late, and never see the kids. This way, longshoring, he'd take a day off and nobody said anything to him. He said, "Longshoring is the best job in the world. The freedom is worth thousands and thousands of dollars."

Bob remembers his first day on the Vancouver docks. The kind of handwork he describes was typical of longshoring in the years before containerization dramatically changed waterfront labor during the last three decades of the twentieth century. This handwork was traditionally called "break-bulk" cargo handling, although Bob didn't use that term.

BOB MCELLRATH

My first day on the docks they needed four more casuals. They put me and a buddy of mine, Rod Kadow, on to go hump flour sacks out of a railcar. The flour came in white gunnysack bags. I did that that day and quite a few days after that. Casual longshoring then was like you get two or three days and then maybe five days. If you got what we called a "ringer," seven days, especially for a guy like me then, whoa, I was in hog heaven.

Bob's longtime work partner, Mike Johnson, recalled his first day on the Vancouver waterfront as well.

MIKE JOHNSON

A friend told me I could go to the Local 4 hall and pick up casual work. I started as a casual during March 1969. You could throw flour seven days a week out of a railcar, turn around, and load it seven more days into a ship. "Pumping flour" we called it. I was one year and three days older than Bob. Kenneth McEllrath, Bob's father, was in a group five years ahead of us. When we were casuals he was a B-man. I was working full-time at the Alcoa Corporation. Bob and I worked together on weekends. I kept casualing. The pay was pretty good. I took a summer vacation and when I came back I quit ALCOA. I worked in ships' holds in 1969 and 1970 and was registered as a B-longshoreman in September 1970. Bob and I worked as partners for twenty-five years.

Bob got his nickname, "Big Bob," early in his years in Local 4.

BOB MCELLRATH

When I got out of high school I was six foot four and about 180 pounds. I did some boxing, fought in some smokers, and continued to work out when I was on the docks. Then I started to lift weights. My heaviest was 268 pounds, but I averaged about 255 or 260. I ran around with this guy with blond hair, Mike Johnson, and they always said, "You know, that blond-haired guy and the big guy, Big Bob." Even now [2018] if people call me on the phone and I say, "Hello, this is Robert McEllrath," they say, "Well, I don't want to speak with Robert, I want to speak to Big Bob." They just know me as Big Bob. Anyway, they gave the name Big Bob to me on the docks real early in my career.

One advantage of working on a job covered by the ILWU is that everyone in the same category earns the same wage. This impressed Bob early on.

BOB MCELLRATH

One day I wound up working right beside my dad in the hold of a ship. We were humping sacks and throwing boxes. Here's my father raised me and he's probably in his forties then and I'm making the same amount of money he is. So I said to myself, "Well, if he can raise a family and buy a house on this job, I should be able to do the same thing." And I just never looked back.

Bob's wife, Sally, recalls the early days of Bob's working as a casual on the Vancouver waterfront.

SALLY MCELLRATH

Bob was so excited about his job longshoring. In the beginning, lots of times there was not a lot of work. Sometimes he'd only work one day a week. Once our friend Gary Hopkins, who was an American Indian, gave us a fifty-pound sack of potatoes. That's what we lived off. But whatever Bob had to do for his job was fine with me. He thrived on the job and loved the union from early on. Some of it was he was proud to work with his dad. So it just was his place.

Bob discusses that place. His remarks highlight aspects of the waterfront's workplace culture.

BOB MCELLRATH

I was still only eighteen years old in 1969, so I took my dad's guidance. He said, "Keep your mouth shut, your head down, and just pay attention. What you hear on the waterfront you never take home. You never mention it, you never say a goddamn word. What you hear here stays here. I don't want to see nothing out of you but your asshole and your elbows."[7] This is what my dad told me right off the bat, right out of high school. I taught my son Pete the same thing. My dad also said, "If somebody comes and bitches that you're worthless, I'll kick your ass. Don't embarrass my name." I never said a word to him. I just went to work. It helped me that my father was there; I can't say it didn't.

In reviewing his early years in Local 4, Bob touched upon the impact of new machines and cargo-handling methods on the waterfront. Automation would be one of the issues he would face as a union officer.

BOB MCELLRATH

In 1970 the local had tons of work. They hired seventy-five B-men that fall. I was one of them. Prior to that I was working casual every day. Never before or since has Local 4 registered that many people at one time. They'll hire fifteen, twenty, or thirty, but never again did they hire seventy-five people at once in that port. In 1970 we were doing a lot of sack humping and manhandling. Then, all of a sudden, it seemed to go the other way with the lift machines and the palletized cargo. This cuts out half your people almost. In the 1980s, when I was dispatching people to work, we had less than one hundred members. Then we averaged about one hundred and eighteen, dipped below one hundred again, and then went back up.[8]

I came onto the waterfront at the tail end of a lot of hand-worked cargo. They used to hand-stack all the lumber. When I got there they just started to stop that. Then what they did was they'd bring the lumber in in packages. We'd take the lift machine and try to get the packages stowed. Sometimes they'd want to stow the lumber tighter, but generally they figured the time it took to hand-stow and then unload and the amount of space that you might lose by just leaving it in the bundles wasn't worth bothering about. Finally they come up with palletized cargo and things really started to change. They'd bring everything in on the pallet and you'd just stow it. That went fast. Things really started to move. There was a lot of hand-handling clear up into the mid-seventies. Then it started to really break.

Bob also vividly recalled other examples of break-bulk cargo handling in his early days.

BOB MCELLRATH

When I went on the waterfront in '69 I was on the bottom end of the totem pole. You didn't even look at a winch job or a lift job.[9] That was for the old-timers. Anything that had to do with picking it up or laying it down the young guys did. Some of my crappier early jobs were working things like tapioca. It's not like tapioca pudding. It was real fine dust in white sacks. I think it was for whitening paper. If the sacks would break, you're all white.[10]

Unloading sacks in a ship, you'd take the wooden hatch covers off the upper deck, roll the tarps, and start handling. Those sacks were loaded right up to the top. You'd go all the way down to the bottom of the hold. It'd take you days to unload that hatch. And then you'd load something in and bring it right back up, cover it up, and the ship would go. You'd be on one of these sack jobs for five, six days. They'd be working that cargo day and night [see fig. 1.1].

Paper rolls used to come into the hold. You'd take the sling off. The old-timers and my dad would say, "We got to get it in that corner." Well, here I'm a young, strong kid. I'd say, "Wow. We going to do that? Damn, it's heavy, we can't pick it up." Of course, the old-timers are letting you try first. Then one would say, "Let me show you how you do it." He'd tip it over on its side. Then he'd say, "When you do that, you take a little two-by-four sticker and you roll it up, and when you do that you can twist it like this [demonstrating]." We'd roll it and we'd push it back there.

Finally he'd say, "Now what you do is we cross our arms and we reach down and pick the paper roll up like this." If you did it right it would slide and it would be tight. You couldn't even get a piece of paper in there. Then you'd do the next one. You'd work yourself right out. The next floor you'd lay plywood down and roll paper rolls back in there and stack them right to the top. You'd put the wooden hatch covers on and go to the next task.

Fig. 1.1. Working sacks in a ship's hold. Handling "break bulk" cargo typified longshoring into the mid-1970s, when containers, huge metal boxes that could be hoisted onto a railcar or the flatbed of a truck, began to replace most hand cargo. In 1969 Bob McEllrath joined his father on the waterfront, wrestling heavy sacks like these. He was eighteen years old. Courtesy of Frank Silva, photographer.

Then there was pulp bails. We used to load pulp up there in Longview, Washington, by hand. These were 450-pound bales of white, square pieces of paper. I'm telling you, that was a job. Me and my buddy were pretty strong, so we were wrestling these things, killing ourselves. But them old-timers knew how to do it. They could stand that bale up, twist it on its corners, flip it, roll it, and get it right in there just like you do with round paper rolls, which were a lot easier than bales. I was amazed. Those old-timers had the tricks.

Bob logged many hours working break-bulk cargo in 1970 before he became officially registered as a B-man that fall. He accrued hours then with an eye to the future. As a union officer he also frequently made decisions with long-term implications in mind. Here he recalls the 1971–72 West Coast waterfront strike as well.

BOB MCELLRATH

Casualing so many hours in 1970 like I did, I got a qualifying year toward benefits and retirement. Right away I knew that if I got the required eight hundred hours and I got registered, it would give me a year. A lot of guys didn't get their eight hundred hours and I did. They said, "How did you get that?" I said, "Well, I went to work and you guys were dinking around."

But the 1971–72 longshore strike ended all those hours and brought tough times. The strike stretched out for a long time.[11] I was on food stamps. It was tough for me and my wife. Our son Jason was born in September 1970, two years after our son Pete, so we had two little boys. I went and got a part-time job pumping gas. I just did anything I could do to keep going and to help on the picket line.

Around the time of the 1971–72 longshore strike, ILWU president Harry Bridges visited Portland, which is close to Vancouver. His speech on that occasion made a lasting impression on Bob, who was there.

BOB MCELLRATH

In 1971 Harry Bridges came to Local 8 in Portland to discuss the longshore contract.[12] My dad said, "Come on, we're going to see Harry." We sat up in the balcony at the Local 8 hall. Harry and the officers came in. They booed and catcalled Harry and wouldn't let him talk.[13] He stood there. I bet it went on for ten or fifteen minutes. Then they calmed down and Harry started talking. My dad said, "You pay attention here, young man." I said, "Yeah." Bridges probably talked for forty minutes. They gave him a standing ovation. I mean the guy was good. At that time there was never one thought in my brain that I would ever be standing in his shoes.

Of course, it would be a long time before Bob would be standing in Bridges's shoes. Yet Bob's union leadership potential began to emerge early, when he was still a B-man. That is revealed in this discussion of the 1970s.

BOB MCELLRATH

In the early 1970s, they allowed B-men to come to the membership meetings because it was a good place to learn. B-men were not allowed to talk unless recognized and asked to speak. Otherwise you had to keep quiet. If they caught you voting, if they saw you say "aye," they would remove you from the meeting. But things would come up, like an issue that affected the B-men. A lot of the guys would ask me if I would say something. If the subject was a good one and warranted speaking about, I might speak after I was no longer a brand-new B-man but two or three years into it. I would raise my hand and ask, "Could I speak on that from our direction?" They'd say, "Go ahead." I'd lay out what we had in mind to give the old-timers some thought process coming from somebody younger. They usually allowed me the latitude to do that. Then I'd sit down. But I was very respectful of the old-timers. I felt good about this. I think my dad had a good influence on that.

Bob's determination to stand and fight, likely carried over from his schoolboy athletic days, is illustrated by this boxing story from the mid- or late 1970s.

I could be a handful in my younger days. They held this boxing thing in Hudson's Bay High School in Vancouver. I'm a heavyweight. I beat this guy and was supposed to get $250. This guy says, "Here's an envelope. Sign here." I got in the car. My wife is there. My two boys are in the back. I threw the envelope back there and said, "Count the money, boys." Two hundred fifty bucks for me back then was huge. They said, "You got $210, dad." I said, "Are you serious?" They said, "Honest, dad." I pulled the car around, pulled up to the side of the gymnasium, and said, "Stay in the car. If I don't come out, don't let nobody in, lock the doors. I'll be right back, leave the car running." My wife, Sally, was not happy. I think she was more scared for me than angry.

I went in the back room. They're counting all the money. There's five of these pretty-good-size men. I threw the envelope on the table and said, "I brought a lot of people in from Vancouver. We could have done this every six months and packed this gym. And you guys cheat me out of forty fucking dollars!" This guy goes, "Kid, you took the forty bucks out." I looked him in the eye and said, "Do you think I came in here to get my ass beat for forty lousy dollars?" I just stared at him. He reaches down and grabs two twenties and goes, "Here, are we square?" I said, "Now we're square." I got my money and out the door I went. Boy, you want to talk about your heart pumping? These guys would have ate me for lunch. To this day my wife says, "You're crazy!" But I went back in because it was the right thing to do.

Bob gained valuable experience when he served Local 4 as alternate dispatcher and then dispatcher between 1980 and the early 1990s. In handing out job assignments, a dispatcher has to be totally fair and trustworthy. People do not hold such a post in the ILWU for a decade, as Bob did, unless they possess those qualities.

I didn't start holding offices in Local 4 till I got my A-card in 1975. In the late 1970s is when I tried to get on the Local 4 Executive Board. In 1980 I was elected to the executive board and the building association board. That November I ran for the position of alternate dispatcher and got it. That allowed me to get a few days in dispatching. In 1983 I was elected dispatcher. When you're a dispatcher in a small local, you learn every aspect of being an officer. Because we don't have full-time officers in Local 4 and the officers and Labor Relations Committee members work on the docks, they'd come in and get a job.[14] If there was a beef, they were allowed to leave the job to take care of it. If there was an arbitration on the job or a health-and-safety issue, they would go deal with it. In the meantime, I answered the phone and when the retirees or the widows came in or somebody came in with a problem, I'd tend to it.

As dispatcher, I went all the way from pension problems, welfare problems, and medical problems to retirement papers. Then when the employers' Pacific Maritime Association [PMA] would call and pitch a bitch, my officers told me, "Well, if you can handle it, go ahead and handle it. Just don't commit if there's a big problem. Get the information and get back to us." A lot of the things I did on the phone with the PMA or the stevedore companies I would work out myself with them. Usually one or two of our officers would stop at the hall at 5:00 and see what was going on. If there was a big problem, I'd get ahold of them right away and they'd come to the hall. But normally I'd say, "I took care of this and this and this and I figured this is what we'd want to do." They'd go, "Yeah, that's perfect." That's where I got my real education. When you're dispatching for a small port, you learn just about everything [see fig. 1.2].

George O'Neil, who was in Portland's longshore Local 8 for twenty years before switching to that city's ship clerks Local 40, has vivid memories of coordinating closely with Bob when they were both dispatchers trying to fill waterfront jobs along the Columbia River. O'Neil

Fig. 1.2. Bob McEllrath as ILWU Local 4 dispatcher, 1980s. A dispatcher is a trusted elected union official who assigns jobs to the members of the local. Bob held that post in Local 4 for more than a decade. *Left to right*: Bob McEllrath, Mel Ingalls, Bob Keels. Courtesy of ILWU Local 4.

has served as Local 8 president and as a member of the ILWU International Executive Board. His recollections suggest that Bob mastered teamwork early on.

GEORGE O'NEIL

My father was a longshoreman. I started on the waterfront on April 12, 1980. I remember the first time I saw Bob. This would be in the early to middle eighties. I can remember him walking down the dock in Vancouver with Mike Johnson and thinking, "Who is that big guy?" Where I really got to know him was when I was dispatching in Local 8 and he was dispatching in Local 4. We dispatched at the same time and I talked to him just about every day. Back in those days, Local 8 was the big dog with the biggest port in the Columbia River area, but we all traveled for jobs. That's why I'm saying when I first saw Bob I was working in Vancouver.

Bob and I made things work as dispatchers. Say a day in Vancouver was just slammed. Portland was busy, too. I would tell Bob, "You call Vancouver first," because Longview longshore Local 21 was slow that day. Then he'd get the majority of the Longview workers. We worked together very well. It's not like he's just a colleague. He's much more than that. Bob is my friend. Today [2014] as ILWU president he's the same down-to-earth guy, just with a lot more responsibility.

Sally McEllrath was a source of Bob's strength throughout his entire ILWU career. Here she describes her views of Bob's union activity.

SALLY MCELLRATH

My father was in the Pulp and Paper Union at Crown Zellerbach Paper Mill in Camas. He went to union meetings and they had strikes.[15] So I knew about that sort of thing. I always encouraged Bob to go ahead and be involved. I'm different from other women. Lots of other women we knew didn't like their husbands to go to union meetings and they didn't like them to be involved or they made it really hard. I couldn't understand why they would be like that. I loved Bob and believed in him. I believed people should always be improving themselves and just keep trying to do something better for yourself and for your organization. When Bob got to be a dispatcher, he just thrived. He was learning a lot of things and he did things for the old-timers. He'd fill out all their paperwork and all that kind of stuff.

Over time, Sally McEllrath carved out her own career. She went to work, attended college, and in the 1990s graduated with honors from Washington State University, Vancouver.

I started at Olson Engineering in 1982. Our kids were teenagers or pre-teens or something. I started there so I could get money for tuition. I went through Clark Junior College in Vancouver and got two degrees. Then Washington State University came to Vancouver in 1989, so I was able to go to school there. I went on my lunch hour. Olson Engineering was not a sophisticated business at that time. The bosses, the two owners, would always go out into the field. But I was an accounting major. I'd say, "Somebody needs to do this task. I'll take this class and I'll do it." My boss, Jerry Olson, was very supportive. He would pay for one of my classes a quarter.

In the 1980s, when Bob began dispatching, Local 4 was hiring under a seniority system. Most ILWU locals used a rotational arrangement. But Local 4 dispatched A-registered workers by five-year increments. There were five-, ten-, fifteen-, twenty-, and twenty-five-year members who had job board plugs in different colors. Twenty-five years was the highest category and carried a gold plug. The system was complex, but essentially it was possible for a senior member to get up to 180 hours of work before a new A-registered member could get dispatched to a job. Bob got involved in a reform effort that led to the installment of a rotational dispatching system. It provided for the equitable sharing of the work among all A-registered members regardless of seniority.

BOB MCELLRATH

In the early to late eighties, when I was a dispatcher, our local was hiring under a seniority system that was brutal. The old-timers had it collared for any time they were below 180 hours a month. If one had 177 hours and a young guy had zero, the young guy still wouldn't get a job. This was not very good and we had a huge political move. Some of the younger A-registered guys that were in my group were going to sue the local. They were going to Portland and getting an attorney. I was always the guy that could get up and speak in front of the membership and try to get a point across. They came to me and they says, "We want you to come in with us and sue the local union." I said, "No way. No, no, no, no, not going to do it." They did their thing and I did my thing.

I got on the phone, called the International office in San Francisco, and talked to Rudy Rubio, the International vice president for the US mainland. I said, "It says in the coast longshore contract we got to hire equally by earnings. This is not an equal earnings hire, I don't care how you do it."[16] He says, "I'll do some investigating and get back to you." It was pretty cool that he even took my call. I kept that to myself, just told a few close friends. Rubio called me back and said, "I did some investigating. I know some people there." He mentioned this guy's name and said, "He says everything is fair." I said, "Yeah, he would, because he's the guy that's got the gold plug. Why do you think he wouldn't think it was fair?" He says, "Well, I'm sorry. You're going to have to just keep continuing to speak at your membership to change it." I said, "No problem. I thank you very much. Don't agree with you, but thank you."

These other young guys kept pushing. Things are blowing up over the Local 4 hiring system. Our leaders called Frank Posey, the local's respected attorney, to come over from Portland and explain things to the executive board. I think it was the same night the International officers had flown up from San Francisco. It was a couple of coast committeemen and Rudy.[17] Posey said, "I've done research on this. If somebody files a lawsuit, the local may lose because the contract says you shall hire equally by earnings. And you guys are not hiring equally by earnings."

Posey said you can hire and have seniority within a bracket. Say me and you had fifty hours. I would let the old-timer go first, that's seniority, that's fine. But you can't say, "You got fifty hours and I got zero hours, then he gets to go first." Posey addressed the executive board, which was mostly older guys, although I was a younger guy on it. He said, "You better fix it. I'm not going to tell you how to do it, but you people have to fix it." That started the ball rolling.

I never said a lot at the executive board meeting about calling the International. I just said, "I have a question. Did you guys down at the International office in San Francisco ever get notified that this was going on? Just wondering." They just stared at me and said, "Oh, no." They knew that I knew and I knew they knew that I knew, but I never snitched them off. I never said, "You're a fucking liar." I understood they got a job to do and it's a tough job. I said, "No problem." Then the San Francisco officers got up and said, "We suggest you listen to Posey and fix your dilemma here." So we did, we changed it and fixed it. There was bloodletting with a lot of our guys, but then we went to a system of a rotating hiring board. It was a tough battle, but I was part of that changing and that history. We just wanted it fair.

Speaking of what is fair, it is reasonable to review Bob and Local 4's stance on Blacks and other workers of color. Situated in rural Southwest Washington, Vancouver did not have many Black residents during the 1970s through 1980s. Bob remembers some members of color in the local, but usually there were no African Americans. For years, some people, including members of other ILWU locals, viewed Local 4 as discriminatory. Still, as Bob recalls, Local 4 was actually more open to diversity than Portland's Local 8, which for a long time was unique in the ILWU for its resistance to the inclusion of Black workers.

BOB MCELLRATH

We had some Mexican people and we had Hawaiians. As far as a local, there wasn't usually anybody Black. We got a lot of blowback as it went into the seventies and the eighties just for that reason. I wasn't discriminatory myself, I've never been, 'cause I played ball, I played sports, and you got to be open. But fingers were pointed at us as north of the Columbia River, all lily-white, discriminatory people. And I got it myself becoming an officer. We did have one Black person back in the early seventies. He was older than me but we were on the same list. You had to feel for the guy because he was in a world of White and he was the only Black.

We did have Black guys come in, travel in, and we'd put them on our dispatch board and put them to work. But I can remember stories how Blacks would show up at Local 8's hall in Portland and they'd give them five dollars for gas and say, "Just move on down the road." Since '69 or '70 we never did that in Local 4, at least not that I observed. It could have happened and I wasn't there, but usually when somebody starts something it goes through the telephone. You tell a longshoreman and they'll tell everybody. That's how longshoremen communicate.

In 1985 Bob participated in another historic Local 4 event that, like the struggle for equality in job dispatching, helped raise Bob's profile in the local. That spring, the Knappton Company chartered a Pacific-Hawaiian Lines barge, the *Sea Islander*, to ship a load of construction equipment to Hawaii for the Kiewit Pacific Company. Additional space on the barge was earmarked for lumber ordered by the Pacific-Hawaiian Lines. Knappton tried to use non-ILWU labor to load the barge at the Columbia Industrial Park dock a mile and a half east of Vancouver.[18] Bob's role in the June 1985 effort to protect the ILWU's jurisdiction from an anti-union attack was among the first high-profile, in-field leadership actions of his career. Over time there would be others. Here he recalls his 1985 experience.

BOB MCELLRATH

A barge pulled in down at the port shipyards, which isn't really where longshore did a lot of work. This was further east on the Columbia River. What they had there was lumber. They were loading this barge nonunion. We wound up with pickets there. We had all kinds of people trying to stop everything. ILWU International President Jimmy Herman shows up with some coastwide union officers. I'm a local officer, a dispatcher, whatever. We're all going to go down there to picket the next morning. Jimmy's going to come down there, too. They took me in the back room and Jimmy and his officers said, "Okay, here's the plan. We got these band cutters and we want you to put them in your pants and under your shirt."[19]

Then Jimmy says, "I want you to be just behind three or four guys up to the front 'cause this is your local." Of course, I had other Local 4 guys there, the older guys and the local's president. They said, "There's probably going to be police and everything else," Jimmy said, "so don't hit no policeman." My local officers are in there looking at me, 'cause they knew me. They says, "Bob, please don't hit nobody." I said, "I won't, I won't. I'll be all right." There was a whole yard full of lumber, three and four bundles high. Jimmy says, "When I step out of line and I look at you, I want you to go cut the bands on that lumber." I said, "Okay, Jimmy."

So the next morning we loaded up and we all go down there and park the cars. We had Local 8, we had Longview Local 21 guys. We had a big turnout with probably a thousand people there. We all got about four or five abreast and followed Jimmy. We're chanting, we are going to go in there. The cops are there and they're seeing this and they just step back and they're looking. They figured everything was going to be fine. We just start getting into the yard. We're going toward the barge. Jimmy looked at me and he goes like that [demonstrating]. I stepped out of line, went in there, and pulled these band cutters out. Everybody says, "What is he doing?" I start hitting those bands on a bundle with that band cutter. The bands are under pressure and they go, "bwang, bwang, bwang."

I hit the next bundle, "bwang, bwang, bwang." Then I go over to the back side of the bundles and push. Once the lumber starts to shift and slide the whole pile crashes down. Guys are looking and I said, "Come on." Then a whole bunch of guys came along. I started popping the bands and they started pushing. We destroyed the whole yard, absolutely destroyed it. Then we got me, Jimmy, and everybody out of there.

The guy from the company comes to Jimmy and says, "Okay, enough. What'll it take?" Jimmy says, "Stevedoring Services of America has been coming down here every morning and they bring a coffee wagon." They gave the contract to SSA, a union company, and said, "Okay, load the barge, only two stipulations. You guys have to restack the lumber and band it." So all the guys went back down there, restacked that whole yard, and banded the lumber. We got the work and we loaded the lumber.

This is how I got to know Jimmy Herman. Later I'd go to ILWU Longshore Division Caucuses. I'd go to rallies, and me and Tommy Hebert would bodyguard Jimmy. When Jimmy was walking a picket line we'd always stay with him and walk with him. Nobody would touch him 'cause we were pretty big boys. We'd take care of anybody that even got close to him. As we walked with him, he'd explain stuff to us like what to watch out for on a picket line. He'd say, "Be careful of this and that."

Don Birrer was a working Local 4 longshore member for forty-two years. He came onto the Vancouver waterfront in the late 1950s and retired in 1999. Birrer spent much of his career moving lumber and sacks and operating waterfront grain elevators. He also served two terms in local office. By 1985 he was one of Local 4's old-timers. Birrer was at the Columbia Industrial Park dock when the lumber bundles broke. He remembered how Bob and "some young guys" spilled lumber that morning.

Bob, who by 1985 had been Local 4 dispatcher for two years, was then emerging not only as a representative of the local's younger people, but also as a leader of the local's whole membership. When Bob was reelected alternative dispatcher in early 1981 he received fifty-two votes. In November 1987, when he ran for reelection as dispatcher for the fourth time, he got one hundred and eight votes. There were only one hundred and eighteen members in Local 4 at the time.[20]

Here Birrer describes what he saw in June 1985.

DON BIRRER

Bob was one of the younger people. That ain't a group I worked with. But you maybe heard about the lumber that was dumped down at the ship-yards? That was one of Big Bob's deals. We were all there. It just happened in a flash. Jimmy Herman and all them planned that. About ten people knew what was going to happen. Big Bob was the instigator of it all. They took some young guys and they just run in and run out. All you do is clip them bands and the top loads went just like that. They were in there and out in twenty minutes, maybe less. It looked like a hurricane had hit the place. By the time the police got there everybody was back out on the street. We went back the next morning, put all the lumber back together, and banded it all up.

By the early 1990s, Bob was quite busy with union affairs. He negoti-ated as representative for the small Northwest ports, worked as Local 4 dispatcher, and in 1991 served as a delegate at the union's Interna-tional Convention.[21] Despite these responsibilities, Bob still had time for a little out-of-the-ordinary fun. Portland's George O'Neil recalled one memorable incident that became a local legend.

GEORGE O'NEIL

Dragon boats are these big racing boats they have at the Portland Rose Festival. They have dragon heads on 'em and you paddle 'em. They have them all over the world. We had a dragon boat team in 1991 or 1993. The longshoremen in Portland did, except we had one longshoreman from Vancouver on the team. That was Bob. He sat directly behind me. I didn't miss a stroke because that big guy would slug me if I did. We ended up winning Portland. We got to go up to Vancouver, British Columbia. Bob was a legend because most of those dragon boats there had little Indone-sians and Asians. These guys all weighed about 120, 130 pounds and here's Bob. Bob probably weighed 240, 250 pounds, but all muscle. They had him up onstage and Bob is flexing his muscles and he has about eight of these little guys hanging all over him. This was before he's International president or anything. He's just Big Bob, longshoreman. They loved him. He was an idol up there.

The only problem we had was that in Portland we had big boats because most of the guys were pretty big size. In Canada they had these real little boats with maybe two inches of freeboard. These little Indonesians just walked on water and they're gone. We might have beat a couple of teams up there but not very many. But we always had fun.[22]

By 1993 things were going along swimmingly, so to speak, for Bob. Life and work in the still relatively rural Northwest town of Vancouver, Washington, had been steady and predictable for some time. But that year David Arian, who followed Jimmy Herman as ILWU International president, asked Bob to fill an important vacant Longshore Division position in San Francisco. This would change the trajectory of Bob and Sally's lives dramatically.

2

"Country Boy with Pencil"

Coast Committeeman, 1993–1999

We were fighting constantly. Bob was the coast committeeman from
the Northwest and he brought us together.

DANNY MIRANDA

Now our story traces Bob's early ILWU career at the coastwide level. In
1993 Bob left Vancouver for San Francisco when he was appointed to
serve at the union's International office as the ILWU Northwest committeeman, one of four officers who form the executive committee
of the ILWU's Pacific Coast Longshore Division. Bob was appointed to
this normally elected post when another person resigned in midterm.
This important committee oversees the Pacific Coast Longshore and
Clerks Agreement covering California, Oregon, and Washington. In addition to the Northwest committeeman, coast committee membership includes the ILWU International president; the ILWU International
vice president for the mainland, or North American continent; and
a committeeman for California. Bob lost his job as Northwest committeeman in a 1994 election. He then went back to Vancouver and
returned to work on the waterfront. But he was elected to this key

post three years later. He kept this position until he was elected ILWU International vice president (mainland) in 2000.

During his Northwest committeeman years, Bob overcame challenges both professional and personal. These are highlighted in this chapter. Out of his struggles to deal with issues as diverse as race relations, internal union politics, and even personal setbacks, Bob emerged in 2000 as a seasoned union official who had matured in office. Along the way, he became a master at building unity inside the union. Indeed, he played a central role in healing a north-south political rift among ILWU regional longshore leaders that threatened the union's cohesion. This, among other things, helps explain his unionwide popularity despite his coming from a small waterfront local in rural Washington rather than from one of the union's large urban port areas like San Francisco/Oakland or Los Angeles/Long Beach.

Several interviewees contribute to this chapter more than once. We first hear from Rob Remar, who was a key legal counselor for the ILWU for many years. He shares his early impressions of Bob. Next, Bob speaks about the problems, including race relations issues, which he faced when first in office at the coastwide Longshore Division level. Then Sally, Bob's wife, provides unique insights into Bob's life and career in the 1990s. Later we hear from Bo Lapenia. A decade older than Bob, Lapenia served as president of Hawaii's islands-wide ILWU Local 142 between 1991 and 2003. He outlines how Bob sacrificed to strengthen the union's cohesion.

Conrad Spell, a former three-term president of ILWU longshore Local 23 in Tacoma, Washington, then describes his association with Bob, highlighting Bob's special qualities for office. Two Los Angeles/ Long Beach Harbor ILWU veteran unionists—Danny Miranda, who was a multiterm president of waterfront foremen's Local 94, and Joe Cortez, who served eight one-year terms as president of longshore Local 13—talk about their experiences with Bob as well. Both remark on Bob's strengthening of the union's coastwide unity. Remar closes the chapter with a story that illustrates Bob's growth in office.

Rob Remar's time as a janitor in the 1970s shaped his resolve to become a labor lawyer. In 1985 he joined the progressive San

Francisco law firm of Leonard Carder. Ultimately, Remar became the lead lawyer for the ILWU, his firm's longtime client, and a close colleague of Bob's. Remar describes his early life and recalls his first impressions of Bob.

ROB REMAR

Margie, my mom, was very political. She was a "Kennedy girl." John F. Kennedy, or his presidential campaign, organized this group of young women to dress up in Democratic Party skirt suits and go around to rallies and promote goodwill and name recognition in support of Kennedy. This was in 1960 when I was six or seven years old. My mom helped me form my politics. She was Jewish, but converted to Catholicism when I was nine. Hanging out with the priests and nuns gave me a way of thinking about life and my place in it. It was a time of liberation theology that said you are here to serve. The priests and nuns were dogmatic and I never converted. But that experience infused in me this left-oriented view and the idea that you have to get involved. That got me involved in the anti–Vietnam War movement and other activities.

I went to UC Santa Cruz when I was nineteen and graduated with a degree in literature. I couldn't get any work anywhere so ended up getting a job as a janitor at Bullock's Department Store in Walnut Creek, California. They treated us like shit in terms of the disrespect and the unchecked power and control they held over us. That convinced me that what I wanted to do with my life was to help workers and to prevent the kind of abuses and indignities I had suffered.

I applied to law school at UC Berkeley to become a union lawyer. When an opening came up at the Leonard Carder labor law firm in 1985, Richard Zuckerman, an attorney there, promoted my application. For years I would pinch myself and say, "Hey, I'm a union attorney." Every time I would go into court where I had to identify myself as Rob Remar, Leonard Carder, counsel for the ILWU, I would get excited. The initial excitement of novelty and youth wears off over time, but the deep satisfaction is still there.[1]

The first time I met Big Bob he was not elected; he was appointed by Dave Arian to be the Pacific Northwest Coast committeeman for the union. Arian was the ILWU International president at the time. This was in 1993. I wasn't the point person of the law firm then. That was Bill Carder and then Richard Zuckerman. I was number three. I still had limited exposure to the different people in the union, so I had never met Bob. I went to meet him in his office, just as a greeting.

He's got a clean desk with one binder. There were a couple of other binders behind him. He's got a pad of paper with a list of things on it and a pencil—no pens, just a pencil. I introduced myself and he was very friendly. In some ways he kind of looked like a deer in the headlights where he was thinking, "I'm not sure what I'm getting myself into." In my memory that day, he was a country boy with a pencil.

I quickly asked him, "Hey, what are you doing? How's it going with the transition? What are you working on?" I was sort of referencing the list. He picked up one of the binders and he says, "I'm going through all of the Coast Labor Relations Committee [CLRC] minutes for the last year to get an overview of the different issues that have been addressed by the committee. I want to understand what's pending now that I need to become familiar with and to make decisions on."[2] This is the first time I've ever seen a union official or even heard of a union official doing that kind of self-study to get prepared. I was really bowled over by that, really impressed.

I said, "So you're going to go through and literally read all of these CLRC minutes, study them, and take notes?" He says, "Yeah, that's what I'm doing. Then I'm going to organize them and have a list of what the issues are or what the coast referrals are that need to be answered that are coming up." I had never seen anybody do their own list that way or do that kind of self-disciplined organizing of the work to tackle it. And I thought, "Whoa, this is a different kind of cat than I'm used to."

This was an iconic experience for me because Bob has proved true to that. He is always that way with the work and with the challenges he faces. He makes a point of learning something, of studying something. He always has his lists. I sometimes tease him about it. He says that he and his wife, Sally, live by lists of what they need to do. One of his favorite things is to check off items on his list. "Did this. Did that. Got this accomplished. Now I can move on to the next thing." His style struck me as kind of funny. It had this contrast. It was so organized and focused—I don't want to say old school—but so antiquated in using a pencil. I never use pencils in our office. Pencils aren't around. We use pens and now, of course, computers. Bob is stuck in his ways about how he's going to go about things, but in a really, really disciplined way.

Bob talks about the role of a coast committeeman.

BOB MCELLRATH

In November 1993 I was appointed as the coast committeeman for the Northwest by David Arian. Rich Austin Sr. had resigned and I took Austin's place. Brian McWilliams was the ILWU International vice president (mainland) and Jim ("Spinner") Spinosa was the coast committeeman for California. Just before this I'd been the rep for the small Northwest ports. You're elected to that position. As small-ports representative, I negotiated for the five small ports on or near the Columbia River: Coos Bay, Newport, Astoria, Longview, and Vancouver. The job function of a coast committeeman is different. There you do the everyday business of implementing the Pacific Coast contract for the union's Longshore Division, including the marine clerks. That is your main subject. You don't organize workers or do anything else, although you support other unions and you support non–Longshore Division brothers and sisters in the ILWU. If you move on to ILWU International vice president, then you become the head of the Organizing Department.

Coast committeemen meet with the employers to help develop guidelines when longshore workers are added to the workforce. Bob recalls such a meeting when he was first in office.

Early on there was a huge buildup with Blacks wanting more diversity within the locals. Local 8 of Portland was trying to get a diversity program going. We were trying to get more Blacks into the local.[3] Arian, Spinner, and I were trying to figure this out at a CLRC meeting with the president of the employers' Pacific Maritime Association [PMA]. We're going on and on with no agreement. The lawyers were all in the room and the way it was going we were opening ourselves up for a huge lawsuit that would go against the Longshore Division.[4] I represented the Longshore Division for the Northwest and I believe that I got set up. If we couldn't agree on a program without getting sued, the problem shifted over to the Northwest Coast committeeman to make a decision—do we try a program?

I'm sitting there and I'm green as hell. I've just been appointed coast committeeman for one year and this is right in the middle of it. I'm thinking, "I can't stick our necks out until I understand everything." So I said we're going to have to vote no to a program right now because the employers didn't want it even if the union did. The next thing I know people said I was a lily-white, discriminatory coast committeeman from Local 4 who didn't like Blacks or minorities. I got people screaming and pointing their fingers at me that I'm a racist and it is far from the truth. As I thought back on it later, I could see that politics played out from our side to the employers to shift the blame so certain people could say, "I didn't make the final decision, somebody else did."

There were repercussions of that meeting, as Bob recounts here.

BOB MCELLRATH

Then we went to the 1994 ILWU International Convention in Los Angeles.[5] Some of the marine clerks and the Blacks asked me to go to lunch with them. I'm thinking, "Oh, shit, I'm in trouble." I can't say no. I went with them and sat down. I'm waiting for them to come unglued on me. But they says, "We just want to tell you that we found out the truth and we apologize for pointing our fingers at you. You never said, 'I didn't do this.' You just took the beating and went from there." I said, "It's awful hard to grab one person. It's a committee and we all try to come to a consensus." So they apologized to me, and I'm thinking, "This is unbelievable." Of course, I was still voted out of office that year as a coast committeeman.

When all that happened, '93, '94, I was receiving letters at my house in Vancouver that were threatening. My wife, who hated guns, did not like what was happening. But I got all kinds of guns myself and we talked about it. I says, "What if somebody kicks in the door, comes in here and wants to beat me up and I'm down in San Francisco? What are you going to do if they decide to beat you up and start slapping the kids around?" So she took a class for five days on how to handle a gun and got a permit to carry a concealed weapon. That's how bad it got and it scared the hell out of me. Then we had a presidents meeting in Vancouver and the problem was still there. This was some time after the 1994 election. They got on me and I wasn't even an officer. Later I was at Local 8 and they got on me there, too. People were still blaming me for everything that happened.

After the 1994 election I went back to the Local 4 dispatch hall in Vancouver. I played the job board and went to work.[6] The first day back I got a shoveling job in ore cars. It was dark black and dusty. I worked with an old-timer named Jack Bridger. It was a hot day and we shoveled and drank cold beer. He was always a character and he gave me a bad time. We had to clean out the edges. I'm on one side and he's on the other. We're trying to clean the corners where the bucket loader can't get in.[7] He makes up a song and goes, "Oh, I was a big shot yesterday and look at me now. I'm shoveling and I'm right back where I started." He was giving me a bad time 'cause I lost the election and I'm back on the docks.

A few months later they had an opening on the lines board.[8] Portland and Vancouver shared the lines. This opening was in Vancouver. The way the lines agreement goes is they don't go by seniority. It reads, "Anybody that wants it, we'll put your name in a hat and we'll draw a name out."

I put my name in the hat and they pulled it out, so I went on the lines board. Working lines, you are tying up ships or letting them go. Sometimes it takes a couple of minutes and you're finished. Sometimes it takes a couple of hours because you're pulling and you can't get things done. I continued on the lines board until I ran for coast committeeman in 1997 [see fig. 2.1].

Sally McEllrath remembers some of the difficulties that followed Bob's losing the 1994 committeeman election.

SALLY MCELLRATH

Bob was really disappointed when he lost that 1994 election for coast committeeman. He was so hopeful. I think it kind of shook his confidence. He just came back home and worked. Then after that he got involved in his own local's politics and he tried again. I've always loved and supported Bob and I've always believed that he had a destiny somewhere. I just knew that he was meant to do something. That's why for a while after that 1994 election I was irritated at him because he wasn't doing anything. He was working tying up ships, but he was drinking and carrying on and he wasn't going anywhere. He had so much potential and I thought he was wasting it. I told him he needed to get his act together.

Bob remembers those stressful days as well.

BOB MCELLRATH

When I was tying up ships I was also working out in the gym with these pro wrestlers. Well, when you get done you start drinking beer. I was kind of a rascal in my day, you know? I used to drink and fight. I'd come home half beat-up and bloody. My wife would shake her head. One time

Fig. 2.1. Lineman, San Francisco waterfront. A lineman ties up ships in port using heavy ropes and other equipment. Bob McEllrath worked as a lineman in Vancouver, Washington, between 1994 and 1997. Courtesy of Frank Silva, photographer.

around 1983 we were sitting there having dinner at my house with her whole family. There's a knock on the door. It's the police. They came to arrest me because I had been in a couple of barroom brawls. I wound up going to court and I got out of it, but I'd been in trouble. Anyway, after the 1994 election my wife had pretty much gotten a bellyful of my running around at all hours of the night drinking. She said, "You got to make a decision. You're destroying yourself. I don't know how much of it I can take." I listened to her 'cause she's a strong woman and I got it. I said, "Okay. I'll switch a little bit of gears." So I backed off of everything and really got involved from that point forward into being active in the union.

Rob Remar recalls Bob, while out of office in 1996, taking a stand against waterfront "side deals," which gave individual workers separate extra earnings outside of the ILWU Pacific Coast longshore contract. In Bob's view, this practice ran counter to basic union principles. Because some influential union members favored side deals, Bob's taking a stand here was courageous and political.

ROB REMAR

In 1996 there was a longshore contract ratification caucus.[9] By that time Bob had lost his reelection bid for coast committeeman, but he was still on the Longshore Negotiating Committee and he was a delegate to the caucus. Bargaining with the employers had already taken place. The caucus was there to review and vote on the tentative agreement. If the caucus delegates accepted it, then it would be passed on to the Longshore Division membership for a secret ratification vote. One of the union's demands in the tentative contract that came up at the caucus was to prohibit the practice of side deals. Side deals are where individuals who are steady workers make special arrangements with their employers to get enhancements that are beyond what the contract provides.[10] They get extra pay or whatever the arrangement is.

The union felt strongly that this practice was undercutting the stature of the union, its representation, and its collective bargaining. People felt that money for the benefit of everyone was being shifted from the bargaining table to this individual practice. This was an offense to the union and to union solidarity. The union wanted the practice stopped and did succeed in getting its demand on the issue accepted. But certain people were benefiting from the practice personally and mightily. Two were on the Los Angeles/Long Beach longshore Local 13 Executive Board and were very influential.[11] During bargaining, they wrote a letter to the president of the PMA [Pacific Maritime Association] saying, "Don't agree to this proposal from the union."

A question came before the caucus about what to do about these two guys and their letter. Bob gets up and says, "I tell you, brothers and sisters, there's only one way to look at this. What these guys did was an act of treason in time of war. When we bargain our contract, our battle is to secure what the caucus and the membership want in our bargaining package and these guys sent a letter to the employers asking them to sabotage that effort. That's treason. They should be severely punished." Bob got mixed applause. It wasn't fully rounded, full-throated support.

Bob's problem was that he was going against people who were influential within the union at a time when there seemed to be a growing sense within the caucus to let bygones be bygones. But I was impressed by how clear the principles were that Bob was laying out. Of course, I didn't say anything to anyone at the time because it's not my place. Still, I was impressed by the strength of what Bob had to say in terms of the character that it reflected and the courage of his saying that we have an institutional duty to do something about this.

At length Bob decided to run for office again. Below, he reviews this 1997 decision and describes a crucial sacrifice he made at the union's International Convention that ultimately helped advance his career as a union official.

When we got to 1997, I said, "I'm going to try for coast committeeman again." I'd always enjoyed working with people, trying to solve problems, and trying to make things work for everybody. Besides, 1994 left a bad taste in my mouth. I wanted to go back and give it one more shot and see if I could do a better job this time. But then the closer it gets to saying yes to running, it's a very hard decision to make for anybody. Everybody likes to say, "I could have been this or I could have been that." It's easy for people to say that. It's very hard to step up and actually do it. So I had a very long conversation with my wife. I said, "If I get involved in this and I do win this election, you have to support me because I don't know where it's going to take us." She said, "I'll support you because you're doing something good." I said, "Okay," and here we are. It was a two-person project.

In 1997 we go to the International Convention in Hawaii. By that time something new had happened. I was given the blessings to be the International vice president (mainland) by the Hawaiians of Local 142, the biggest local in the union. If Local 142 says, "We're going to nominate Bob," that's a pretty big endorsement. I'd been a past officer, I'd worked with Local 142, and they liked me. They liked me for whatever it is, your personality or half personality and half brains, whatever. Then a couple of days go by and Spinner says, "I'm running for vice president." I said, "Spinner, you're supposed to run for president! I'm going to be the vice president, that was the deal." He said, "No, I'm running for vice president." So I go back that night to Local 142 with Bo Lapenia, the Local 142 president, and all the Local 142 officers. There's a lot of guys there. I said, "Hey, Spinner's running for vice president so I'm going to hold back and I'm going to run for coast committeeman." They go, "What? We already told you you'd be the vice president. Everybody's going to vote for you."

Bob's choice here was based on his evaluation of the internal politics of the union. He prioritized reinforcing the cohesion of the union over his personal interests. There was a north-south split among ILWU

Longshore Division leaders in the 1990s that threatened the union's West Coast unity. Coastwide solidarity had been the source of the union's bargaining strength since the 1930s. However, the north-south split became a cause for concern after Los Angeles/Long Beach replaced San Francisco/Oakland as the biggest port complex on the Pacific Coast. Personality conflicts, too, worsened the split by the early 1990s.

BOB MCELLRATH

I said to the Local 142 guys, "Look, it isn't about me, it is about this organization getting back on its feet and getting some unity." There'd been a lot of turmoil with a north-south split in the Longshore Division on the West Coast, and Spinner was from Local 13 in Los Angeles. I said, "We're almost to a split. It isn't healthy. I can wait three years and see how it works out." The room got quiet. Then Bo Lapenia said to me, "I like that. When you're ready to run let us know 'cause we got your back." He told the guys, "There's a guy that's not self-serving." I said, "Thank you, Bo, but I just want this union to work." My stock went up a thousand percent that night. Everybody's happy and now the Hawaiians wanted me to be a coast committeeman.

As president of Local 142, Lapenia's opinion carried great weight with his constituency and beyond. Here he describes his early years in the union, meeting Bob, and developing the relationship with him that would help Bob strengthen the union's internal unity and overcome its north-south Longshore Division split.

BO LAPENIA

I was born November 9, 1942, on the island of Hawaii. I worked on a plantation doing herbicide spraying, carrying a forty-pound herbicide tank to kill weeds. Management wanted to make me a management trainee. I said, "No, I'm not interested." I couldn't see myself being some kind of a supervisor and telling my friends what to do, "Do this, do that." My dad was a laborer. He told me, "You know, boy, before the union I worked from sunup to sundown. Even if you're sick, you got to go work." I said, "Wow, a hard life." I became a steward, a unit vice chairman, a business agent, a division director, and in 1991 president of Local 142.[12] I retired in 2003 to take care of my dad, who needed help.

I met Bob at one of our conventions, either in Seattle or Portland. After that we became good friends and maintained that relationship. Bob and I just hit it off. Somewhere along the line we had the chemistry and we trusted one another. We always talked about what was happening in Hawaii and up in the mainland.[13] Bob always said that if I needed help that I should let him know. He was always there if we needed him. He never bullshitted me and I never did bullshit him. That's how trust works. I could call on him and he could call on me. One time when we had a lobbying effort in Washington, DC, I had Wesley Furtado from Hawaii and Big Bob with me. I forget what bar it was. Wesley later became the ILWU International vice president for Hawaii. That time at that bar I encouraged them. I said, "You guys are young. You folks have to take over one day." At first they said, "No, no, no, we cannot." I said, "Hey, bullshit."

Sally McEllrath provides added insight into Bob's relationship with Bo Lapenia and Local 142.

SALLY MCELLRATH

Bob made good friends with the Hawaiians. He'd go out and drink and carry on with them. They're kind of a male-oriented society. So the males all just kind of hung out. I think the Hawaiians just liked Bob. Bo Lapenia was his main Hawaii person way back. Bob's always been really close with Wesley Furtado, but Wesley wasn't there early on. Bo and Bob were good friends. They both liked to drink and talk about politics. I think they liked to strategize. Bob is excellent about seeing way far away. If there was a war or anything, you'd sure want him to be planning it out.

He sees the whole picture. He thinks, "Well, if this happened here, what would happen there?" I think he and Bo might have spoken that way while they were drinking. Of course, I wasn't ever there. They were out until probably 6:00 in the morning. They were just wild men, you know?

Bob reviews what happened to his lineman job after the 1997 coast committeeman election, puts the union's crucial need for Pacific Coast Longshore Division unity into historical perspective, and comments on his efforts to keep that unity intact.

BOB MCELLRATH

The Longshore Division Caucus was the next week after the 1997 International Convention.[14] Nominations for coast committeemen would be taken there. I was nominated, ran, and won. After the 1997 committeeman election I had to wait to get sworn in by the ILWU Executive Board. A guy from the PMA called me at home. He says, "You're going to have to resign from the Local 4 lines board." I said, "Oh yeah? There's a Section 13 in the Pacific Coast longshore contract that says you can't discriminate against a guy for taking a union position. I don't have to resign. I will stay on the lines board. Under the lines agreement it says you can rotate that job every ninety days. Don't ever call me at my house again. If you want to relay a problem, relay it through the local Labor Relations Committee and take it up with the union."[15] He never did call again.

I am still to this day [2013] on the Local 4 lines board after twenty-one years. They rotate my job. The guys say, "Oh, I got Big Bob's job for this three months." They tie up ships and then they're back to the hall and somebody else will get the job. I still have that position. When I go back to Vancouver after I leave office in San Francisco, I'll only work one day on the job. I'm going to go to work for my son Pete, who is a foreman and president of walking bosses Local 92.[16] I'm going to be drinking on the job and he will have to fire me. That's just something traditional. You get fired. Then I'm going to collect my pension and go home.[17]

As I said earlier, there was a time in the 1990s when we were split north and south. We were even talking about getting rid of the International. Well, Harry Bridges put this union together in the 1930s with a coastwide longshore contract. That was what made our unity so tight. If it was not for the coastwide agreement, I think we would be totally disarrayed. You'd probably have some local Northwest contract and you'd have something in LA and we wouldn't even hardly be associated. The employers would absolutely destroy us. It would only take a couple of years. Soon as they pieced off LA, gave them everything they wanted, then they'd crush the rest of us and the next time they'd come back and crush LA.[18] So I've always protected that coastwide contract. Even when I was a coast committeeman I protected it.

Bob emphasizes how he always kept a keen eye on the internal politics of the union. To many people the ILWU is best known for its support of social justice issues. This reputation is well deserved, but without internal union cohesion and strength, not much impactful social justice action is possible.

BOB MCELLRATH

All while I've been in office, that relationship of the north, the south, and even Hawaii was being brought together again. I was getting along with Local 142. I also got along with Local 13, all of their officers, and I got along with the guys out of Local 10 and obviously a lot of guys from the smaller ports in the Northwest. I made friends from LA and San Francisco all the way to Canada, Alaska, and Hawaii. This is one of the things that has helped me so much.

Tacoma, Washington's Conrad Spell, an influential ILWU leader in the Northwest and a friend of Bob's for years, describes his career on the waterfront and then points to the basis for Bob's broad appeal to the union's membership.

CONRAD SPELL

I was born in 1960 and grew up in Lakewood, Washington. In '62 my dad started working on the waterfront in Tacoma as a casual. I can't tell you about the first day I went to the Local 23 longshore hall in Tacoma because I was hanging around there since I was a little kid. I always jumped at the opportunity to go down on the docks with my father. When I was young I said, "Dad, I want to be a longshoreman when I grow up." Around high school Christmas break of 1976 I got to go down for my first day of work on the docks. When I got registered as an A-man I thought I would like to get involved with the local. I got elected to the local's executive board in '93, shortly after I got my A-book. A labor relations spot came open about '96 or '97 and I ran for that and did two terms. I liked the job because you were helping the brothers in the union. I became president of Local 23 in '03 or '04 and did three terms.

I saw Bob for the first time in about '94. He was campaigning for coast committeeman and had come to our local in Tacoma. I was on the local's executive board then. I thought, "Who is this monster?" He got up there and I still tease him today [2014] because he said, "I can work with anyone." Every time he gets frustrated I remind him of that.

One key to Bob's success is that his political base was very, very wide to begin with. If he was a guy from LA, he would have got his power base right in his own front yard. What helped mold Bob is that he understood that his power base was everywhere, that it had to be everywhere. It couldn't be just right at home in Local 4 because home was only two hundred guys or less than two hundred guys.

Danny Miranda, a Los Angeles/Long Beach Harbor longshoreman and waterfront foreman, became acquainted with Bob in the mid-1990s. Miranda eventually became part of Bob's ILWU-wide network. He outlines his own career on the waterfront and describes his early impressions of Bob.

DANNY MIRANDA

My mom was born in California and my father in Las Cruces, New Mexico. They are of Mexican American background. I was born on May 9, 1957, in Harbor City, California. My father was a longshoreman when I was born, so I've been a longshoreman my entire life! My uncles, my cousins, my son, and several other members of my family are all long-shoremen, all in Los Angeles and Long Beach. In 1978 I got my first longshore casual card. My ambition was always to be a longshoreman like my father. I got registered as a B-man in longshore Local 13 in 1985. I worked in the hold or lashing a good twelve years straight.[19] Then I got crane trained, winch trained, and became a steady crane operator for two and a half years. In Local 13 I was a business agent, a longshore caucus and convention delegate, and secretary-treasurer. I became a Local 94 foreman in 2000. I was put on the safety committee in 2002 and was elected president of Local 94 in 2003.

I met Big Bob when he ran for coast committeeman in 1994. He came down to LA for his election campaign against Glen Ramiskey, who was from Local 24 in Hoquiam, Washington. Being the Local 13 night business agent, I was asked by someone who knew Bob, "Can you drive Bob around?" I gave the offer to both candidates. It was a weekend and that day I was a relief business agent. Glen I took around that day. That night Bob came and I drove him to all the docks. That's the first time I sat in a car with Bob, got to talk to him, and got to know who he was.

But Bob didn't win in 1994 and I didn't see him for a few years. Then I met him some time later. He said, "Hey, how you been?" He never forgot me. I still got an original "Vote for Big Bob for Coast Committee" button. Then we just became really good friends off the job as well as on the job. He was a longshoreman that impressed me. He was a hold man like my father and me. That's where I came from.

In 1997 I was secretary-treasurer of Local 13 and I was negotiating the gear man supplement.[20] Bob and Ray Ortiz came walking into the union hall. They had just been elected as the two coast committeemen. I said, "Bob, I got an issue here. Hey, you're a coast committeeman now, tell me how to fix this gear man thing." We were talking about wages. There must have been twelve gear men there. Bob said, "I think what you ought to do is to go to this percentage and I think you guys will make out." I put that in the contract bid and we got it. After that I looked up at him and I said, "Wow." What's amazing about him was at that time we gave him some numbers and he didn't even write it down. He figured it all out, "snap," and told us exactly what it was.

If you're ever around Big Bob and you go to dinner with him, no one could add up the numbers of the tab or do the percentage of the tip faster. There is no way you're going to compete with that. I'm telling you, he can do numbers so fast. I mean, he's gifted, he just has it.

Bob recalls a rewarding encounter with Cleophas Williams during Bob's second term as a coast committeeman. Williams was the first African American president of ILWU longshore Local 10 of San Francisco and Oakland. Initially elected president in 1967, he served four terms in that post. Williams, an impressive speaker who emphasized unity, appealed to both Black and White Local 10 members during the turbulent 1960s and early 1970s. He became one of the ILWU's legendary figures.

BOB MCELLRATH

We had this huge problem back around '97 when I was reelected coast committeeman. It went into '98. There was an amendment to our pension plan that relieved the employers from putting in so much money. It dated from ten or fifteen days before I was sworn into office. In a pension plan there's lots of things that you got to do. I was trying to explain to people how this works. The employers were putting in so little. I said, "This will come back and bite us in the ass." I went to the pensioners' meeting at Longview, Washington, in 1998.[21] I spoke on this issue and explained and explained it. All the old-timers looked at me, relatively a young kid, and said, "Bobby's being political." But I wasn't. I just gave facts and figures for them to digest.

Cleophas Williams was in the crowd. I have tons of respect for Cleophas, who was a president of longshore Local 10. He is a very intelligent man and a very eloquent speaker. Well, they broke for lunch. I've got a lot of stink on me and nobody wants to sit with me. But Cleophas walked up to me, put his hands on my shoulders, and said, "I'm gonna tell you something, young man. You keep speaking, you did a good job. Believe me, people are listening." He patted me on the back. I said, "Thank you, Cleophas," and he walked off. That was hugely uplifting for me 'cause I felt like I was on the bottom of everything at that time. He came up and boosted what I was trying to say. I'll never forget that. He really helped me.[22]

Miranda characterizes how Bob used his communication skills in working to overcome the north-south split in the ILWU's West Coast Longshore Division.

DANNY MIRANDA

It is special that Bob can communicate with anyone from the basic longshoreman to the president of a high shipping company. It's the democracy of our union that someone who has common sense, will, a lot of heart, and intelligence can succeed. And Bob is a very smart guy. I think those combinations is why a small-port guy from a little local they used to call "the country club" back in the day shot to the top.

Communication is a key point here, too. When I first became a caucus delegate from Local 13 in 1997, '98, right around that time, we from Local 13 in Southern California did not even talk to the people from the Northwest and we were fighting constantly with the brothers from Local 10 in San Francisco. At my first caucus, Local 10 sat in front of us. We all stood up and they turned around and it was super hostile, like we were going to fight each other. But I'll tell you, Bob was the coast committeeman from the Northwest and he brought us together. He said, "You guys got to meet these guys."

So we met the Local 4 guys and we started having a good time going out with them and with the Local 8 guys from Portland. There was Lee Braach from up in Tacoma who we met with. Then Willie Adams and Conrad Spell, freshmen delegates from Tacoma, and myself met. There was also a guy from Local 63, the LA/Long Beach ship clerks. Little by little we broke those barriers. Pretty soon instead of us going our separate ways and not talking, we started going out and having a couple of after-hours beers. That's how Bob made it because he's the one who started bringing us all together with his "Hey, you guys got to meet these guys," and "I brought you all here to make friends."

Another thing about Bob, he's never late. We can go out all night long and drink every kind of booze there is to buy, but he will always be there the next day before time.[23] If he says he's going to do something, he'll do it.

Joe Cortez, a longtime president of longshore Local 13, reviews his own waterfront career, remembers Bob maneuvering to overcome the north-south West Coast Longshore Division split, and describes how Bob won over the large Southern California longshore local to his cause.

JOE CORTEZ

I was born in 1946 and was raised in the Los Angeles Harbor area. My parents are both Mexican American. I started longshoring around '63, '64. I was about seventeen when I started. In the 1960s, I worked at a place called Vegetable Oil, which was in ILWU processing and packaging Local 20. They had just become organized and I was lucky that I was there because I seen how the union works. In 1969 I was elected to be a convention delegate for Local 20. When I got into Local 13, first I sat back and watched the old-timers. Around 1985, '86 I decided to get involved and was elected business agent.

There was a difference of opinions between the north and the south around 1990, but I didn't agree with that way of thinking. So what happened with Bob was that he was a young caucus delegate when we hooked up. We just met each other at the bar. We formed a friendship and went on from there. Then as the different years of the caucus came there was more young guys elected. Change was happening, Bob opened up to Local 13, and we really got attached to him. That's when I got real close to Bob. Then when I started getting younger caucus delegates coming up, I'd say, "Before you guys leave, go down to buy a round, start mingling." And it resolved to be good.

In 1996 there was a hard contract caucus. There was an issue with our crane operators. The caucus came up with a pay formula that wasn't right. One night we were in caucus at the Cathedral Hill Hotel in San Francisco. We went to two in the morning and it got pretty heated. When we got back home to LA, Local 13 voted that contract down, but it passed on the Coast. Later our negotiating committee met with the PMA and they're finalizing everything else in the contract. But I was the Local 13 president and I appealed to the negotiating committee to correct the wrong on this formula for the crane operators. Bob was on the committee and he is excellent with numbers. He heard what I was trying to say and he wrote it down. Still, the committee negotiator told me to go pound sand, the contract was done.

Cortez emphasizes how Bob used his skill with numbers at the right time during the 1996 contract negotiations in a way that improved the contract for crane drivers while solidifying his own political position with what was the biggest longshore local in the union.

JOE CORTEZ

Then I went and talked to the employer group from the PMA. They said, "Well, we know this formula is wrong, but we can't do anything about it." Meantime, while I was talking to the employers, Bob persuaded the negotiating committee that they screwed up. They ended up rectifying everything. Bob really backed me up there. I let the Local 13 membership know too what Bob did in '96. I said, "Bob did this, he's all right." And if the Local 13 members know you did something good, they're going to stick behind you.

I think 1996 was the turning point for Bob with Local 13.[24] Then with Bob becoming president I think it was just a matter of timing. He probably could have made a push for International office at the Hawaii convention in 1997, but he decided to step back. He went for coast committeeman instead then.

Conrad Spell sums up many of the characteristics that helped Bob rise to high office in the ILWU.

CONRAD SPELL

Bob has done all these terms in union office. It is very unusual for someone from a very small port of two hundred to get to where he's at, but he is an unusual man. Guys like this don't come around every day. I think that the rank and file of this entire union saw that. First of all, Bob's a good worker. He's got a good work ethic. He's likable. He's very social, people like to visit and be around him. That's what starts to open doors. He's very competent. The guy's got vision. He's very fair, too.

One of his other strengths is listening. He's a very good listener. Most people of his stature or in his shoes don't listen. They think they know everything. But you'll even see Bob onstage at these longshore caucuses and he's got his book out. As resolutions are being read, he's studying them and he's listening to the debate 'cause he knows that's what puts the package together that forms our arguments with the employers. Of course, you could have all those qualities and still never get ahead. He's also a very sharp politician. The guy understands politics and he understands people.

Bob here returns to his old concern with race relations in the Pacific Northwest. He recalls how he dealt with a problem from the past. He also remembers how Conrad Spell aided him on another occasion.

BOB MCELLRATH

Around 1999, 2000, Local 8 needed to register longshore workers, but they also still needed diversity.[25] So I sat back and learned what I'd done right and what I'd done wrong. We met with the employers. We got to the agenda and the employers said, "Okay, first thing on the agenda." So I said, "Spinner"—he was the chairman—"we're not going to number one, we're going to go down to number eight." Number eight was registration in Portland. I says, "We're going to number eight and we're not getting off of number eight until we solve it," because I already had the okay on this from Spinner. The employers looked at me. They said, "What do you want?" I said, "I want registration and I want a diversity program to put Blacks into Local 8."

The employers said, "Well, you know, it's not that easy." I said, "Fine, then we're done. We're not meeting until we solve number eight." Three days later we had a program. They had a barrel full of Whites' names, a barrel full of women's names, and a barrel full of Blacks' names. They drew so many Whites and so many Blacks. We've got a new system now, but that's how it was done then. My point is that I did go back and clean something up that was real sore in my career back in '93 and '94. I've never gone to the Black members and said, "Look what I did." But, for the record, I refused to move the agenda until that was done and we got it done.

Another time when I was a coast committeeman I went to Tacoma. This would be around 1998. They had a huge lawsuit going on. It was a Black and White issue and they were being sued. There were twenty-five Local 23 guys who could vote on this. They voted thirteen to twelve to continue the lawsuit. I said, "You people can't be serious. If there's going to be one vote that's going to change the outcome of whether we're going forward or backward, I'm going to be that vote and we're not taking this lawsuit any further. We're going to settle it." I go back to San Francisco, but things I didn't hear about got changed and then the local felt that I had betrayed them. A couple of weeks later we get a letter, an individual letter to all four officers. It said, "We'll see you at the next stop-work meeting to explain yourselves."[26] Only I showed up. I stood there for an hour and I got blasted. I was called everything but Bob. It was just fucking horrible. The guy that saved me was Conrad Spell, 'cause Conrad was in the room when the deal was cut and then the deal was changed when I left. Now Conrad stood up and defended me.

In going to Tacoma to meet with the local's members under challenging circumstances, Bob strengthened his political position with that local.

BOB MCELLRATH

After that we settled the suit and today [2013] you know which local probably supports me more than any other local? Local 23, because they say, "You came up here and you addressed us. You didn't hide. We appreciate that whether we agree with you or not." To this day I got Local 23 guys coming up to me saying, "Thank you for showing up those fifteen years ago."

Beyond internal union issues, over the decades it has been a tradition of ILWU people to support social justice causes and to help other unions in need nationally and abroad. Some have done more than others, but many have participated. ILWU officers, active members, and pensioners frequently raise money, sign petitions, write letters to editors, and attend marches and demonstrations.[27] This is in keeping with the union's official slogan ("An injury to one is an injury to all") that traces its origins to the radical Industrial Workers of the World (IWW) of the early twentieth century. Bob followed this tradition as coast committeeman, International vice president, and International president.

In 1998 the Patrick Stevedore Company of Australia fired hundreds of its unionized workers and planned to replace them with nonunion subcontractors. The company, with government backing, employed security guards with attack dogs to chase union workers from its docks. An ILWU delegation led by International president Brian McWilliams that included Bob, then a coast committeeman, entered the Australian consulate offices in San Francisco to demand that the Australian government stop interfering with union rights and cease colluding with Patrick. San Francisco police arrested eight ILWU members who refused to disperse, including McWilliams, Vice President Jim Spinosa, and Bob.[28]

During January 2004 Bob, then International vice president, and the ILWU Coast Committee donated five thousand dollars and lent the services of the union's law firm to the United Food and Commercial Workers (UFCW) during a major Southern California grocery strike. Later that year, Bob presented a six-thousand-dollar check from the ILWU to the San Francisco Labor Council to help 4,300 locked-out hotel workers of Unite Here Local 2, an affiliate of the recently merged Union of Needletrades, Industrial, and Textile Employees (UNITE) and the Hotel Employees and Restaurant Employees International Union (HERE). Many of the Local 2 members were people of color.[29]

In March 2005 Bob led a march of 1,500 unionists in San Francisco to protest President George W. Bush's plan to privatize Social Security in the interests of his corporate constituents. Bob also recalled being arrested, detained for four hours on a police bus, and jailed in San Francisco when he was International president for demonstrating for the Unite Here hotel workers again during their 2010 contract struggle. In 2014 Bob spoke against death squads then attacking Honduran dock workers. He headed a protest march to the Honduras consulate in San Francisco and, despite a police presence, led ILWU members into the consulate building where he insisted on addressing Honduran officials directly (see fig. 2.2).[30]

Fig. 2.2. San Francisco Unite Here hotel workers and their supporters demonstrating in 2010 for a better hotel contract. Bob McEllrath periodically joined social justice actions. On this occasion he was detained by police and arrested. *Center, left to right*: with raised fist, ILWU vice president (mainland) Ray Familathe; with clenched fist, ILWU International president Bob McEllrath; California Labor Federation secretary-treasurer Art Pulaski. Courtesy of Anne Rand Library, ILWU.

Besides noting social justice actions, there are a few more comments remaining in this chapter about Bob's early career as an ILWU coast committeeman. Conrad Spell describes first meeting Bob and examines what he learned.

CONRAD SPELL

The first time I actually met Bob, Local 23 was involved in a lawsuit. It was either a racial lawsuit or a gender-based suit. One of the two. This was about '97, '98. Lee Braach, our local president, sent me down to the Tacoma courthouse to take notes on what was going on. He told me, "Your coast committeeman, McEllrath, will be there. You know, the big guy that came to the local that time." I remember going into the courthouse, which was in the old Union Station. I look in the middle of the foyer and here's that monster in there. He's got a little briefcase with him. So I took notes and so on. It turned out that we had about forty-five minutes to go have a bite of lunch. As I was leaving the courtroom, I said, "Hey, Bob, I know a place where we can get a sandwich." That's how my relationship with him started. We went down to this little place on Pacific Avenue across from the courthouse. It was just a beat-up old storefront where they had a little shop with soup and sandwiches.

I remember our discussion. The theme of our conversation was the walking bosses. My father was a walking boss then. I was telling Bob that I would never in a million years go do that. Bob said, "Conrad, it's important that good union men go do that job. Don't beat up the bosses so bad, okay." That's ironic 'cause in his area they're as hard on the bosses as anywhere. Somebody goes walking boss and he's like a traitor because then you become an extension of management and some bosses forget where they came from. But it was very interesting to hear Bob's perspective on it. So that was my first meeting with Bob. He and I did have one rough year once, but we got over it like two friends should. We have had a good relationship for a long time.

Finally, Rob Remar recalls an incident that illustrates Bob's development in office.

ROB REMAR

When Bob was a coast committeeman for his second term, after being elected in '97, he and Ray Ortiz, the California coast committeeman, were up in Portland, Oregon, or Vancouver, Washington. This was in the late nineties. After the union meeting, they went out to a local bar or restaurant. I wasn't there, but I heard about this soon afterward from Ray. Bob was familiar with the place. He knew the regulars who went there. This longshoreman—a big, aggressive dude, I don't know the guy's name—comes up to their table, stands over Bob, and starts picking a fight with him. He says, "Oh, you think you're such a big man now. You think you're such hot stuff because you're at the International office, you're a big committeeman. Well, I think you're just a pussy, a phony, a nothing." According to Ray, the guy was really drunk, was very belligerent, and clearly wanted to start a fight.

Bob, in response, tries to get the guy to leave without immediately engaging. He sees that the guy's drunk. The guy leaves and then he comes back and starts to make a move on Bob. Ray says before the guy knew what was happening Bob springs up and at the same time takes a swing and hits the guy solid. Blood comes flying from the guy's face and across Ray's shirt. Ray is sitting there in complete shock. The guy is lying there. Bob stands over him, then kneels down to talk to him quietly. He says, "I don't want any more trouble from you. Look, let's just call it a night. If you want to continue this, I'm going to lay you flat again."

What's important about this story is that in some ways that's the last occurrence of the old Bob. In the old days before he got into union politics, when he was just a working stiff, he had a rough-and-tumble life and lived in a rough-and-tumble world in a small port in the rural area of Vancouver, Washington. People in his culture used their fists to resolve their differences, and Bob had a lot of experience with fights and bar brawls. He'll tell you that when he became a union officer, he knew that he had to consciously purge that from himself and he did, he really did.

But that only goes so far. You can't change what you grow up with. You can't change your fundamental constitution. This is another element, I think, of Bob's power and his authenticity. When you're working with Bob, you get the sense that if you push too hard, too far, that element of his could come out. I've never seen it come out. I've seen him get close to it and I think he sometimes taps into that to use that as sort of a strategy. I don't mean that he actually threatens people. He doesn't do that. It's more the energy, his body language, that you get. This guy knows how to fight, can fight, and if you challenge him on that level he will fight and he'll kick your ass because he's got the experience, he's got the strength, and he's got the size to do it.

I think Bob was unhappy with the incident that took place in the bar that Ray Ortiz told me about. He didn't want that to happen. It's important to him to not get to that level. At the same time, I believe that he has no problem getting into it with people when it's the only thing that can be done.

By 2000 Bob had grown in office. He had overcome challenges both personal and professional. As Northwest Coast committeeman he had dealt effectively with issues ranging from race relations to an internal ILWU political division that threatened the union's coastwide unity and its coastwide contract, which were the foundational corner-stones that had served the Pacific Coast longshore workers well since Harry Bridges's day. It is possible to argue that by reestablishing the union's internal unity Bob had saved the ILWU from potentially imploding. Bob's role was widely recognized by key regional ILWU leaders and by rank-and-file union members. It guaranteed that he would become a major ILWU leader despite his small-port origins. He was now ready to move on to the post of ILWU International vice president (mainland) with the confidence that experience and success on the job provide.

3

"Going to Shake Hands"

International Vice President, 2000–2006

Wow, who is this big old redneck down there?

WESLEY FURTADO

At the May 2000 ILWU International Convention in Portland, Oregon, Hawaii's Bo Lapenia nominated Bob for International vice president (mainland). Joe Cortez from Los Angeles seconded the nomination. So did delegates from the Pacific Northwest and Alaska. No one sponsored another candidate. Nominations were closed to a standing ovation.[1] Bob soon took office as International vice president (mainland) and director of organization.

While vice president between 2000 and 2006, Bob refined his leadership style as he dealt with organizing in Hawaii, internal union problems in Alaska and Portland, relations with the East Coast's International Longshoremen's Association (ILA), and an extremely threatening West Coast longshore industry lockout. During these years, Bob also prioritized strengthening the ILWU's ties of solidarity with overseas maritime unions.

As this chapter opens, Bob looks at organizing in general. Then International Vice President (Hawaii) Wesley Furtado, Bob's wife, Sally, and Bo Lapenia explore Bob's outreach to the Islands since he was especially supportive of organizing there. Along the way, Clayton W. Dela Cruz recalls Furtado's early organizing days in Hawaii. Next, Conrad Spell and Rob Remar comment on a vexing Alaskan issue. We also hear from Walter "Pee Wee" Smith and Bob on a separate Alaskan question. Sally and Remar then compare the ILWU to the East Coast's ILA. Remar and Bob follow with discussions of the 2002 coastwide longshore lockout and the Portland issue. Finally, Bob, Furtado, Sally, and Paddy Crumlin and Jimmy Donovan from the Maritime Union of Australia, Joe Fleetwood of the Maritime Union of New Zealand, and Terri Mast of the ILWU-affiliated Inlandboatmen's Union (IBU) review Bob's role in strengthening the ILWU's international connections.

First Bob talks about his experience as ILWU vice president (mainland).

BOB MCELLRATH

As vice president you become head of the Organizing Department. I will be honest and forward: I really don't know shit about organizing as far as organizing goes. Organizers go in and talk and then they get cards and sign people up. Wesley Furtado is probably the best and I've seen a lot of people in my day. He knows how to organize a campaign and how to get it on the ground running. My strong points are after that's done, you want to fix a contract, and you want to bring people together. I've always been pretty good at organizing by going out and meeting people.

When you talk about organizing a group, I did a little bit of organizing. In the Port of Vancouver we had what we call "port mechanics." They'd work with everything except longshore equipment. I said, "Look, we need to get these guys organized," because they were nonunion. I went after them as coast committeeman. I think it was '93 and '94. I couldn't get it done because they weren't working on stevedore-handling equipment. The PMA [Pacific Maritime Association] was watching me. They said, "Bob, if they were working on stevedore-handling equipment we'd bring them in as mechanics but they're not. They're working on a road grader for the pile butts or they're putting up a light pole for the electricians or something like that."[2] I said, "Okay." We went and carded the mechanics as part of longshore Local 4 and gave them like a 4-B or a 4-A.[3] Then we said, "We're now the bargaining agents for the port guys," and the port just about died. At the time the port was a PMA member.

I says, "If you're a PMA member, you have to employ ILWU longshoremen." As soon as I done that everybody seen the play. They made them ILWU 4-A. We got them a great contract because if they didn't get one they'd picket and we would honor it. That was one organizing project that I was involved in. It was very small but I thought it was a strategic move on the docks.

The next one we did, I put together a plan with some of my guys to organize the security guards. It was right there; we had it. But one of our guys in Local 4 was too close to the port. He went and told the port, the port gave them a raise, and they turned their backs on us. To this day [2013] the guards are not organized. We'd never vote for that guy again, never put him in office. He never ran again. It was very sad. He opened his mouth. That's about my direct organizing extent.

Of course, I've been involved in trying from that level, vice president, or president, which ones we should go after. Now when you talk about organizing a department or organizing an office, people will tell you I'm pretty good at that. I'm good at organizing a budget, making the budget work, saving money, and finding a leak in the payroll. When I was vice president they'd call me "Fast Firing Bob," because I moved some people around. I know it was against some people's objections. But as an organizer I leave that up to other people that have a lot better and more experience.

Like I said, Wesley Furtado was one of the best. He's got thirty-some years right now [2013] and he only worked on the docks for about eight or ten years. Then he went to work for Tommy Trask, the Hawaii regional director, and he's been organizing ever since and he's good.[4]

Wesley Furtado reviews his background and describes his early career as an organizer in the Islands.

WESLEY FURTADO

I was born in Honolulu in 1955. My dad was Portuguese, my mom Japanese. Dad was a foreman on the docks. The whole family was raised on the ILWU. My dad went to ILWU caucuses and he knew Harry Bridges, Jack Hall, and those guys.[5] When I started on the docks I was twenty-two years old. I started in the hold as a basic longshoreman and became a shop steward and a longshore unit vice chairman. I ended up becoming a regular winch man and drove as the years went by.[6] Then I started driving hammerhead cranes.[7] I'm fifty-eight years old now and this year [2014] I think I have thirty-six years combined with the waterfront and the ILWU International.

In 1986, after I had ten years on the Honolulu docks, Tommy Trask says, "Wesley, you have family on Kauai?" I said, "Yes, a lot of my dad's family are still on Kauai." He says, "We're going after organizing a hotel there. How would you feel about trying to organize?" I said, "I don't know. I'm newly married and I got a two-year-old daughter. Organizing takes a lot of time." He says, "Well, maybe just try it out. We'll teach you the process of organizing."

He sent me to Kauai and we started on an organizing project. I knew people and talked to them till today I run the Organizing Department in Hawaii. I found a passion to help people that need to stand up as equals to the employers. That's what still keeps me driven to run this department. We tell the employers what we think we deserve and we deal as equals. Anyway, in 1986 Tommy sent me to Kauai. I got into it and never came back home for a year and a half. We got things rolling and then Tommy calls me and said," We have a big problem on the Big Island of Hawaii, come to that area." I went over there and spent almost two years organizing. We carded over 4,500 people.[8]

The ILWU International Organizing Department in San Francisco's tough 'cause you have a lot of people spread out on the US mainland;

you're like a needle in a haystack. In the islands, Kauai was tighter and smaller, with my family, my friends, with people I grew up with. I walk into town and they go, "Hey, Wesley, you with the ILWU." They tell me who I am. We went to the Big Island. It's bigger. You got Hilo, Kona, it's a lot more spread out. But every island had a uniqueness of how people act. Organizing, you got to blend in with the community. You got to be able to work with the people and they got to trust you before you tell them about the ILWU.

Clayton W. Dela Cruz remembers Furtado's early years as an organizer. Born of Filipino and Japanese parents in Waimea on the Island of Kauai in 1947, Dela Cruz worked in the sugar industry, became a full-time business agent in the early 1980s, and was Local 142 Kauai Division director from 1994 to 2010.

CLAYTON W. DELA CRUZ

I worked with Wesley when he first came into the union and they assigned him as an organizer to Kauai. He was assigned to our island for quite a while. If you organize, you have to go find people in bars, you have to go find people in all different kinds of places. Wesley's a little bit younger than I am, but we all went out together and tried to organize all the hotels. Wesley was a guy that could get along with all different types of people. He was a very nice guy, always smiling, always joking around. Wesley had family on Kauai. He had a way of talking to the local people who work in hotels and in other industries. He'd say, "Hey, you guys want to have a few beers? What's your job like?"

After organizing on Kauai and then on the Big Island, Furtado did similar work on Maui and served in other positions before winning election as ILWU International vice president for Hawaii in 2000. He describes those posts and then recalls his first impressions of Bob.

WESLEY FURTADO

I went to Maui after the Big Island. Then I was still a rank-and-file organizer on leave of absence from the docks. I was going to go back to the docks after organizing. I won an election for full-time business agent for Local 142 in 1989, but six months into my three-year term Tommy wanted me to organize some more. Jimmy Herman, the ILWU International president, was Tommy's boss; they turned around and offered me an International representative position. As International rep, I took on full-time capacity with the union. So I was a rank-and-file organizer from '86 to '89 and an International rep from '89 to 2000. Then from 2000 to current [2014] I've been International vice president for Hawaii.

When I was still a rank and filer I never knew Bob. But I was up in San Francisco for a Longshore Caucus. I heard a commotion outside the Cathedral Hill Hotel on the main road, Van Ness Avenue. I opened my window and looked down. I seen Bob holding somebody by the shirt collar with his neck up against the wall. I was like, "Wow, who is this big old redneck down there?" Then when I got to the caucus Bob came in with Jimmy Herman. We met and we became good friends after that.

Sally McEllrath recalls Bob's close working relationship with Furtado.

SALLY MCELLRATH

Wesley is a very calming influence. He is really smart. Wesley does the same kind of thing Bob does, thinking and strategy, but his manner is different. He kind of takes care of Bob or watches over him. Bob likes to travel with him, but I don't think Wesley is as wild as Bob is. I don't think he drinks as much.

Furtado here analyzes Bob's inclusive leadership style.

WESLEY FURTADO

At the time Bob became president of the ILWU his local had 140 members. Who would think someone from a small port like that would be able to run the International? But when he won as a coast committeeman for the Northwest, Bob proved hisself on a bigger scale. He's a guy that looks at everybody. Bob doesn't care about ethnicities, where you live, what's your position. By doing that people looked at him with his style and his leadership abilities, which took away the fact that he came from a small port.

Bob sold hisself as a leader that would work with everybody and could deal with the diversity of the membership. He has a lot of support in Southern California. We always thought, "Jimmy Herman was a marine clerk. President Brian McWilliams was a clerk." Everybody was thinking, "Man, Bob can't be president. You got to be a clerk or whatever." But he proved that he would work with the clerk issues, the foremen's issues, the Hawaiian issues. I'm telling you, he brought Hawaii close to the International. He really did.

Bo Lapenia, like Sally, commented on Bob's connection with Furtado.

BO LAPENIA

During Jim Spinosa's International presidency [2000–2006], Big Bob was a vice president, head of organizing. Wes was organizing here in Hawaii and they had to work together because Big Bob was in charge of organizing for the International and we came under the umbrella of the International.

Furtado describes the development of his working relationship with Bob.

WESLEY FURTADO

Bob was coast committee but when he went to International vice president him and I worked side by side and built good relationships. I took him to the Islands. I had him sit in negotiations with me when I'm doing hotels. I'd have him sit there and listen to the worker committee's arguments. Bob would say, "Wesley, maybe we should walk out 'cause it's kind of intimidating for them with us being in the room." I says, "Yes, that's fine." So we walk out and he was like, "You know, now it's a different makeup." But he would come in and say, "You got my support." That's big.

When he was president he came in and sat in on a couple of negotiations with me, too. He could have went and laid on the beach at Waikiki. No, he comes right in. He's very punctual and he takes his work very seriously. Him and I just had lunch today [during a caucus break] and we're walking back and he says, "It's five to 2:00," and he's trucking. I'm like, "God, Bob, you're sixty-three years old and you're racing back." He said, "No, 2:00 on the nose." That's the way he is.[9]

In the past, the president of the International sitting in San Francisco just looked at Hawaii as, "Ah, well, we'll keep in touch with longshore because predominantly we're longshore up here." Election time, Hawaii's got more tourism member votes than anybody else. But it wasn't political for Bob and that's what I respect about him. It was like, "Hey, here I am."

Bob became vice president for the mainland at the same time I became vice president for Hawaii [2000]. Bob was my lateral. Jim Spinosa was the new International president. So Bob and I were looking at the budget and we're looking at the trustees and we go, "Oh, God, we don't have money in our organizing." The whole deal was that 30 percent of the

International per capita would go into organizing.[10] But what happened is they were using that money to run the International and not plunging it into the Organizing Department.

Bob calculated the per capita. He's good with math, good with numbers. Bob's very good as an administrator. I mean he itemizes and categorizes everything. He says, "Wesley, I don't know how to organize a dog catcher into the union. You got that." I said, "That's not a problem." He says, "I'll work on this side to make sure we can afford to pay for the organizing program." In about a year and a half we were in the black with a separate account for organizing.

We took our organizing program in Hawaii to a different level. I was able to put on more people where it was needed. It paid off for the International 'cause we put a lot of new Hawaii members in there. That's paying more per capita, and then we could continue to run organizing programs.

During 2000–2006, Hawaii's Local 142 added nearly two thousand new members to its ranks despite employer delaying tactics and intimidation of union supporters. Most of the new members were in the hotel-related tourism industry.[11]

In addition to partnering with Wesley Furtado to help facilitate organizing projects in the Hawaiian Islands, as vice president Bob used his leadership skill to solve problems inside the union. Tacoma longshore Local 23 member Conrad Spell and ILWU lawyer Rob Remar recall how this worked during a serious early 2000s crisis in Alaska's Local 200.

CONRAD SPELL

When he was vice president Bob used to get sent up to Alaska a lot by Spinner (President Jim Spinosa) to try and fix the crap up there. I shouldn't say it like that, but they had problems. Bob would go up there and he would call and tell me, "Oh, my God, you wouldn't believe what happened today." Some of the things he'd tell me would be mind-boggling.

Bob's responsibility as vice president was to deal with Alaska in general. He was the point person for the officers in that region. They were having big problems, what I would call a civil war, among the different Alaska units in all the different ports and cities within the state. It had to do with John Bukoskey, who was a member of the International Executive Board. For years he had been a major organizer for the International for that area. He had become the appointed, not elected, administrator or business agent for Alaska Local 200, which was the umbrella local for all the different Alaska units. People either loved him or hated him. He became the issue over which people fought in Local 200 to the point where there were moves being made by different groups to separate and form smaller locals or different organizations. There were even rumors about disaffiliating from the ILWU.

The whole thing was collapsing on itself structurally up there. Bob called a meeting with the representatives of the two warring camps to see if he could work out some sort of resolution. We're in this meeting in a small conference room in the International building in San Francisco. There's a huge table in there with very little room to move around. People are yelling at each other. The two sides are lined up on opposite sides of the table. Bob and I are in the middle. At some point Bob finishes saying something and Pete Danelski from Alaska stands up, points his finger at Bob, and says, "You're a fucking liar, you motherfucker." Danelski is almost as big as Bob. He was a big, loud, boisterous, aggressive character. Bob gets up slowly from his chair, turns to him, and says, "Nobody calls me that without having to fight for it."

Bob immediately proceeds to walk over to where Danelski is. The message from Bob's body language and tone of voice was "Get ready because I'm going to fuck you up." Danelski proceeds to walk toward Bob. Everybody in the room felt, "There's going to be blood on the walls. These are two big men and it is going to get ugly." Fortunately, because it's so cramped and hard to maneuver, it was easy to block them with the people between them. They started yelling at each other; then they cooled off. Bob and Danelski got separated. Then Bob had separate conversations with the two camps and we got a deal. What happened was that the confrontation broke the tension and broke down some walls.

For reasons that to this day I still don't quite understand, the confrontation empowered Bob in the eyes of the Alaskans. It said he was in charge and wasn't going to take shit from anyone. He was willing to go to physical battle right then and there. That gave him the bargaining power necessary to force both sides to compromise. We ended up creating a new organization called the Alaska Longshore Division. We helped the Alaskans put together their own bylaws with a lot of compromises built in.[12] I still don't know how calculated that was on Bob's part, whether it was raw reactive emotion or whether there was also some strategy. At the time I thought it was raw reactive emotion, but as I've worked with Bob through the years I've learned how strategic his thinking is. I've seen him do similar things, not nearly as extreme with potential for violence, but where it's part of a choreography or strategy for getting to a solution.

Around the same period there was a shortfall in the welfare fund of union retirees from Southeast Alaska. Beginning in 1998, ILWU pensioner Walter "Pee Wee" Smith, a Vietnam War veteran who had worked as a commercial fisherman, logger, and longshoreman in Alaska, pushed to have the shortfall made up. Smith recalls Bob as vice president traveling to Alaska to negotiate a solution to the welfare shortfall.

WALTER "PEE WEE" SMITH

Big Bob came up on the next negotiations. He negotiated a fifty-cent increase. I do not know how that got by the employers because to this day [2014] they are walking the walls going, "We did what?" Because you are looking at five hundred thousand hours, for example, this year [2014]. That is a quarter of a million dollars going into a fund and this fund can only be used for our welfare.

Bob remembered solving the pensioners' problem by using fifty cents from the wage increase he negotiated to seed what became known as the "Pee Wee Fund" to help the Southeast Alaska retirees. In 2018 he called this "one of the best things I did."[13]

During his interview, Smith added a general comment on the ILWU leadership and spoke about the organization's tradition of union democracy and about Bob.

WALTER "PEE WEE" SMITH

People will come up to me and say, "How in the heck do you guys maintain what you get? You get healthcare after you retire, you even get bumps up during the year. How the devil? We do not get that stuff when we retire." I says, "It is really simple. Our generals are not from West Point, our generals ain't hand-me-down, heir-apparent bean counters from Harvard. Our generals have hit the bricks with us. Our generals do not sit back two hundred miles in a tent and say, 'Take that hill!' Our generals head up that hill and say, 'Follow me.' Our generals are one of us." That is what makes us different. I put Big Bob in that category big time. He could have sainthood in our state.

The ILWU has long been celebrated by unionists like Smith and by others for its consistent record of clean governance and rank-and-file control. This is frequently emphasized when comparing the ILWU to the East Coast's International Longshoremen's Association (ILA), which Harry Bridges and the West Coast longshoremen belonged to in 1934 but broke away from to form the ILWU in 1937. The relationship between the two unions was tense through the 1950s, then eased over time. Here Sally McEllrath compares the two organizations. Her comments provide the context for a Rob Remar story that sharply illustrates the difference between the two groups. That difference has made dealing with the ILA problematic at times for ILWU leaders, including Bob.[14]

There was a difference between the unions. The way that they run things out there is different than we run things. Ours is so democratic. One time we were invited to go to an ILA convention and we went to Puerto Rico.[15] They had the employers there speaking to the people. The workers, the rank and file, never would get up and argue or say anything like they do here, where they get up on a microphone. Everything was just a presentation and they just took it all.

Bob made friends with the ILA's Daggett, kind of.[16] I mean they were friends for a little while. Now [2016] they are talking again. Bob says that the unions are so different, that the philosophies and everything is just so opposite. I don't think the ILWU wants to be like that because the organized crime was always hinted at back there on the East Coast. So I think that they think of themselves on the West Coast as being purer.

ROB REMAR

Around 2000 there was a meeting with Governor Jim McCreevey of New Jersey. We were on the East Coast in Washington, DC, or at an AFL-CIO function in Florida. Al Cernadas was the International vice president of the ILA. He was trying to woo the ILWU officers into a closer relationship. Ever since I've started, since 1985, I have seen that. The ILA's always wanting to bring the ILWU into some affiliation arrangement. ILWU officers have always resisted without being impolite.

Governor McGreevey, then a big rising star for the Democratic Party, was pals with Cernadas. We showed up for dinner. It was Al Cernadas, me, Spinner, Bob, Governor McGreevey, and the governor's aide. The conversation was dominated by the governor and Al Cernadas. The three of us—me, Spinner, and Bob—were wide-eyed and appalled at the stuff we heard. Their relationship was about cronyism and to some extent political corruption in the sense of "I scratch your back, you scratch mine," in ways we don't see or do here in the ILWU.

Cernadas tells this story of having to deal with the Waterfront Commission, which is set up by the states of New York and New Jersey to ferret out corruption and to keep criminals off the docks and out of the ILA. Al was telling the governor how there was some hearing or proceeding. He and others from the ILA had to testify or do a response. The governor says, "Why didn't you call me? I could have fixed it for you. I know those guys on the commission. I could have sent one of my people there to keep them in check." We were blown away by the blatancy of it. There was no shame or even concern that they were discussing this in front of us, we being strangers to them and of a totally different mindset and set of values. Within a few months of that meeting McGreevey had to resign his office because of various scandals and Cernadas was indicted and went to prison for corruption.

Another situation involving the ILWU and the ILA merits review. In early 2000 peaceful pickets from ILA Local 1422 protested a Danish company's employment of nonunion longshore workers at the Port of Charleston, South Carolina. A fight broke out between the police and pickets from the predominantly African American local. Five Local 1422 men, four African American and one White, were arrested and held on felony rioting charges that might have resulted in long prison sentences. Protests arose across the country against what looked like excessive and politically motivated accusations. ILWU longshore Local 10 in San Francisco initiated a call for funds for the defense of the "Charleston Five." Contributions from ILWU constituents amounted to thousands of dollars. Finally, after a long trial, in November 2001 the Charleston Five were freed of all felony charges. The five were released on misdemeanor charges instead that included a one-hundred-dollar fine and no jail time.[17]

Below, Bob describes how the ILWU aided Local 1422 and the Charleston Five. Local 1422 was atypical within the ILA. It was led by Ken Riley, a progressive African American activist who sometimes pushed against the ILA top leadership. As Bob recalls, when the ILWU sent funds directly to Riley and Local 1422, ILA International president John M. Bowers was displeased.[18] Bob also contrasts the ILWU and the

ILA and reveals how he worked to deal cordially with ILA officers even before Bowers retired in 2007 and the more flexible Harold Daggett became ILA International president in 2011. As might be anticipated from Bob's record of bringing ILWU sections together, Bob bid for an improved ILWU association with the ILA by cultivating personal relationships within the ILA.

BOB MCELLRATH

Spinner was the president.[19] We were very involved with the Charleston Five. We marched with Ken Riley of Local 1422. Riley came to our Longshore Caucus and we gave him money. He went to Local 10; he went to 13. They wrote him checks. They had another big rally down in his 1422 hall. We had an open war chest here. We put it all in a fund. Spinner, Ray Ortiz, Joe Wenzel, and myself go to this function in South Carolina and had a rally and walked.[20]

The ILA is involved in this, right? Johnny Bowers is the ILA president. We got up and gave a check to Ken Riley and gave a little speech. The ILWU International gave him $50,000 and we gave him $50,000 from the Longshore Division. Then we gave him another $137,000 from all the locals that had donated into the fund we had set up. So it was money from the brothers and sisters on the West Coast to fight this battle in court. We gave them the check and everybody's clap, clap, okay, we did our thing.

A month later Spinner and I are at an International Transport Workers' Federation meeting in London. Bowers sits on the ITF Docker Section at the time. I went up and shook Mr. Bowers's hand. He was pissed off. He said, "Kid, you disrespected me. You didn't give me that check. You gave it to Ken Riley and I was completely out of control. I don't want to talk to you anymore." I said, "Mr. Bowers, I'm sorry. Nobody tried to disrespect you." He looked away and walked off. I said to Spinner, "We got a problem. Bowers just chewed my ass out about giving Ken Riley that check."

So Spinner had to get up and we went to lunch. We sat down and talked to Bowers and broke bread. We apologized. But the truth of the matter is this. The ILA International never gave Ken Riley a dime through that whole thing. Never helped him a bit. Had we given Bowers the money, we don't know how much would have siphoned down to Riley and to his local.

I've been to dinners with ILA officers as ILWU vice president and as ILWU president. They've brought up joining with them a couple of times. Al Cernadas brought it up, others have. They said, "The ILWU ought to come back into the ILA." But you'd have a political war on your hands, right? My first impulse is obviously the answer is "no," as long as I'm the ILWU president. I would not want to go back in with those guys. I've been back East and watched how they function. Our membership would go absolutely crazy. How many people get up and speak at our conventions? Tons. By the end of the day our microphones are melted down. I've been to ILA conventions several times. Their microphones are never used. Their delegates don't get up and they don't speak.

But because of myself and Harold Daggett, the two unions have become visible as partners in the news media. We support each other, we're vocal about that. It looks good, it sounds good, it's a good sound bite for these papers to pick up. Even before Daggett became ILA president I'm building relationships with all their vice presidents. I'm meeting them all over the world, constantly talking to them. Me and Harold hit it off pretty good. So we built relationships. They're going to do what they got to do, I get it, and it doesn't do any good for me to put anybody on the spot or call anybody out. Right now the relationship between the ILWU and the ILA as I sit here today [2013] is probably as good as it's ever been. Still, the best thing I think we could do is to be closer together as partners yet with separate organizations.

Beyond issues of union democracy and interunion relations, in 2002 a serious crisis emerged when Bob was vice president. It threatened the very existence of the ILWU. In many ways it dwarfed the problems Bob had already faced in office. This was a PMA lockout of the union's entire West Coast Longshore Division. The whole ILWU Longshore Division has only engaged in major strikes a few times in its history.

These include the Big Strike of 1934 for survival, a peaceful rehash of that violent confrontation during 1936–37, a strike in 1948 when the union's leadership and its hiring hall came under attack, and a strike in 1971–72 over wages and the concern of some union members that shipping company employment of "steady men," or full-time employees, threatened the ILWU's hiring hall principle. There was also lingering concern about automation in 1971–72 that dated back to Bridges's and the unions' agreement to accept containerization in the early 1960s in exchange for certain concessions. As a similarly major waterfront employer initiated work stoppage, the 2002 lockout was unique.

The lockout occurred a few years after the PMA appointed Joseph Miniace, who had a reputation as a union buster, as its president and chief executive officer. US president George W. Bush's administration was in the early stages of its "War on Terror," the US military was in Afghanistan, and Bush was gearing up to invade Iraq. The wartime atmosphere seemed an opportune moment for the PMA to push the union hard. Bargaining lasted for five months before the PMA initiated the lockout. Negotiations stalled largely because the PMA attempted to suppress the union's jurisdiction by refusing to guarantee that newly computerized ship clerk positions would remain ILWU work.[21]

As Rob Remar explains, the lockout posed an existential threat to the union that had not been seen in years. He vividly re-creates the feeling of that challenge, which during prelockout negotiations saw Bush's conservative Republican administration forcefully take the employers' side without even a cursory nod toward neutrality.

ROB REMAR

We were at war, we were in the trenches of the war, and the trenches weren't moving. It was so exhausting physically, mentally, and emotionally, twenty-four seven. I was constantly working even when we weren't in meetings. I was either doing research, writing, or doing proposals for the next day's meeting to review internally. None of us were sleeping very much and we were under tremendous pressure from the government in ways that I don't think anyone can fully understand who wasn't there.

In the midst of this war fatigue, we were faced with the possibility, maybe in our minds, that we were going to lose this thing. It wasn't just losing our position on a contract, but that the government was going to come in with troops. This was their threat. They were going to militarize the ports and we knew that our people were not going to let that go lying down. People were going to be killed. When that would happen there was the real prospect of the ILWU being destroyed as an organization by the government.

We were not quite sure whether the threat of war with Iraq was real or whether that was a tool of manipulation. It turns out it was real. But the government men sure were in a mind to be very belligerent with us. Their answer was, "We're going to war in Iraq. We need to have the ports secure for that. If we have to step on you guys to make that happen, that's what we're going to do." We took them seriously. All of that created this reality that we were going to lose everything. The thing for me personally that I cared most about and that I had worked all this time for was going to be destroyed. Well, it didn't happen. We actually came out victorious.

The lockout lasted for ten days. President Bush stopped the lockout by invoking his power to do so under the Taft-Hartley Act. This activated an eighty-day "cooling off period" during which work was supposed to return to normal. The ILWU feared that the PMA would charge the union with an illegal slowdown and that an injunction and extremely severe fines or worse might follow. Nonetheless, in the end the government did not militarize the ports or severely damage or destroy the union, and according to the contract that followed the lockout, the PMA agreed to the idea that all new computerized ship clerks jobs would come under ILWU jurisdiction (see fig. 3.1).

The ILWU had won an important point, which was not easy to do considering that by precedent the employers had the right to employ new technology going back to wording in the 1960 longshore agreement and even in the 1934 contract. It was disturbing, too, that over time the employers did not always live up to the 2002 lockout

Fig. 3.1. Workers demonstrating on the Tacoma docks during the 2002 Pacific Coast longshore lockout. George W. Bush's Republican administration, then planning to invade Iraq, wanted the waterfront open. Before the lockout, Washington, DC, had sent a federal official to San Francisco in an unsuccessful effort to intimidate ILWU officers into signing an inferior contract. Courtesy of Anne Rand Library, ILWU.

settlement on jurisdiction in practice.[22] Some traditional clerks jobs were lost to the introduction of new technology, although the workers affected were given other waterfront employment. Still, the union won increased pension rates and maintained complete employer-paid health coverage in the agreement, which was ratified by an 89 percent vote of the union's Longshore Division membership.[23] As a follow-up, shortly after the lockout the ship owners fired Miniace as their PMA president and CEO.

Remar here describes the government's threatening prelockout behavior in chilling detail.

ROB REMAR

Before the lockout Tom Ridge, the secretary of Homeland Security, started making threats. Then the Bush administration sent out this guy,

Andrew Siff, who was an attorney from the Department of Labor. He's the guy that did most of the talking to us about the threats. He represented a White House task force made up of top people from the Department of Defense, Department of Commerce, Department of Labor, Department of Transportation, and the White House itself. It was designed to figure out how and when and to what degree to intervene in our bargaining. Siff, who was based in Washington, DC, says at one point, "I need to meet with your guys directly on behalf of the entire White House task force."[24]

We set up this lunch off-site at the Wok Shop Café on Sutter Street in San Francisco, just a couple of blocks from the ILWU International office. That way we could easily walk away. This was with the Longshore Coast Committee. Bob was there. We meet Siff and he starts off by giving us this Gestapo routine where he starts telling us things about the union and about us as individuals that he knows from their intel. Not so much me, but the officers. He turns to Bob and says, "I know all about you. Your father was a longshoreman. You live in Vancouver, Washington, and you have a son that's a longshoreman there. You were a dispatcher at Local 4 and I know that you and your wife, Sally"—all sorts of details about Bob's personal life. You could see Bob's hands on the table. It was one of those moments like when he got into it with Pete Danelski over Alaska.

I wasn't sure what Bob was going to do. It was possible that he was going to leap across that table and wring that guy's neck or punch him out. Fortunately, he had the self-discipline not to do that. It felt like this is what Siff wanted Bob to do. Bob didn't take the bait. That was hard for him because I know it was really hard for all of us to sit through it and listen. It really was a classic intimidation tactic of, "I know where you live and where your people live and I can get you any time I want."

Bob too recalled details of the 2002 lockout and of the meeting with Adam Siff. He recounts some of those impressions.

When Donald Rumsfeld, the secretary of defense, called us up here you know what he called us? Economic terrorists! This was prior to the lockout. Then they sent some little guy, suit and tie, and he had lunch with us. We sat and talked to him. The guy must have had myself pegged. I said, "Well, I'm from—" and he said, "Don't you tell me where you're from. You're from Vancouver, Washington, your dad was a longshoreman, he's passed away, your son is a longshoreman, your wife's name is Sally, and we know what your address is." I sat there and Rob Remar was there and everybody's looking at me. That's like a threat.

I just as soon got up and drug his ass around the bar a few times and knocked the shit out of him. He'd have never got back on the airplane. But I kept my cool. I just sat there and stared at him. This is what he told us: "Look, the government ain't got time to screw around with you guys. We're going to war. You are going to accept this contract that's on the table." I said, "No, it's a bag of shit."

In 2002 the PMA was headed by Joe Miniace. He had a grandiose plan. We went to the PMAs for mediation and there was guys standing in that hallway with guns! We walked out of that mediation. Anyway, down probably five, six, or seven of the days of the ten-day lockout, I'm at the PMA again. I'm walking to the bathroom. Miniace is coming out. He said, "Bob, you know, we planned this lockout. I want you to know that this is by design." I said, "Well, I want to thank you for everything you've done. Not since 1971 have I seen one man unite so many people and you did it in one day. Thank you, Joe." He just stood there and looked at me. I went back and told our negotiating committee what I told Joe. They all laughed.[25]

There's that poster I used in our seventy-five-year anniversary in 2009. I said to Gene Vrana, our director of educational services, "I want old and new," 1934 and recent.[26] One great photo we put on the poster used to have Local 10 on there, but I made it generic so any one local wouldn't be upset. That picture was the 2002 lockout. The struggle continues after seventy-five years.

Rob Remar remembered another phase of the lockout that illustrated Bob's leadership qualities.

ROB REMAR

We were in bargaining. It was October and the employers had instituted the lockout. The White House proposed a thirty-day extension on the contract, which would stop the lockout but would also stop the union from being able to do anything that's considered economic activity to put pressure on the employers. The government was also threatening Taft-Hartley and, of course, "If you guys act out and don't comply with the injunction of Taft-Hartley we'll militarize you guys."[27] Me, Spinner, and Bob report to the bargaining committee, about twenty-plus observers, alternates, and hangers-on. The decision is in front of them: Is the union going to agree to the thirty-day extension or take our chances? After I give my report, I say, "My legal recommendation is that you say yes." Then I gave all sorts of reasons about how it could help and about the evils it would prevent. Spinner says, "I agree." They go around the table. "Yes, yes, yes, yes." Maybe three-quarters of the way through it landed on Bob.

Bob says, "No. We're too far down the road. Agreeing to the thirty days is giving up. We lose all of our steam and momentum. We lose the ability to keep the membership focused and all the pressure on the employer gets released. We'll have to start from scratch and they won't let us build the kind of pressure we've got now. We have to fight." Then everybody else following Bob says no. It comes back around and pretty much the whole room uniformly says no. This one speech was remarkable, and Bob doesn't make long speeches. It was pithy and to the point. He had a clear vision of what needed to be done strategically. I still feel badly about giving the advice I gave. I learned that sometimes you have to risk losing everything in order to win the fight, especially at such high stakes as West Coast longshore contract negotiations with the government poised to get involved militarily.

At other times during the lockout, Bob did have disagreements with Spinner about strategy and some of our bargaining proposals. Without drama or getting emotional and raising his voice, he would tell the bargaining committee what he thought. Then, if he lost on it, he lost on it. He was always a good soldier in the sense that, "Okay, this is the majority decision so that's what we're going to be fighting for and what I'm going to be fighting for with everything I can as best I can." He's a soldier and he values that as an attribute for anyone that wants to consider themselves a good union member.

Finally, Remar described another incident from the lockout, revealing that, despite the extreme tension and pressure of the moment, Bob could still act humanely toward an adversary when the circumstances called for it.

ROB REMAR

In 2002 bargaining, we would have these marathon sessions. We would go all night or bargain formally and then break up into smaller groups for less formal discussion. Sometimes there was discussion off the record over dinner or while drinking after a meal. On one of these occasions I left before they started drinking, but one of the PMA attorneys stuck around. By the time they were done it was 4:00 in the morning. This PMA lawyer was completely drunk. He pulled out his keys and was ready to get in his car. Bob stopped him and took him under his wing. He escorted him away, called a cab, got him in the cab, and got him sent home. That was a good turn. Here we are fighting it out, both sides hating each other and trying to push concessions, yet Bob does this humane, kind thing.

Remar also assessed how Bob resolved a far less dangerous but still challenging negotiating problem involving the Powell's Books workers of ILWU Local 5 in Portland, Oregon. The company is an independent bookseller with several city outlets. In dealing with Powell's, Bob employed some conventional union bargaining lessons for Local 5's unconventional members. Negotiations took place in 2003, not long after the organization of the Powell's workers into the ILWU during 1998–2000.[28]

ROB REMAR

Bob is the point person, he's the vice president of the International. He's responsible for helping Local 5 and Powell's Books employees win their second contract.[29] It looked like the company was making a move to destabilize and decertify the union through their hard bargaining and if not successful in that their concession prize would be, "We'll weaken the contract and weaken the union going forward."

Bob came in to help the local and he was amazed and appalled at what was going on. He calls me up and says, "Remar, Remar, we're in deep shit here, I need your help. This Powell's bargaining is really bad. They have bargaining in a theater and they're on a stage and there's an audience that watches. Not only that, our people don't have a list of what the issues are to be bargained for or a list of what their agenda is. I need help organizing these people. It's like herding cats, Remar." He kept using it, "It's like herding cats."

So I fly up there and meet Bob. We were meeting in this basement of one of the Portland hotels. They had the bargaining table on the stage with seats set up. There were fifty to seventy-five union members sitting there watching. People would come and go, eat their popcorn or whatever it was. Because of the open theater aspect you couldn't get anything done. There was no way to have frank discussions. There was no way to do things that you normally need to do to break deadlocks and move things along.

Bob slowly but surely got the Local 5 people organized. One of the first things he did was he pulls out his pencil. He's still using his pencil, not a pen. He says to the group when the employers aren't there, "Let's make a list. How about this? Let's make a list of what you guys have accomplished so far. Then we'll make another list of what needs to be done. Then we'll make a third list about what are the priorities of what needs to be done." Basically he's teaching them bargaining 101 and he's moving them along in a very friendly way. Of course, they're all ears. They know they're in deep shit, that they've been spinning their wheels. They're frustrated and it's looking bad and the rank and file is getting upset.

So they're looking to Bob to be the savior and that's what happened. Slowly but surely we ended up having more and more private meetings. We ended up going to a coffee shop with just a couple of committee members—me, Bob, and Mary Winzig, the president of the local. The counterculture element in Local 5 was strong, too. It was so different from the way of the world at that time. The members were like the remnants of the hippie sixties thing combined in this punk/Goth, Queer Nation, transgender thing with a lot of ink and metal in people's bodies. There were a lot of free spirits with weird incestuous sexual relationships going on among people on the committee. We were really amazed. We also loved working with them and learning about a totally different segment of culture. And they did finally get a contract.

Bob, too, remembered the circumstances surrounding the negotiating of Local 5's second contract with Powell's Books and commented on that process and its outcome.

BOB MCELLRATH

I helped the Local 5 people bargain their second contract. I sat down with people that got green hair and blue hair. They got earrings in their eyebrows and tattoos. I know we got guys with tattoos, but it was quite the deal when I sat down and looked around the room. They were from a different culture, different than the way I was brought up or raised. But I said, "Let's help the brothers and sisters." It was no problem after I moved in there with them.

Their bargaining was quite an eye-opener for me. I had never seen bargaining like that. There's a whole roomful of people. They come and go. When they want to take a caucus or break, the employers would stand up and start to leave. The whole crowd would stand up and start chanting, clapping, hollering, whistling, and doing all this stuff. I'm not used to that. I'm used to [hitting hand on desk], "Here's how you're supposed to do it," and you're not going to be interrupted by everybody in the peanut gallery. But that was their system.[30]

So I said," Let's sit down and figure out where we're at. Where's your master sheet? What have you agreed to and what have you taken down?" They just kind of looked at me. Someone said, "The employers are keeping notes over there." I'm going, "No, no, no, no, we're not going to do that." So I got ahold of Rob Remar and said, "I have a problem here. This thing is pretty much out of control. I think it's inexperienced as to what they're doing. Before, when they got their first contract, I think Peter Olney helped them.[31] Now they're in there by themselves and they're all over the map." Rob says, "I'll be there." I told these guys, "Okay, stop the bargaining. I'll be here Monday and I'll have my attorney." We finally got 'em down to two pages of what was left and a page or so of what we'd agreed to. Then I had everybody sit down and said, "Now you see where we're at? You focus on this. Is there anything we're leaving out?" Remar was there to help me.

Of course, they'd bring up stuff and Remar would say, "You can't do that, that's a law, you can't do this, can't do that." I wound up meeting with Mr. Powell, the guy that owns the bookstores. It was me and him, Mary Winzig, and somebody I can't remember. Powell said, "How do we fix it? What do we do?" I said, "There are some things you want and some things I want. I'm sure there's some place in the middle we can go and make this thing work." Within a couple of days we went back and forth and we got an agreement. The members voted it up. We went along three more years and got another agreement. Of course, the Local 5 people were babies in 1998, 2003, and now [2013] they're mature and things are going along better.

Besides overseeing organizing, dealing with a threatening lockout, and taking care of internal union issues, while ILWU vice president Bob developed a keen interest in international solidarity with dockworker organizations around the world. As the process of globalization accelerated during the late twentieth century and the early twenty-first, it became clear that dockworkers everywhere served the same shipping companies and could help each other greatly in times of crisis. In recognizing this and pursuing his interest in it, Bob used the skills for making and cultivating friends and allies that he had relied upon successfully earlier in his career. He would continue to work at this conscientiously throughout the rest of his years in union office.[32] Bob, Wesley Furtado, and Sally McEllrath comment on these matters.

BOB MCELLRATH

We have always supported the Maritime Union of Australia (MUA), the Maritime Union of New Zealand (MUNZ), everybody around the world. Australia and New Zealand are very close. They always come to our conventions. I made good friends with these guys. People got to understand internationalism. Internationalism isn't you read a book or you pick up a phone and say, "Hi, this is Bob," you talk a little bit and hang up. You have to make your presence there. You have to look at them face-to-face, eat dinner with them, go out and have a beer with them, go to their meetings, sit around and exchange ideas. That's what internationalism is all about.

People say, "Oh, well, Bob, you travel all over the world." Yeah, this job has given me the huge opportunity to go all around the world, but when you go there, you have things to do. Traveling is not that easy. It's pretty tough on your body. You're tired, you're not eating right, you're not doing a lot of things right. But that's the way you build solidarity internationally. You go to their rallies and they come to yours and you support each other. When I got arrested during a strike in 2011 there was people from all over the world that came over with their flags waiting to see what they were going to do with the president of the ILWU. This was great, great support. We try in turn to do that.

I can tell you about when I was the vice president and Jim Spinosa was the president. He'd travel but he didn't travel a lot. He traveled whenever

Fig. 3.2. Bob McEllrath, *left*, and Wesley Furtado sharing a laugh at the 2006 ILWU International Convention in Vancouver, British Columbia, Canada. Bob worked closely with International vice president (Hawaii) Furtado for years on organizing in the Hawaiian Islands and on developing overseas maritime union solidarity. Courtesy of Anne Rand Library, ILWU.

he could. He said, "I need you to go here, I need you to go there." That's fine. I said, "Okay, I'll tell you what I'm going to do, Jim. From now on I'm not going to go by myself, I'm going to take Wesley Furtado." Me and Wesley had been friends for years. So I took Wes and we've gone all over the world. Every time I have a meeting, have something to go to, I always take Wes. And he's made a lot of friends. I took him to Japan several times, to New Zealand, Australia, over to Europe, Argentina, South America, Panama, you name it. That's how you build it. By taking Wesley there I also think it's built a really strong relationship between the state of Hawaii and the West Coast [see fig. 3.2].

So you gotta go meet these people. They'll come and meet you and show hospitality. Then when you pick up a phone and say, "I need help," they know what to do, they come and help you. And we do the same thing for them.

Bob basically opened the door for me to travel internationally when Jimmy Spinosa was president. Now [2014] we go to do global solidarity work with Australia, Japan, Taiwan. We went to Buenos Aires and I flew with Bob. We felt that dockers would support dockers more than like the AFL-CIO, but I'm not going to get into that. Anyway, if we were on those trips everything was set so we would take care of business. We're going to shake hands, we're going to talk to people, we're going to build alliances.

Bob used to go to Japan with Jimmy Spinosa and the coast committee. Then Jimmy didn't like to sit through all of that ceremony and he would go, "Ah, Bob, you get it, you get it." Bob was going by hisself. So Bob approached Jimmy and said, "You know what, I'm going to take Wesley with me." Jimmy goes, "Why take the Hawaiian vice president?" Bob said, "Hey, he's a vice president, he's my lateral. I'm going to go, he's going to come with me."

SALLY MCELLRATH

Bob has friends in England, friends in Australia, his little group, and friends in Japan. The other night he was sleeping and he was yelling something about the longshore union in Japan because he just came back from there. He has said that there's only a few shipping companies, they just have different entities but they're basically the same shipping company. He would talk to the other countries about what's going on there and what's going on in ours.

Over time Bob developed a close relationship with Paddy Crumlin, the national secretary of the Maritime Union of Australia (MUA). Crumlin's position is equivalent to the presidency of a major American union. He was elected national secretary of the MUA in 2000, the same year Bob became ILWU vice president for the US mainland. The

CHAPTER 3

ILWU connection with Australian waterfront workers goes back to the days of Harry Bridges, who was originally from Melbourne. Bridges and Jim Healy, the legendary leader of Australia's Waterside Workers' Federation (WWF) between 1937 and 1961, used to maintain direct communications.[33] The relationship between the two unions slackened briefly around 2000. But it grew especially strong during Bob's period as vice president and then president of the ILWU. Here Bob characterizes Crumlin's leadership and Crumlin reviews his own background before exploring the ILWU's international outreach under Bob's guidance.

BOB MCELLRATH

Paddy Crumlin is probably the greatest labor leader I've ever seen. That guy has been to more countries, more little unions, and has tried to help more people by working through the International Transport Workers' Federation (ITF) plus the MUA that he is the secretary of.[34] He is very talented, smart, and articulate. There will be books and books written about that guy.

PADDY CRUMLIN

I was born in 1955 in Sydney. My father is a merchant seafarer. I was a surfer, surfed all over the world, so I was a bit of a greenie and environmentalist. But when I finally went to sea in 1978 I was politicized by our very strong, militant, progressive, maritime trade union, the Seamen's Union of Australia (SUA). In the mid-1980s I relieved [served a turn] in the SUA office. Taffy Sweetensen, an old Welsh marine fireman, was union assistant secretary. He said, "I took union office because I realized there's not many things in life where you can make a difference. But in this job you can. You can find someone a job or save someone a job or get someone worker's compensation. It's a very rewarding way to live your life."[35] Once he said that I knew I was a goner. By 1993 I was the second in charge, the deputy secretary of the Seamen's Union.

The year 1993 saw the amalgamation of the SUA and the WWF into the MUA.[36] After the merger, Crumlin became the MUA deputy national secretary. In 1998 he served for six weeks on the MUA picket lines in West Australia during the major lockout of the waterfront by the Patrick Corporation. Two years later he was elected national secretary of the MUA. Below he traces the early development of his working relationship with Bob.

PADDY CRUMLIN

The guy who was MUA national secretary before me, John Coombs, was very close to ILWU president Brian McWilliams. Because John was such a good friend of Brian's, when Spinner won for ILWU president over Brian in 2000 there was a separation. Everyone was aware of it, even Bob, then the new ILWU vice president. I'd just been elected MUA national secretary myself.

Of course, Bob reached out. Bob and I, we're like siblings politically. We sat down and had a chat about internationalism. In Australia we put on a big Maritime and Mining Conference at Newcastle.[37] This was in 2002. That was really our first indication of supply chain organizing because we were linking the situation into the mining company Rio Tinto at the time, down the trains, into the ports, and into international destinations.[38] I had formed a very strong friendship with ILWU longshoreman Willie Adams, who had invited me to speak in Tacoma in the early days when he used to run Black History in Labor there.[39] He was there for the strong political friendship we'd formed. Ray Familathe had been an ITF Inspector. He was there because of the work he and his wife, Cathy, had done supporting the MUA in 1998 on the *Columbus Canada* picket line in LA.

The *Columbus Canada* sailed to Los Angeles from Australia with scab-loaded cargo during the Patrick Corporation's 1998 lockout of dock workers in several Australian ports. The company had sought to reduce its workforce by fiat. Los Angeles ILWU members picketed the *Columbus Canada*. It was forced to return to sea without unloading. Bob, then a recently elected coast committeeman, recalled much "behind the scenes work" on the *Columbus Canada* case. He spent hours on the phone along with coast committeeman Ray Ortiz, ILWU vice president Spinosa, and Rob Remar because the situation was so tense. With any misstep, he said, "the ILWU could have been sued big time."[40]

Crumlin here continues his discussion of what transpired at the 2002 Newcastle conference.

PADDY CRUMLIN

Bob was there at the conference. Bob and I sat down and said, "What are we going to do about international dockworkers so we can reform and unify them into a militant internationalism?" We were both strongly of the view that if the employers hadn't busted the Liverpool dockers in 1996 they wouldn't have done Patrick's.

The ILWU strongly supported the Liverpool, England, dockers during their bitter dispute with Mersey Docks and Harbour Company over firings. The confrontation lasted from September 1995 to January 1998. When the *Neptune Jade* arrived in the Port of Oakland in 1997 carrying scab cargo, ILWU members picketed it for three days. The PMA attempted in court to force activist Robert Irminger to name the *Neptune Jade* picketers. He refused.[41]

Later ILWU workers picketed the vessel in Vancouver, British Columbia, Canada. The *Neptune Jade* returned to sea unloaded. During most of the Liverpool dispute, Bob was out of office and working on the Vancouver, Washington, waterfront. But after the English dockers' struggle was over he traveled to Liverpool, where he "wanted to help anyway" and joined a picket line set up to confront a different issue.[42]

Now we return to Crumlin's 2002 Newcastle discussion with Bob about international cooperation.

PADDY CRUMLIN

Bob and I agreed that the ITF had become too bureaucratic. We felt that their bureaucratic approach to internationalism was more educative than it was geared to organizing or formulating campaign structures. I said to the old London ITF bureaucrats, "You've never had an organizing strategy since the US State Department withdrew funding after the Cold War. And now we've got to rebuild." Bob and I and the group, the leadership in my union, the leadership in New Zealand, and the leadership of the ILWU sat down and said, "Okay, what are we going to do?" So we decided to get together at a more grassroots level with our delegates and talk about supply chain organizing, which then translated into Bob leading the dockworkers section of the ITF and subsequently me becoming president of the ITF. The last eighteen years (2000–2018) have seen a reformation in the ITF and Bob has been front and center on every part of that.[43]

Jimmy Donovan of the MUA went to work on the Sydney waterfront in 1962. By the mid-1960s he was a WWF rank-and-file committee activist. He served as an officer of the WWF Sydney Branch and was national president of the WWF before its 1993 merger with the SUA. He then became the MUA's first president. He retired in 1999.

Below, Donovan recalls the evolution of Bob's relationship with Crumlin and how this has helped struggling longshore worker organizations around the world.

JIMMY DONOVAN

Today [2016] I'm the national president of the MUA Retired Veterans in Australia and keenly attend all meetings and pickets. I see from the sidelines the wonderful relationship between Paddy and Bob that has developed even to a higher level than existed under all the previous leaders. The relationship started long before our Patrick dispute of '98. But it grew with strength from '98 and it's grown even stronger because of the ties and because Paddy is now the national president of the ITF. Had the ITF come to the help and rescue of the Liverpool dockers in the mid-1990s, then the rest of the dockers throughout the world wouldn't be in the uncertain position they are in today. But world docker unionism has been strengthened, strengthened by Paddy being there and by the support of Big Bob.

Bob and Joe Fleetwood also developed a strong relationship during the latter's years as the leader of the Maritime Union of New Zealand (MUNZ). When interviewed in 2018, Fleetwood was general secretary of the MUNZ. That position is equivalent to the presidency of an American union. Fleetwood describes his background and characterizes his coordination with the ILWU and with Bob through the ITF.

JOE FLEETWOOD

I was born in Wellington, New Zealand, in 1965. I first shipped out and come to sea when I was fifteen and have been in the union ever since.[44] I joined the union like my dad. I'm fifty-three now, so that's thirty-eight years of going in the union straight. This is my third four-year term elected as the MUNZ general secretary. I was the vice president when we first amalgamated and created the MUNZ in 2002 from the New Zealand seamen's union and the wharfies.[45]

The advantages of international cooperation are so much. We're probably the only industry in the whole world with the same employers. We have Maersk in New Zealand, Maersk in Australia, and Maersk on the West Coast and East Coast of America, and all around the world. That's where the ITF comes in. It's the only global union federation that can stop anything. Every six months we meet in London and we coordinate through the ITF. I might have to fly somewhere and Bob's there too and we deal directly with him. Other than that, everything's dealt directly through the ITF. But I've probably been dealing directly with Bob for the last fifteen years on international campaigns. We fit into the ILWU and they fit into us, just like we fit into the MUA and they fit into us, too. Your struggles are our struggles.

The Inlandboatmen's Union of the Pacific (IBU) is the Marine Division of the ILWU. Terri Mast became the IBU national secretary-treasurer in 1993. During 1981 she had been a member of Seattle-based ILWU Local 37, a mostly Filipino organization. In season, the local dispatched members to Alaska salmon cannery jobs. Mast was active in a reform movement that stood in opposition to the local's corrupt president, Tony Baruso. She was married to Silme Domingo, a prominent reform leader in the local. On June 1, 1981, Domingo and his fellow reformer Gene Viernes were shot to death by order of Baruso, who was working in consort with a Seattle gang and with Ferdinand Marcos, the notorious dictator of the Philippines.

In a heroic stand following the tragedy, Mast challenged Baruso in Local 37 meetings. She was soon elected vice president and then president of the local, which merged with the IBU in 1987. After the merger, Mast became regional director of the new IBU Region 37. Mast also campaigned along with others for justice for Domingo and Viernes. Ultimately, the gang members Baruso had employed to assassinate the two reformers, and Baruso himself, were sent to prison.[46]

Mast recalls her early struggles before describing the value of the ILWU's international outreach under Bob's guidance.

TERRI MAST

The first meeting after the murders, Baruso was trying to take credit for the work we had all done as the reform movement. What gave me the strength to oppose that was that Curtis McClain, the ILWU International secretary-treasurer, was there. He was sent up from San Francisco to see what was going on and how he could assist. We were asking ILWU president Herman for help. Baruso did have the Tulisan gang in there armed and trying to intimidate us. What helped me was the strength of my union, knowing that the International was behind us. It was the community that we had built that also supported us. The old-timers from Seattle ILWU longshore Local 19 would come up and sit in the hall with us.

After the killings I raised our two children. I have no idea how. When you're young you just do things. You do it 'cause you have to. I had a lot of support with my family, my mother. During the funeral people gave money. Some of my close comrades gave money and helped in that way. A year later my union office became a paid position. It paid enough. It wasn't much, but we weren't doing it for the money, right?

I remember meeting Bob and seeing him around when he was on the coast committee. He had a presence about him. When he was ILWU vice president he engaged with the IBU a bit. He came to our conventions a couple of times and offered assistance. I think he spoke at our convention in those early years. Once, we had some financial hardship in the IBU and Bob approached me to talk about it. He was more than willing to work with us. Bob was more concerned about how do we get out of our situation than he was about taking any measures against the IBU. He said, "Hey, locals go through that. We're not all longshore."[47]

I sit on the ITF Women's Committee. It was ILWU president Brian McWilliams that first nominated me to be on that board. But Bob always supported that position as well. When Paddy Crumlin was first running as the ITF president, I told them if they needed me to step up and run for ITF Executive Board, I would do that if that would help. Bob asked me to do it and I did.[48] I think Bob does recognize the role of women in our union, the role of women's leadership, and the need for the ILWU to place people on committees or boards.

I've been to the MUA conferences with Bob's delegations a couple of times. Overseas participation gives us a sense of what's happening internationally because what happens to trade unions there is usually going to come this way, if it hasn't already. It helps us understand what global capital is doing and how to structure our union to be prepared to fight back. Especially with the MUA, they've lost their cabotage, something like our Jones Act, they don't have it.[49] They are constantly under the gun, under attack. I think we've learned a lot from them about why our protections are so important.

It is especially important for the ILWU Longshore Division to see that because it protects the IBU, the IBU in turn protects them. International exposure provides a better understanding of some of the labor laws, some of the things that we do have that sometimes we take for granted that can be easily taken away. As to longshore, they share the same employers internationally, so that international solidarity is very important. For all of us, international travel is always an eye-opener to see that workers everywhere face the same situations and can learn lessons from each other. That's an important thing that Bob has brought.

By the eve of the 2006 ILWU International Convention, President Spinosa was ready to retire. Having helped the union advance its organizing objectives in Hawaii, solve its problems in Alaska and Portland, survive threats as serious as the 2002 lockout, and strengthen its international maritime solidarity position, the time seemed right for Bob to move on to the union's International presidency.

4

"I Got a Plan"

International President, 2007–2009

Technology is coming. You can't stop it. Technology's coming whether you and I like it or not.

BOB MCELLRATH

The ILWU met in International Convention at Vancouver, British Columbia, Canada, during May 15–19, 2006. Joe Cortez from longshore Local 13 in Los Angeles nominated Bob for International president on May 19. Nate Lum of Local 142 in Hawaii, Fred Pecker from warehouse Local 6 in Northern California, and Tom Dufresne of longshore Local 500 in Vancouver, British Columbia, seconded the nomination. There were no other candidates. Retiring president Jim Spinosa then moved that nominations be closed. Bob, now assured of the International presidency, got a standing ovation and a lei from the Hawaiian delegation.[1]

In his speech nominating Bob for International president, Local 500's Dufresne, who was also the president of ILWU Canada, touched in general upon some of the main reasons for Bob's unionwide support and for his elevation to the union's top leadership position.

I have come to appreciate [Bob's] dedication to this union, his hard work, his ability to stay and work as a team, not to fall apart and have things all divided up. Bob is a builder. He's a builder in building consensus, building solidarity, and keeping the union together and keeping everybody focused. Wherever there is a beef, whether it be in Alaska, Liverpool, Australia, Canada, people recognize Big Bob, and not just in the Longshore Division, but in longshore, warehouse, hotel. Whatever there is a beef, people know that they can call up and they can get Bob McEllrath on the phone and that there is going to be some action taken.[2]

Bob's popularity with the union's locals was affirmed in the balloting after the convention. He received 7,564 votes, 660 more than the next highest count among the three other candidates who ran unopposed for titled officer positions in 2006. It can be difficult to judge popularity when a candidate runs unopposed. But Bob's vote counts ran high in locals large and small along the West Coast and in Hawaii, Alaska, and Canada.[3]

Most of this chapter is taken up with Bob's efforts to keep things together, to echo Dufresne, first in dealing with internal challenges involving discrimination and then in handling issues related to the union's negotiating its 2008 Pacific Coast Longshore and Clerks Agreement with the Pacific Maritime Association, the employers' bargaining representative. In negotiating with the PMA that year, the question of automation on the waterfront was paramount for the union.

The chapter begins with Rob Remar and Bob commenting on sensitive questions about race and same-sex marriage. Then Remar, longshore Local 10 president Melvin Mackay, and Bob recall issues arising from an ILWU May Day shutdown in 2008 during the Longshore Division bargaining season. Next, ILWU benefits plan director and Local 10 veteran John Castanho, Remar, and Bob recount how Bob worked to develop unity within the union's Longshore Division

Caucus as it approached bargaining with the employers. Castanho and Remar then review aspects of Bob's negotiating style. Former ILWU benefits plan director George Romero and former coast director for the ILWU-PMA Alcohol and Drug Recovery Programs George Cobbs add comments.

Remar, ILWU Canada president Tom Dufresne, Bob, and ILWU longshore maintenance and repair specialist Tom Hebert follow with an assessment of the important challenge of automation on the waterfront and how Bob sought to deal with it. Former ILWU Local 10 president Lawrence Thibeaux adds his observations. Bob then remembers dealing with a pension funding problem. Next Melvin Mackay discusses funding in general. Bob then compares the union's recent contracts and recalls a difficulty stemming from 1993. Romero adds a comment about the 1993 problem. Bob recounts a money issue from the 2008 recession. He then revisits an ILWU Warehouse Division organizing drive that failed and recalls a hard decision he made. Finally, Remar describes an extraordinary confrontation from the ILWU's 2009 International Convention.

Early during Bob's presidency, a group of African American longshore workers complained vehemently of discrimination in things like tests for lashing containers to container vessels. Lashing, using heavy metal equipment, is dangerous and physically demanding. Tests were timed.[4] Here Rob Remar reflects in general on Bob's ongoing predicament with some of the union's African American members. Then Bob recounts how he dealt in his own unique way with the immediate challenge that was before him in 2007.

ROB REMAR

I remember Bob saying and feeling that he was being misjudged and that there was a particular bias against him as a person and as one of the officers. And there clearly was, he didn't just make that up. The way Bob put it was, "They see me as this redneck country boy, this White guy from a small port that doesn't have a lot of diversity. So they assume that's all I'm about and that I'm, therefore, racist and insensitive to their issues. It's so not true and so unfair. It pisses me off that they think that way and I'm not sure how to respond. But I'm not going to go out of my way to prove them wrong just for the sake of my own reputation. I'm just going to do the right thing." The other thing that came to me from experiences with Bob was seeing how sincerely opposed to discrimination in pretty much any form that the man is. It's not a political opposition or a philosophical one, it's more like a basic sense of what's fair. It's a shame that people don't see that.

BOB MCELLRATH

In 2007, as soon as I got in as president, there was another upheaval with the Black coalition. I was getting all kinds of letters and comments. Some militants out of Seattle traveled down here to San Francisco to meet with me. There were some from Portland and other places, and San Francisco. I had my committeemen and Rob Remar with me. These Black guys came in and they started. I listened to them for a long time. They said, "We want you to write a letter and we want you to do this and we want you to say this and do that." I said, "I ain't writing no letter." They go, "What?" I said, " I am not writing any fucking letters."

I said, "I have been an officer. I knew Harry Bridges, I worked for Jimmy Herman as a bodyguard, I worked under David Arian, I worked under Brian McWilliams, I worked under Jim Spinosa, and now I'm the president, and every time one of them wrote a letter that had anything to do with the problems that you guys are bringing up, you used it against them. You turned it, you took it out of context, and you used it against them." I says, "I ain't writing no letters. I don't care what you say."

They all sat there and looked at me. I said, "I'll do you one better." They said, "What's that?" I said, "You keep yelling at my officers and you keep telling us what the problem is and you think it is my fault. You think that the officers in this administration are the ones that are doing this to you. It ain't us. It's the boss man. It's the boss man down there on Market Street that's doing it to you.[5] It ain't me. You don't want to believe it, but it ain't me." I said, "Wait right here. I'll fix it for you. I got a plan."

I got up and came in my office and called Jim McKenna, the head of the PMA. I said, "Jim, we got a problem. I got all these Black people. They're very upset. They don't like what's going on in Seattle-Tacoma and other ports. They'd like an audience and I'd like you to listen to them." He says, "Well, I can do that. I'll give them one hour and we'll go from there." I hang up the phone and go back in there.

They said, "What are we going to do?" I says, "You guys liked to bitch at me and tell us what the problem is. I'm going to give you an audience—it's never been done before—in front of the CEO of the PMA, Jim McKenna. You can sit in front of his officers and tell them exactly what you're telling me. He's an Irishman like me. Tell him to get fucked if you want. You got the floor. They said, "You'd do that?" I said, "Ten tomorrow morning, the PMA. Be there at 555 Market Street." Rob says, "Wow, that's pretty good." I said, "Yeah, well, let's see how this goes. I've been here doing this a long time and I've never seen this happen, so let's do it."

The next morning we meet. Everybody goes in the PMA boardroom. I went back and got McKenna. I said, "Go ahead," and they took off. They vented, they yelled, they hollered. The PMA people, who had their attorneys there, answered all their questions. They said, "This is what we're going to do." Then Jim says, "Well, we're done. I got another meeting to go to." The PMA got up and left. I shook everybody's hand and was going to leave.

There's one Black guy out of the Seattle area that's a very militant guy. He said, "Bob, I don't say 'thank you,' especially I don't say 'thank you' to a White guy, but I want to say this: 'Thank you for what you did today. I have a lot of respect for what you did." I said, "It's my job. No worries about that, but thank you," and out the door I went.

I tried my best all along. I learned from '93–'94. Then I knew what we had to do for Local 8 and I knew what happened here. It's a tough situation. There is no direct right answer. You're damned if you do and you're damned if you don't, but you try to make it fair. That's all you can do is take the color out of the man's skin, or a female, or whatever, and move on.

Some good came out of that meeting at the PMA because the local Labor Relations Committee up north got the message from McKenna and they relayed it and they stopped doing certain things and started complying. If a guy takes a lashing test and he's a White guy, everybody's just kind of talking. A Black guy takes a lashing test, they're, "Oh, you made a mistake here, you did that," making it harder on them. We told them, "This type of shit's got to stop," and it did. Things got straightened out.

In discussing fairness, Rob Remar added comments on Bob's handling of same-sex marriage and the union's Longshore Division pension plan. His testimony affirms that Bob's approach to fairness was consistent.

ROB REMAR

Another thing that relates is Bob's dealing with same-sex benefits, same-sex relationships, and couples marriage under the longshore plan. There was an issue with the Pension or Benefits Committee of the Longshore Caucus about what position to take. This was when Bob was president. It was probably around the 2008 longshore contract negotiating time. There were several strong voices among our delegates that were opposed to the idea of providing benefits to same-sex couples. Bob's approach to any group meeting is to let other people speak first and to hold his fire. If it comes out the way he thinks it should, then he doesn't feel the need to come in. If it's like it's organic to the group, fine, works for him, let's move on. If it doesn't work for him, if they're going in a different direction, then Bob will speak up.

It was this kind of a meeting where he was really quiet for a lot of the discussion. Then, when it felt like the voices against same-sex coverage were starting to build, Bob did something he normally doesn't do. He said, "Wait, I want to tell you guys what I think about this." I remember this clearly. He says, "This is discrimination. I don't care what form it is, it's discrimination and it's wrong. I don't know about you guys, but I'm not putting my name on something that discriminates against a certain group of people, period. If you guys want to do it, you're going to have to get somebody else to sign it."

It was really short, didn't give a lot of details, didn't have the rhetoric or speech about gay rights. It was just very clear and solid: It's discrimination, it's wrong, and I'm not going to have any part of it. That shut the whole thing down. Everybody turned to Bob and there was silence. Then people who were speaking said, "Well, wait. We're not necessarily saying this is what we're going to do." There was a lot of backtracking and pretty soon it was like, "Okay, we're not going to make a distinction with same-sex couples. They're covered." That was very impressive. It was a beautiful moment. I wish everybody in the union was there and able to see it.

In 2008, not long after Bob took office as International president, the ILWU's Pacific Coast longshore contract came up for renewal. Bob had served on previous coast longshore contract negotiating committees, but this was his first as International president. Shortly before the negotiations began, members of a left progressive group in San Francisco's longshore Local 10 pushed for a May Day waterfront shutdown to protest America's unpopular wars in Iraq and Afghanistan. May Day is significant for its symbolic value. It is celebrated in many countries to honor workers. Its origins in America date back to labor's long battle for the eight-hour day in the nineteenth century that reached a high point with a major 1886 confrontation in Chicago.[6]

May Day, with its special overtones of struggle and militancy, was intentionally selected by the Local 10 activists for their protest. Their move was reminiscent of 1984, when San Francisco maritime activists staged an eleven-day boycott of South African cargo in protest of apartheid in that country. Six years later, Nelson Mandela publicly credited the boycott with helping end South African apartheid.[7]

In January and February 2008, during an ILWU Longshore Division Caucus, the Local 10 activists introduced their idea for a May Day work stoppage. The caucus, made up of elected delegates from the West Coast's longshore locals, was meeting in preparation for the division's 2008 contract negotiations. A motion was introduced to hold the shutdown during the day on May 1 as a "stop-work" meeting. Stop-work meetings were held periodically for training and other concerns. The motion passed with a strong vote. It seemed possible to view the proposed protest as a stop-work meeting because such meetings could be valid under the longshore contract. Unfortunately, the contract required the PMA to agree to any stop-work meeting during the afternoon shift. The PMA denied permission. Consequently, when an eight-hour coastwide longshore shutdown occurred during the day shift on May 1 it was a violation of the contract.[8] This gave the PMA cause to threaten a lawsuit.

Rob Remar recalls how events unfolded.

ROB REMAR

Around the time of 2008 longshore negotiations, Local 10 passed a resolution to shut down the Port of San Francisco and call for all other locals to shut down West Coast ports coastwise on May Day in protest of the Iraq War. The International wasn't involved in this. In fact, they were opposed to any local-initiated, ad hoc move, or what I would call random initiation of any work stoppage during bargaining. This was because it could and would only be seen as related to bargaining. Even if it wasn't seen that way, it would have the effect of triggering responses in government, among politicians, and in the general business community affecting our bargaining.

This would be bad because any kind of government intervention necessarily has the impact of manacling the union's bargaining power. It would restrict the union's ability to do what it needs to do and is allowed to do under federal labor law in the form of concerted economic actions or job actions that seek to promote the union's bargaining positions and pressure the employer to accept them. The union held that whatever job actions or economic actions that were to be done during longshore contract negotiations were a matter to be controlled by the bargaining committee itself. It has been a long tradition of the ILWU that once bargaining starts it is under the exclusive domain and judgment of the bargaining committee as to when, how, and why any job actions or economic actions take place.

CHAPTER 4

So Local 10 did this resolution to shut down the coast for May Day 2008. Bob was faced with what to do about it. He could try and shut that down, or override it, or preempt it, or he could work with it and run with it. What he decided to do was to use it as a strategy or as a tactic for the 2008 bargaining. My understanding is that he talked with the other locals and with the bargaining committee and they basically picked up the sword on this, ran with it, and said, "Okay, we're going to let the shutdown go forward."

It was pretty clear and based on history with Local 10 that Bob wasn't going to be able to stop it anyway. So Bob was faced with the real political question of, "What do I do with this unstoppable resolution?" He decided to run with it and to turn it into not just a thing against the war, but into a pointed jab at the employers to enhance our bargaining power. The PMA, of course, got wind of this, made threats, and said, "This is a premature job action. We still have a contract, it's in place, and it won't expire for a couple of months, on July first. A May first shutdown is unlawful and we're going to go into court to sue you guys. We're going to get damages. If we get an injunction and you guys go forward then there's going to be high consequences to pay."

Bob comes to me and says, "We have all these threats. I'm still going forward. In many ways the PMA threats make it even more necessary that we go forward and not be stopped." He says, "Remar, do what you can do," because I'm telling him we got no legal ground to stand on. We have a contract in place. There's a no strike clause. It prohibits this kind of thing. They're going to get their injunction. Bob tells me, "I don't care. If they put me in jail then do what you can to get me out. But I'm going forward. Damn the torpedoes, full speed ahead." So that was an extraordinary thing with a lot of pressure on the lawyers to do what we could to protect the union and to protect Bob and the other leaders that were putting their necks out.

At this point Remar digresses to explain how the union customarily evaluated the potentially heavy cost of lawsuits or leadership imprisonments if it broke contracts while supporting social justice causes or antiwar campaigns.

ROB REMAR

This is a much broader issue that's faced by the ILWU all the time. Since the start of my career with the ILWU as counsel in 1985, the union's leaders regularly face this question. They factor in the potential for high money damages and take it very seriously, but usually they decide that's just the price of being a militant union and exercising what bargaining and economic power they have. I think in some ways that's what makes the ILWU different than other unions. That's their willingness to take on those risks and those liabilities and see it as one important factor but not a factor that's going to stop them necessarily. Sometimes it does. They will look at this on a case-by-case basis.

Remar went on to explore the unpredictability of some of the ILWU's actions and to relate this characteristic to the union's much-celebrated practice of union democracy.

ROB REMAR

Whenever the ILWU does something that's unpredictable or that's outside of what other mainstream unions do, it reinforces the notion on the other side that they cannot predict us, that the ILWU is fearless in many ways, and that they're dealing with an entity that cannot be subject to well-orchestrated schemes that the employers or even the government may have about how to corral the ILWU into submission. But it's not like people sit around and say, "We're going to do things that are unpredictable." It's more the nature of the full force of democracy within the ILWU that makes it so that things happen and, often surprisingly, without anybody fully being able to predict it.

After these revealing digressions, Remar returned to the challenge of the 2008 May Day shutdown.

ROB REMAR

We went forward. Ironically, the PMA filed their papers late in court to get an injunction for May Day. They went to the judge and said, "Judge, you've got to stop everything you're doing, listen to our motion, and issue a broad injunction against the ILWU so they don't do any kind of job action here in San Francisco or elsewhere." The judge was Claudia Wilken in the US District Court for Northern California, sitting in the Oakland branch. She was very peeved. According to the papers that the PMA filed, the PMA had known about this for some time and for whatever reasons delayed in getting things filed until the last minute. So the judge held an emergency hearing on the same day that the PMA filed. She did this by telephone. I think she made a point in scheduling the telephone hearing at the end of the day. It was 5:00 or 6:00 because I remember doing the call when I was at home.

Wilken says, "PMA, do you really expect me to be able to read all of the papers, declarations, evidence, and arguments you filed within an hour or two and issue the extraordinary remedy you want? I had a full day today. I can't possibly do that. I'm going to have to kick this over for hearing after I have time to read the papers and give the ILWU an opportunity to respond." Well, I had made a point of filing because I knew this was going to happen. We had prepared papers that we filed with the court and that just added to the thickness of paper that this judge had to read to deal with what the PMA wanted done in just one day.

Our filing helped me focus on what the defenses were to make it clear to the judge that there were serious legal issues in dispute and this wasn't a cakewalk for the PMA, although personally I felt it was a cakewalk for them. The judge threw up her hands and said, "These issues are in dispute. I'm going to put this off. I'm not issuing an injunction. I'll hear the

Fig. 4.1. San Francisco's "Raging Grannies" rallying in support of the ILWU's 2008 May Day West Coast port shutdown to protest the wars in Afghanistan and Iraq. Coming during Longshore Division contract negotiations, the shutdown presented Bob with challenges. Courtesy of Anne Rand Library, ILWU.

motion next week." Well, next week was after May 1. May 1 comes and Local 10 shuts down.

On May Day 2008 the ILWU shut down all twenty-nine of its West Coast ports on the day shift in protest of the wars in Iraq and Afghanistan (see fig. 4.1).[9]

Remar continues his story.

ROB REMAR

By the time the court calendar allowed the PMA to make their motion it was too late. The PMA decided that it was better strategy for them for getting a contract to leave the thing alone. So they withdrew the case

CHAPTER 4

rather than seek punishment. They could have filed for money damages for violation of the "no strike" contract clause in another lawsuit or amended the current one, but they chose not to.

Melvin Mackay was president of Local 10 during the May Day strike. He recalls the 2008 shutdown. Mackay is a mechanic with much experience repairing waterfront equipment. His father and grandfather were active in the Brotherhood of Sleeping Car Porters, the famous African American union founded in the 1920s. Mackay was a member of the Boilermakers Union and the United Auto Workers before joining the ILWU in 1991. He has served multiple terms as Local 10 president.

MELVIN MACKAY

We were in negotiations. I was the president of Local 10 and I was on the negotiating team. Bob and the coast committeemen walked over to Dolores Park in San Francisco and spoke. Big Bob didn't particularly like moving to strike, but since the local did it he wasn't discouraged about going down there speaking. When it came to me that we're not going to work, I expressed to the negotiating team, "We're not going to work, guys." Nobody was taken aback. They understood it. There was other locals that stopped work as well.

Bob also recalled the coastwide shutdown of May Day 2008.

BOB MCELLRATH

Right in the middle of bargaining Local 10 brings this May Day thing. The dissidents are putting out flyers, "We're going to shut down on May Day." They're putting it on emails, they're putting it on every website they can get. Now I had already told my bargaining committee to disclose it:

"No one will work May Day. You are not to dispatch one person on May Day for eight hours. This isn't about shutting down the West Coast, this is about how much power I got with my guys, with our guys looking at PMA to call our bluff. If we lose this, this is going to be crucial for the rest of negotiations."

The PMA hears wind of it, so they come after us. They had all the flyers, all the emails, they had everything. It was simple for people to do nothing, to listen to the president and the negotiating committee that relays it back to the locals—twenty-nine of 'em—and say, "Don't take a job." Nobody knows, right? It just happens. So what does PMA do? They come up here to the International office and they says, "We're going to Kagel, we demand that you do this, we demand that."[10] I said, "Get out of my International. Let me show you the door and don't let it hit you in the ass. I'm not doing a goddamned thing." They went to the judges. Our officers said, "Bob, what are you going to do 'cause they're going to get this restraining order?" Remar's sitting there. I said, "The officers are staying here. Me and you, Remar, we're going to go to the judge." Remar said, "Okay. Then what are you going to do?" I says, "Well, you're going to tell me when I stand up how to politely tell the judge to go fuck himself 'cause we ain't working May Day."

Remar said, "They'll throw you in jail." I said, "Good. When they throw me in jail that's even better. Can you imagine what will happen then? We'll shut down for a week." He said, "Oh, that's not a bad idea." I said, "Yeah, that's what we're going to do. We're not going to blink." Okay, the PMA takes it to the judge. It was a Friday afternoon. The judge said, "What have we got here?" The PMA said, "They're going to shut down May Day." The judge said, "That's not until Monday. Nothing's happened yet so come back to me when you have a problem." The PMA said, "Well, it'll be over by then." The judge said, "Then you won't have a problem." It was just lucky.

Before moving on to look at the specifics of the Longshore Division's 2008 contract negotiations with the PMA, it is helpful to consider Bob and the union's general approach to bargaining. John Castanho, the union's benefits officer, reviews his own background and then describes how Bob routinely functioned as president during Longshore Division Caucuses held to determine the union's bargaining priorities weeks or months before negotiations with the employers began. Recall that the goal of the Longshore Caucus is to get a diverse group of democratically elected delegates to agree on a list of demands in going into bargaining with the PMA.

JOHN CASTANHO

I was born in 1967 in the little town of Crockett, California. Crockett was a C&H Sugar Company town.[11] My parents immigrated there from Madeira Island, Portugal. My grandfather came here first. He was a member of ILWU warehouse Local 6. I'm third-generation ILWU and my son is a fourth-generation member. My father became a member of ILWU Longshore Local 10, San Francisco. I was nineteen when my dad passed away. I got registered in Local 10 under the Child of Deceased Rule. Then I was able to help supplement my mom's income.

On September 1, 1986, I started on the waterfront in Local 10. I was elected secretary-treasurer of the local in 2003. In July 2007 I started the job I presently have as ILWU coast benefits specialist. I had served on the union's Pension and Welfare Committee from '98 or '99 until I was hired for this position. I got interested in pension and welfare as a result of the struggles I saw my mom go through after my dad passed away.

Back then the benefit structure was different than it is today [2017], especially for surviving spouses like my mom. Under the old rules a person who died had to have twenty-five years of service for their surviving spouse to be eligible for ongoing healthcare coverage. That has been changed. Now it's five years. My dad had twenty-one years. Mom was only allowed welfare plan coverage for four years. After that she had to pay Kaiser medical premiums out of her own pocket. So I promised myself that if I could get in a position to help people like my mom I would do whatever I could. As coast benefits specialist I work in conjunction with the union trustees overseeing the implementation of healthcare, pension, and disability benefits and Medicare and Social Security enrollment.

I'm also involved in collective bargaining for issues around pensions and healthcare. I've learned a lot from Bob and not just in the context of working together at the ILWU. I've been with him going on ten years. He's been a great mentor and has taught me how to talk to people, how to listen to people. Bob has a tremendous amount of respect up and down the coast. He's earned it over the years. What he says at these caucuses carries a tremendous amount of weight. He does a very good job of not asserting his opinions on every matter because he likes to hear from the rank and file about what their feelings are. That is a very responsible thing for a person to do, especially when they know they have a lot of influence.

Bob could easily speak on ten different subjects and probably have 85 percent of the room agree with him. But what he likes to do is pick one or two really important matters he feels strongly about and speak on them. Even then he'll wait until after all the rank-and-file delegates have had a chance to speak at the caucus. Most other issues he'll just set aside and let the rank and file debate the issues and not offer an opinion unless he is asked.

Rob Remar recalls Bob's heading of the ILWU Negotiating Committee during 2008 longshore contract bargaining. His remarks echo John Castanho's characterization of Bob's leadership of the Longshore Division's pre-negotiations caucuses.

ROB REMAR

Bob's style of leadership was played out in full in 2008 bargaining. His approach consistently was building consensus, getting the bargaining committee members to throw out ideas. He's got an idea of where he wants to go, but he lets others start first. Sometimes people would have ideas that were similar to Bob's. Then Bob would help facilitate the discussion and facilitate consensus. Other times there would be discussion about an approach that was different from Bob's. He's got an open mind enough to know that neither he nor any one person has all the right answers. Then he might go, "Wow, this is a better way to go." Bob would speak on it toward the end and that would be the consensus.

Other times during 2008 the discussion would go in a direction that Bob thought was bad. He would wait to make his move and say, "Hey, people, I think we need to look at it a different way. Here's my thinking." Nine times out of ten people would follow that because of the power and validity of what he was saying. Sometimes they would follow it because of the reputation and the creditability Bob had built over the years. He's an extraordinary negotiator and strategist and a very shrewd guy. Oftentimes people would just defer to that reality.

Bob too outlined his approach to building a unified stance on the negotiating committee while at the same time accommodating the concerns of the various regional locals of the Longshore Division.

BOB MCELLRATH

Everybody gets to send somebody to negotiations. The wants and needs of somebody in San Francisco may be entirely different than what somebody wants out of Seattle or LA. When everybody comes together we start at caucus with resolutions and debate them. Then we move to the negotiating table with what's left. Everybody has gotten their share of what they want, how they want it done. No matter if it comes out of Aberdeen or San Francisco, there's a reason it is on the table and you have to understand it. I try to understand everybody's issues.

John Castanho described how Bob dealt with the PMA during 2008 longshore negotiations themselves. He reviews Bob's overall approach and then recalls one particularly vivid incident from 2008 bargaining sessions.

JOHN CASTANHO

I met Bob years ago, but I didn't really know him that well until I started working at the International in '07 and got to see how he approached and interacted with Jim McKenna of the PMA during the 2008 negotiations. What I found about Bob not only through collective bargaining but just in general is that he is a much smarter person than people give him credit for. He's like a chess player. Bob has the ability to see two or three moves down the road. He is able to formulate strategy based on what he anticipates employers or adversaries will do. It's a very unique set of skills that he has that I haven't seen in too many people.

I got a really good one from 2008. We're sitting there bargaining healthcare. Chiropractic coverage was being discussed. Much like they do so often, the employer trustees were complaining of what they perceived as fraudulent billing related to claims. The union put forward a demand where the group of chiropractors that members would be able to see under the plan would be restricted to a defined number of providers enrolled in a network known as a PPO, preferred provider organization. This was our idea. Bob is sitting on one side of the table. Jim McKenna's on the other side. But because this was the healthcare portion of the plan, Michael Wechsler, the PMA's chief finance officer, was doing all the talking and interacting with Bob.

Wechsler is also an employer trustee on the welfare and the pensions plan. Bob slides our demand across the table. It says we'll select a PPO our guys have to go into. It'll save the plan money. There'll be more oversight, so we'll address the PMA concerns about possible fraudulent activity. It'll be better for our members because it'll get away from fraudulent billing, collection notices, and that sort of thing.

Wechsler takes a look at the paper. He sets it aside very casually, didn't give it much thought. He says, "We don't feel like we need to get involved with any chiropractic networks." Bob said, "So you don't want it?" Wechsler says," No, we don't need it." Bob's face starts turning red. He reaches across, slams his entire arm on the table, grabs the paper, pulls it back, and crumples it up. He said, "Fine, it's off the table. What's next?"

At that point Jim McKenna had the foresight to think, "Let's take a time out." The employers caucused for a long time, I think the rest of that day. We got back together the next morning. Apparently they made some phone calls to the plan consultant and to some network providers. They found that this was actually a good idea. It was a cost-saving measure to the plan and it was beneficial to our members. When we sat down Wechsler was quiet. Jim McKenna took over. Jim starts asking about our idea. Bob was very coy. He goes, "What are you talking about? That is off the table. You guys had that yesterday to discuss. Remember, I crumpled that thing up and threw it away. We're on to the next subject now." Jim persisted. He said, "We think this may not be a bad idea."

Bob said, "Fine. Put it back on the table as an employer proposal but you're going to have to buy it now." So they took another caucus and we ended up getting a really nice improvement in our vision benefits for glasses and contact lenses. This was a quid pro quo. The tradeoff was that this network would be implemented in exchange for an improvement in our vision benefits. Nobody anticipated the employers saying "no" out-of-handedly to something when we were trying to address their concerns and the concerns of our members at the same time. Bob handled it perfectly. He made a show where he was visibly angry, but on purpose to demonstrate to their negotiating committee that their guy didn't know what he was talking about. I'll never forget that one. It's one of the best negotiating moves I've ever seen.

Remar also discussed the anger strategy that Bob sometimes used in negotiating with the employers during 2008. His comments resonate with Castanho's recollections. McEllrath's 2008 approach is reminiscent of how he dealt internally with the ILWU Alaskan crisis he faced as International vice president in the early 2000s.

There were a few occasions when the employers did or said something in bargaining that so pissed off Bob that he blew up, chastised them, called it the way he saw it, stood up, and said, "I'm outta here." Then the whole ILWU committee would get up and follow him and we would lose a day of bargaining or we would go back to our internal caucus meetings. I would always be surprised when that would happen. I would not see it coming. But it was very clear to me, either in talking with Bob or in observing what was going on in the aftermath of those occurrences, that all of it was strategic and planned out. When Bob gets mad and does something extraordinary like walk out, it's not because his emotions have got the better of him. Instead, it's because he's decided that using his emotions, which are always authentic, is a good tactic to bring forward what we need to get done and to put pressure on the employers.

George Romero was president of ILWU longshore Local 10 during the early and middle 1990s. In 1998 he became the union's benefits special-ist. He held that position for ten years before John Castanho took over the job. Romero was at the 2008 Longshore Division negotiations. His brief comments echo what Castanho and Remar remember.

GEORGE ROMERO

Bob is good at dealing with the PMA. He doesn't seem to let them get him offtrack. I think he manages them well and he's pretty firm with them. They know that he's not going to give anything up. He realizes that this is his legacy and he doesn't want it messed up by some bad deal.

George Cobbs, an African American longshore worker, became a Local 10 member in 1965. He was a widely respected pioneer in the field of alcohol and drug recovery. Cobbs worked for the ILWU-PMA Alcohol and Drug Recovery Program, first as Northern California coordinator and then as coast director, between 1980 and his retirement in 2003. He then served as an officer of the ILWU Pacific Coast Pensioners' Association. Like others quoted, Cobbs observed the development of Bob's leadership over time.[12]

GEORGE COBBS

I wasn't always impressed with Bob. Then I learned as he become the president how valuable this man was. He was smarter than I gave him credit for. Today [2016] we have a really good relationship. I've helped Bob with arbitration. I know a lot about alcoholism and drugs and I know the ins and outs of the rules. One case, Bob was scared to move it forward until they interviewed me. Bob was smart enough to listen to see if you blowing smoke or if you really know what it is you're talking about. He heard the things I said. Then he said, "Yeah, let's move it ahead."[13]

The other good thing about Bob, he a fighter, he like to fight. That's not a bad thing to have about your leader. If it's something that is worth having, then I think it is worth fighting for.

We now turn to the main industrial issues of the ILWU's bargaining with the PMA in 2008. Rob Remar was close to the union's negotiating for its Longshore Division contract that year. In what follows he puts the key issues of 2008 and Bob's role in bargaining that year into perspective.

ROB REMAR

Our 2002 bargaining dealt with marine clerk automation. By 2008, when Bob was president, he as well as the Longshore Division itself through its caucus wanted to focus on automation as it affected traditional longshore jobs. Things had occurred in technology between 2002 and 2008 to make it apparent that the next wave of technology was going to affect long-shore workers more than clerks. One of the primary objectives of ILWU bargaining for 2008 was to secure protections related to work that's left over from the introduction of new technologies.

What we were looking at was what we were calling the third wave of mechanization in the longshore industry. Following containerization, the big change was the internet and the ability of the employers to process their information and their inventory in the terminals by means of networked computers. That was what 2002 bargaining was about. By 2008 we were looking at robotics, the idea that a machine was going to be man-less, to use an old-school term, and this technology was going to replace operators of machines. Most of the longshore jobs in container ports involve operating different types of cranes. In looking at the new technology and the consequences of it, it was clear to us that the jobs that would be left over would be the mechanic jobs [see fig. 4.2].

That is to say that robotics would replace the people that used to perform the jobs. So what's left? Servicing the robotics, that is, doing the mechanical work for keeping the robotics in service, maintained, and repaired. From our point of view the mechanics became the direct successors of the crane operators. We took the position in bargaining, and this was one of Bob's main priorities, that there was going to be a quid pro quo for the employers to introduce robotics. From Bob's perspective and philosophy there was nothing we could do in reality to stop robotics, nor did the union really want to because the Longshore Division in the last ten or fifteen years had come to the understanding that taking a bargaining position to stop technology is an unwinnable and self-defeating position. You also lose creditability with the outside world. So you have to ride the wave of technology and get what you can. That was the approach with 2008.

The idea was that the union would agree to free rein for the employers to introduce their robotics. In exchange, the ILWU gets all of the remaining jobs plus all of the new jobs created from this new technology to the extent that the new jobs are functionally equivalent to the long-shore jobs that are being displaced. This basic concept got adopted in the 2008 contract. We took many weeks of hard bargaining to hammer this

Fig. 4.2. Longshore crane driver, container overhead, San Francisco waterfront. By 2008, with robotics threatening to replace waterfront machine operators, automation became an important topic in ILWU longshore contract negotiations. Courtesy of Frank Silva, photographer.

out and get the contract language that is now part of Section 1.7 and some related letters of understanding, which we call LOUs.[14]

The disruptive side of accelerating automation looms as a major challenge to all workers in the twenty-first century. The speed and degree of automation may be new, but the elemental danger to workers of technological displacement is not. In the Pacific Coast longshore industry, the ship owners first got the right to introduce labor-saving devices in Section 11(d) of the federal arbitration award that followed the 1934 strike.[15] That principle carried over to the Mechanization and Modernization Agreement of 1960 that Harry Bridges sponsored and his membership voted for. "M and M" allowed the ship owners to introduce containerization unimpeded in exchange for certain concessions. This peaceful revolution in seaborne freight transportation replaced hand-worked, "break-bulk" cargo handling with a big metal box shipping system. The containers, called "cans" by the workers, ultimately became standardized at twenty to forty feet. They are lifted on and off ships by huge cranes. The cans are transported to and from the waterfront by truck and rail.[16]

Because containerization promised to reduce the waterfront workforce, M and M included guaranteed job security for current registered workers and incentives for early retirement. As part of the arrangement, the union gave up many of its hard-won work rules, which returned much dockside power to the employers that they had lost in 1934. Once M and M was in place, the employers increased the weight of formerly limited sling loads of traditional break-bulk cargo, making an already demanding job harder and more dangerous. Still, early retirements plus the increase of cargo tonnage during the Vietnam War hid the immediate impact on job opportunities of increased productivity under M and M.

In 1966 M and M was renewed. It included a controversial clause that let the employers hire some permanent workers, nicknamed "steady men," who did not have to report to the union hiring hall for job assignments. Activists worried that this could undermine allegiance to the union. This problem, recognition around 1970 that now there were fewer jobs on the waterfront, and general dissatisfaction with M and M helped lead to the major coastwide longshore strike of 1971–72. Finally, with containerization taking over the waterfront almost completely by the late 1970s, it was clear that productivity had increased tremendously while job opportunities had fallen precipitously. [17]

M and M remained controversial for years. Some people still question certain sections of the two contracts, including the 1966 "steady man" clause. Many feel denied by the decline of waterfront jobs. Had there been a better way to soften the blow of technological change? The union fought the employers tenaciously in the early years. There were major strikes over important principles. There were numerous short-term work stoppages. Between 1934 and 1948 there were 349 longshore industry shutdown days.[18] Would resistance and guerrilla warfare have staved off containerization or gained more for ILWU members in the 1960s? This option worked in the short run for the ILA, which resisted the forces of change and hung on to its traditional large work gang structure as long as it could. But before long the ILA too had to accept wage guarantees in return for granting the employers greater flexibility. Within a few years containerization dominated East and Gulf Coast ports of the US as much as it did West Coast ports.[19]

The 2008 contract was supposed to provide that all new jobs created by automation would be ILWU jobs. Thus the union saw the protection of waterfront mechanics jurisdiction as key. Still, within a decade of the signing of the 2008 contract, the employer move toward the use of robots to totally automate ports seemed suspect. It was not even clear that robots were more productive than good crane drivers. But robots did have the potential to eliminate union people. Some observers felt that this was the employers' main concern. In response, the union enlisted community support in an effort to stop a Port of Los Angeles permit the Maersk Shipping Company requested to totally automate its big Pier 400 terminal. Maersk's move threatened to cost hundreds of ILWU jobs and to depress the economy of the Southern California Harbor Area. ILWU longshore Local 13 president

Mark Mendoza proclaimed, "Automation is not good. It's not good for the community, it's not good for labor, it's not good for America."[20]

ILWU officers and rank-and-file members, leaders from various non-ILWU local unions, small-business owners, and even some area politicians went on marches, attended packed meetings, and spoke against the idea of trading jobs for robots. Regardless, in mid-2019 the Los Angeles Board of Harbor Commissioners voted three to two to move forward with automation at Pier 400 despite Commissioner Diane Middleton's strong voice in disagreement.[21] It was a close call, but even a spirited appeal to the community could not hold back technological "progress," at least not in this case.[22]

In retrospect, the responses to technological change that the ILWU took in 1960 and even 2002 and 2008 look practical-minded, the idea being to get what you can while the getting is good. This was the case even if those responses provided only partial and at times controversial answers to the ongoing problem of "the machine" and even if some aspects of the resulting contracts could be vexing.

Since the longshore industry is a global enterprise, members of the autonomous ILWU Canada located primarily in British Columbia began to worry about advanced port automation in roughly the same era that Bob did. Tom Dufresne went to work on the Port of Vancouver, British Columbia, waterfront as a casual longshoreman in 1971. He was twenty years old. In 1982 Dufresne became a full member of ILWU longshore Local 500. He subsequently served as president of the local and then, between 1996 and 2013, as president of ILWU Canada. His observations about automation parallel those of his fellow ILWU unionists in the US.

TOM DUFRESNE

In my opinion, and in a lot of people's opinions, what we are seeing nowadays [2013] with the conversion to greater automatics is that the hours are going to be in the trades in the repair and maintenance of equipment, computers, and what have you. We have to be able to seize those jobs for our future. We went from hand-held sack cargo to forklifts to bigger sling loads of palletized lumber and then to packaged lumber. It is the changing nature of work. There was resistance to those ideas when they came along, but like anything in that nature, it is going to prevail. But you have to make sure that you can secure your work.[23]

Following up from Remar's and Dufresne's comments, Bob discusses technology and his part in the union's 2008 longshore contract negotiations.

BOB MCELLRATH

I bargained mechanics in 2008 because technology is coming. I get a kick out of people. They said, "Oh, we're not going to allow it." I got on the docks in 1969. If we said we weren't going to allow it, we'd still be picking up wooden hatch covers.[24] It's not feasible. You can't do it. I wasn't around, obviously, but when they put the 1960 Mechanization and Modernization Agreement in, acceptance took quite a while. I've read about that. I'm sure there was a lot of angry people on that one saying, "Harry sold us out," and all this stuff. Perhaps Harry could see it coming. I could see it. That's why in 2008 I says, "We want all the work because mechanization is coming again and I want all the electrical work, mechanics work, all the IT work. I want all the work 'cause we're losing jobs." Some people are saying, "You got to fight technology and you got to fight mechanization." I got up to give a speech one time and I says, "Technology is coming. You can't stop it. Technology's coming whether you and I like it or not."

Bob had been thinking about the future of waterfront maintenance and repair work (M and R) done by mechanics for some time before negotiations for the 2008 contract started. Former San Jose State football player and M and R pioneer Tom Hebert recalls his background and early career, his precontact conversations with Bob, Bob's support of mechanics, and the results of the 2008 contract negotiations.

TOM HEBERT

I was born June 1, 1951, in San Pedro, California. My father was a long-shoreman. He worked as a gear man and on the waterfront.[25] When I was going through college I worked as a casual longshoreman and as a mechanic. There was no money in coaching and teaching. I went back down to Southern California and became an International Association of Machinists (IAM) mechanic in December of '74. Then the ILWU had openings. This was in January 1985.

When I got into the ILWU they said, "Would you like to help us with M and R?" I said, "Okay." I was working at American President Lines as a mechanic. I became a steward at APL in the power shop and worked there from '85 to '92. In 1992 I ran for business agent in longshore Local 13 and won. I was also the M and R representative. That was a volunteer thing. They didn't have anybody taking care of M and R. It was in its infancy. We had a committee and negotiated our own supplement and I was always the chairman.[26]

In M and R we only hired people that were qualified. A lot of them came from the IAM. We got them from the surrounding industries. A lot of IAM guys wanted out of the IAM. They didn't like the way it was run because their officers are appointed, they weren't voted in. Ours was a democratic group. Now [2014] you have close to a thousand ILWU mechanics. I have been professing for years that the mechanics will be more and more important. Even when I left Local 13 in 2000 and became a Local 63 marine clerk, I still was involved with M and R.

I met Bob in 1989. Big Bob and I have been huntin' and fishin' partners for years. You couldn't ask for a better leader. He knows how to handicap a situation, and he can do it quickly, especially when it comes to pensions and monies and the way the employer thinks. He has something very few people have. The best contract Bob got through was the six-year 2008 contract where we secured so much jurisdiction, especially in M and R. The only problem we have is the employers have used every scam in the world to get this work away from us.[27]

Bob too asserted that the employers engaged in bad faith by failing to adhere to their agreements with the union regarding technology. Below he outlines this feeling, which includes concern for employer infringement on the union's contractually guaranteed jurisdiction over waterfront jobs recently altered by technological innovation.

BOB MCELLRATH

They haven't done it in good faith. The problem with the 2002 clerk's thing is that we've got a framework for automation, but by the time you have a meeting and you explain to the employers that you've caught them—maybe management's doing the job or somebody else is doing the job—they say, "Okay." Then by the time you get to arbitration they've changed the whole file and they do it another way. We show them where we caught them but they've fixed it and they go, "Where is it at?" They're terrible, they really are.

With maintenance, repair, and fixing these huge pieces of equipment, that's where we're constantly in a fight with the employers. If something breaks, they want to bring in somebody and say, "This is under warranty" or "Take it off the dock and have 'em fix it and bring it back." We say, "You can't do that. We can fix it." But they always like to say that we don't have the capability to fix it, which is completely wrong because we've got great mechanics, we've got people that are great electricians. We can do it all.

Despite sharing Bob's concerns about employer bad faith, Tom Hebert remained upbeat in summarizing his view of Bob's contribution to the union's efforts to deal with technological change.

Bob had the vision to take the ILWU into the modern age. He had it way back and we talked about it. Bob was always behind me in M and R. We would discuss it, study it, chew it up, and spit it out, what we should do, what we shouldn't do. We'd go fishing, we'd talk about M and R. We're drinking a couple of glasses of wine, having cigars, and we're talking about the union, what we're trying to do, and where we're going in the modern age.

In the period around the 2008 longshore contract year, ILWU organizer Peter Olney advocated that in addition to securing M and R, the union should aggressively expand unionization along the product supply chain. He saw as a precedent the union's organizing of waterfront and then uptown warehouse workers in the 1930s to protect against the ship owners recruiting low-paid, unorganized freight handlers as strike breakers during any longshore labor dispute. In later years, the union undertook two major long-term organizing efforts in California that reflected Olney's thinking. The first, at the Blue Diamond Almond Growers facility in Sacramento, failed in 2008. The other, at a big Rite Aid Drug Company distribution warehouse in Lancaster, succeeded in 2011 after a long struggle.[28]

Lawrence Thibeaux, a former secretary-treasurer and president of ILWU longshore Local 10, has been active in the ILWU Pacific Coast Pensioners Association since he retired in 2009. He also thought strategically. In his 2016 oral history he connected technological change and organizing.

LAWRENCE THIBEAUX

When we were doing handwork we had control over production. How are you going to cope with this information technology (IT) thing when you don't have control over the program? You have an agreement that says trucks are supposed to stop here, do this, do that, but then you don't have control over the program to make that work under your contract. In fact, the IT guy can bypass all that. And as long as you don't have control over the production, you don't have anything. My fear is that we're losing the control over production. The bottom line is that there's a human being somewhere that's bypassing us and that's the guy we need to be looking for so that we can organize that guy into the ILWU.

Unfortunately, isolating and organizing the right person or even the right group of people along the supply chain is not often simple or easy, especially during an era when labor law is not in your favor. After the loss of the Blue Diamond campaign, which was costly and took a long time to bring to an NLRB [National Labor Relations Board] election, Bob decided that very expensive, multiyear organizing would not be undertaken anew while he was still in office as ILWU president.

One of Bob's goals as president that proved readily attainable, though, was the significant upgrading of the funding the employers had to contribute to the union's longshore pension fund. Bob recalls how that came about in 2008 and after.

BOB MCELLRATH

The employers had gotten relief on the pension plan. They paid $19 million one entire year.[29] That is when you rob Peter to pay Paul. We had to catch up. I maintained that the employers were going to put money in. The employers want to pay the minimum that they have to spend. Well, they stepped up and they had to put in. They were putting in from the 2008 contract moving forward certain amounts of money and I made sure they kept at it. They were putting in between $45 and $55 million a month. I wouldn't let them up.

The employers had to double up, triple up, and quadruple up their monies to catch up for what they had gained back there. And I wasn't going to let 'em up. I told them, "You're paying. You're paying or we're coming," and they did. We'd been in the forties, low-forties, mid-forties percent funding level. With the help of ERISA attorneys and myself and pushing the employers, today [2018] we're at 98 percent.[30] I feel that if I did anything, I feel good about the pension plan.

Former Local 10 president Melvin Mackay comments on Bob's leadership as well as his handling of ILWU Longshore Division finances.

MELVIN MACKAY

Big Bob goes out of his way to assist. We don't see eye to eye on every issue, but for the most part the man has been a great leader in my eyesight. Bob knows how to assemble and read people and he wants to help. He'll help Local 10, Hawaii, Canada. The man is also very conscious about the structure of the union. I can tell Bob about the problems I have in Local 10. If they have coastwise significance, he'll say, "Let's go for it." If it's a detriment, he'll tell me, "No." He's also brought the forefront of the waterfront to a different plateau. When Bob took over we didn't have much money in our coffers. By hook or by crook, we have money now [2017].

In looking back at the 2008 coast longshore contract while being interviewed in 2013, Bob compared that agreement to past contracts he had helped negotiate. Notably, the 1999 contract reduced the number of years a worker who died had to have on the waterfront to qualify a surviving spouse for long-term medical coverage. This adjustment eliminated the kind of medical coverage problem John Castanho's mother faced when her husband passed away in 1986. In the 2008 contract, too, Bob managed to correct what he considered a mistake dating back to 1993.

BOB MCELLRATH

The best two contracts since '87 and '90 were the two negotiated in 1999 and 2008. They cleaned up a lot of medical stuff and we didn't have to give away everything. The 2008 was the only contract that was voted up unanimous at the caucus. The '99 agreement there were a few "no" votes. But the 2008 was 100 percent voted up. Made me feel good. In 2008 we got the good pension, we got good welfare, and medical benefits—teeth and all, and glasses. And in '99 we got a good one. We straightened up a whole bunch of things. For example, if you were on the waterfront for twenty-three or twenty-four years and you died, your spouse only got medical benefits for four years. My mother fell into this. When my father passed away she only got medical the next four years. If you had twenty-five years, then your spouse was carried on the books. In 1999, there was 176 widows and partners on the list that did not have medical benefits and my mother was one of them.

We gave the employers a sheet with the 176 listed. I watched them. It went like one page, two page, and then they went like this [demonstrating] and they went to the "M's," and there's my mother, Rosemary McEllrath. So they were working me, right? During the break I'm in the hallway. Miniace, the PMA president then, says, "I see your mother's on there." I go, "Yeah." He says, "So, is this kind of like for your mom?" I says, "No, it's for all 176 of them."

I said, "My mom's on there and I'm going to take care of her just like you're taking care of your mom." Miniace flew his mom here to San Francisco from where he was from and had her at the Sutter Home for the Elderly. I knew that. I said, "I'm doing the same thing you're doing." He goes, "Okay." He just walked away. I knew we were going to succeed. We changed the rules from twenty-five years to five years. Now if you're married and you're on the waterfront and you've got five qualifying years and you die, your spouse is cared for. Those were some great things we did in '99.[31]

The worst contract was the one in 1993. I was still negotiator for the five small ports on the Columbia River and so I sat at the coast longshore contract negotiating table. That's when they took away the inter-port travel pay up and down the coast.[32] I think we could have kept that and still got a pension increase. That's when ILWU president David Arian went from thirty-nine dollars per year of service for pensions to sixty-nine dollars. To get to there we gave away all the travel, inter-port travel. It's still a sore spot in a lot of people. I was asked to sit on the coast committee, like I told you earlier, in 1993 and '94, so I came to San Francisco. David had to go down to Local 10 and I went with him. I didn't think we were going to get out of there. I really thought it was coming. Finally some guys escorted us to the parking lot and into the car to get out.

George Romero recalls this situation vividly.

GEORGE ROMERO

In '93 I was the president of Local 10. But I wasn't negotiating. I was busy trying to be president of the local. Ralph Rooker [a Local 10 activist] was always watching what was going on. He came down and told me, "Hey, George, they're talking about taking away our travel time." We got ahold of Dave Arian, who was the International president, and had him come down and meet with the executive board. He told us, "They're not going to take your travel time." Well, it turned out that they gave us this transition trust. It used some formula that didn't provide as much. It was only supposed to be there for the life of that contract. So they did take our travel time basically. What the Longshore Division got for that travel time was a major increase in the pension. That did not go down well at all. Oh, the membership was hostile.

Bob recounted how things played out.

BOB MCELLRATH

I'd voted for giving up the travel pay in 1993. I didn't like it. It's one of those things in your early days if you look back, you think, "I wish I hadn't have." It really didn't affect a lot of us where I represented in the Northwest. I thought, "A bridge toll, that doesn't affect me, I just go to work." It really affected more of, obviously, San Francisco. Every time a worker there gets a job located in the East Bay it costs five or six bucks for the toll to come across the Oakland bridge. Well, in 1993 I was a young guy sitting there and I'm thinking, "It doesn't really hurt us." It was a big fight with David Arian in Local 10 though. But in 2008 we got their toll back. Every time they get a job they get five or six bucks for the toll and if the bridge toll goes up, the toll payment goes up.[33] I've tried every year to get that thing back. So we did that in 2008.

Another 2008 contract-related issue arose shortly after the ILWU and the PMA signed the Pacific Coast longshore agreement in July. Soon the American economy took a serious downturn known as the Great Recession. Expressing financial concern, the shippers asked for relief from their pension obligations. Bob recalled his response.

BOB MCELLRATH

The employers wanted $350 million back from the pension plan, to not have to pay into it. I called for a two-day Longshore Division Caucus. I gave a speech about what the employers wanted. Then I told the caucus, "I'm going to tell the employers, 'No, you're not going to get it back.' I want you guys to tell me why I should say 'yes.'" So I reversed it. By the end of the two days, everybody said, "We agree with you, Bob, tell them 'no.'" And I told them "no." About six to eight months after I told the

PMA's Jim McKenna "no," that I wasn't going to give it back, we were having a lunch or a dinner and he told me that it was probably the best move I ever made. He said, "It was the right thing for you to do."

Things, though, do not always turn out right for any person. As noted earlier, in late 2008 the union lost an important National Labor Relations Board union certification election at the Blue Diamond Growers of Sacramento, California. This followed a four-year effort to organize what was the largest almond-processing facility in the world. With eight hundred employees, including five hundred hourly workers who were eligible to vote, the plant was an attractive target. The plan was to organize the Blue Diamond workers into ILWU warehouse, processing, and distribution Local 17 of West Sacramento. Victory there promised to strengthen the union's Warehouse Division, which had suffered declining numbers in recent years, and to establish an important beachhead in the product transportation supply chain.

Worker grievances were real enough. Hourly employees were poorly paid and company contributions to worker health insurance were meager. The company made the eligibility requirements for paid time off for illness and vacations so difficult to meet that few workers could qualify. One worker with twenty-eight years of service could not qualify for time off for a decade. Blue Diamond also would not identify harmful chemicals its employees were exposed to when workers inquired. Regardless, in response to the ILWU's organizing effort, Blue Diamond mounted an aggressive union-busting campaign. The company engaged professional anti-union consultants to intimidate the workers, half of whom were Latino, in one-on-one and captive group meetings that were lawful under Taft-Hartley.[34]

In 2006 a federal judge ordered the company to rehire two workers it had fired for union activity in violation of the National Labor Relations Act. Yet Blue Diamond still threatened people with dismissal well into 2008 if they joined or supported the union. When the NLRB election was finally held, it went 353 to 142 against Local 17.[35]

A few years later, Bob commented on what had happened at Blue Diamond. As may be recalled, he emphasized that costly, long-term organizing drives would henceforth be avoided while he was ILWU president. Here he reviews the detail of his thinking.

BOB MCELLRATH

Blue Diamond started when I was the vice president and head of organizing. I listened to a lot of people around me. Blue Diamond goes on and on and on. We flew all over the world trying to get support for Blue Diamond, wherever the nuts are going or not going. We spent thousands and thousands of dollars on that and came up short. I think a four-year campaign is just way too long. If you go in and you're going to organize and you get the people rolling, you should call for the question six or eight months into it. Four and a half or five and a half years of organizing will never happen again as long as I'm president.[36] If you haven't got them figured out and you can't card them in eight or nine months, then we're out 'cause you lose that surge, that thing, the way to go.[37]

During June 2009 the ILWU met again in convention, this time at the Westin Hotel on Fifth Street in Seattle. Bob had one last internal crisis to deal with as his first three-year term as International president came to a close. That crisis might seem to have its humorous side in retrospect, but it probably did not seem very funny to Bob at the time. Rob Remar recalls that occasion.

ROB REMAR

We're at this hotel. A lot of people are there and the ILWU members are a pretty rough-and-tumble bunch, right? They work hard and they live hard. They can be pretty rowdy, especially when they congregate with libations. Well, one night there was a party in one of the hospitality rooms, which is simply a big guest room that is designated for gatherings, parties, food, and, of course, alcohol. The place was packed and we were really loud. The whole idea of having a hospitality room among the guest rooms is a problem. But that's how the hotel had designated it instead of having us use a business or conference room on a different floor from the guest rooms.

So you're getting to 10:00, 11:00, 12:00 p.m., and a lot of guests in nearby rooms were complaining to management about the noise. Apparently—I didn't see the beginning of it—the hotel security came up and told people to quiet down, be cool, stop making noise. That didn't work. Then they came back and started barking orders. Now I'm sure hotel security is used to people following orders, behaving, and being submissive. Their approach didn't work too good for our group, who were pretty well toasted. Some started barking back at them. Bob comes out into the hallway where there was a yelling match or something. I'm pretty sure there wasn't anything physical. I follow Bob. He doesn't ask me to go, he's doing his own thing. But I want to see if I could help.

Bob's trying to calm things down. He says, "Look, everything's cool, we're good. We'll get the party calm." The security guards say, "No, no, it's too late for that. You all have to leave the hotel now. We're kicking you out." Bob's trying to convince them otherwise: "No, that's crazy. We're in the middle of this convention. We've got a contract with you guys. You're not approaching this correctly!" They said, "We're calling the cops." So some cops come. Bob talks to them and says, "I get it. The guests want their peace and quiet. We're really sorry. We'll stop making noise. Let's deal with this down in the lobby."

Everybody goes toward the lobby. In our group there must have been 150 people. We get to the lobby and there's about a dozen police officers with their batons out. They're shoulder to shoulder with all the hotel security guards, which must have been another dozen. They formed a line in the lobby and tried to corral us into a corner. There's yelling and screaming back and forth. The police are saying, "We're going to escort you to your rooms, but you're all going to get out now. If you don't leave the hotel, we're going to arrest you." There's a few Hawaiians in our group. These guys were fighting mad and ready to have a brawl with the police. There's a lot of "Fuck yous, you're not going to kick us out. We've paid our money. You're going to have to make us. Come on." I was near Bob on the front line. You could see close up that the police were terrified and so were the security guards. That terrified me because when a person has a gun and they're scared, it's very dangerous.

Bob says to the cops, "Okay, we'll go. Let me just talk to my people, but I want privacy. I want to tell them what needs to be done." They say, "Okay, okay," and stand back. Bob says, "Everybody follow me." He walks deep into this corner of the lobby where we were corralled. He says, "Do exactly what I say. No questions, no delay. Everybody with me?" They say, "Yeah." I'm wondering, "What is Bob going to do?" He says, "When I say 'go,' everybody run to the elevators and the escalators and run to your rooms. Lock the door, don't come out. They'll have no idea who you are and where you are." We come out of it like it was a big football huddle. Bob says, "Go!" Everybody runs in different directions and leaves. The cops are all nervous but they're not doing anything.

The next day we congregate at the scheduled time for the convention and continue the proceedings. Nobody gets kicked out. They were going to have to kick out everybody because they had no names. They had Bob's name, but once things settled down and I think with the morning they decided not to press the thing. But I don't believe this hotel is ever going to allow for an ILWU event again!

Rob Remar was probably right that the hotel confrontation was dangerous. Obviously, the Westin Hotel incident showed again that Bob could come up with a plan, and quickly, if need be. What he and Rob could not know that evening was that Bob would have to call upon that skill again before long when faced with some even more threatening challenges.

5

"Seeing Where People Are Going"

International President, 2010–2012

> Everybody was watching to see what would happen, to see if the strength and the power of the ILWU still remained intact.
>
> WILLIE ADAMS

At the June 2009 ILWU International Convention in Seattle, Bob was nominated for a second term as president. Given the broad-based support he now enjoyed within the union, he was again the only nominee. Still, the union's democratic procedures were carried out. Joe Cortez of Los Angeles/Long Beach longshore Local 13 nominated Bob. Cortez emphasized one of the familiar refrains of Bob's administration. The president, Cortez said, had "continued to bring solidarity, and one of the most important is that of international solidarity."[1]

Nate Lum of the union's largest local unit, Local 142 from Hawaii, seconded Bob's nomination. Tom Dufresne, the president of ILWU Canada, also seconded Bob. Repeating the international theme, Dufresne highlighted the way Bob "handles himself internationally when he is on the road representing this great union." Richard Cavalli of San Francisco ship clerks Local 34 delivered a third second. Cavalli reminded everyone how Bob had risen "like a Phoenix from the ashes" after his 1994 election loss and applauded his handling of the difficult 2008 longshore negotiations. With no other nominations offered, Cavalli, acting as chair of the proceedings, announced that Bob's name would appear alone for president on the union's official ballot. The assembled convention delegates then treated Bob to a standing ovation.[2]

Shortly after the convention, Bob and the union faced a series of daunting new challenges. Remar, Willie Adams, then ILWU International secretary-treasurer, and Bob recall the lockout of an ILWU local in rural Southern California. The resolution of that dispute illustrated Bob's ability to negotiate with his own people as well as with employers. Adams, Ray Familathe, the ILWU International vice president (mainland), and Bob then discuss the union's struggle to secure a contract at a major drug company distribution warehouse nearby.

Next Bob reviews the amalgamation of the Panama Canal Pilots Union with the ILWU. Joe Fleetwood remembers the ILWU's aid to the Maritime Union of New Zealand during a 2012 Ports of Auckland lockout. Around the same time, the ILWU renewed a mutual aid pact it had with the All-Japan Dockworkers' Union. These instances are good examples of ILWU international outreach during Bob's tenure in office. Finally, Wesley Furtado tells a humorous tale that still contains a serious message about international solidarity, and Remar contributes a story that reveals much about Bob's character.

The first crisis was a 105-day lockout of the 450 members of Local 30, an ILWU miners' affiliate isolated in the small Mojave Desert town of Boron, California, 90 miles southeast of Bakersfield and 120 miles northeast of Los Angeles. The workers' employer, Rio Tinto Corporation, operated a huge open-pit borate mine in Boron that was the biggest of its kind in the world. With offices in London, England, and Melbourne, Australia, Rio Tinto did business on six continents and was one of the world's largest mining conglomerates. The company was also known for exploiting native populations, its own workers, and the environment. For example, in the 1970s and 1980s, Rio Tinto's copper mining on the island of Bougainville in the Pacific contaminated the soil and degraded regional agriculture. When protests and an uprising followed in 1989, the company sided with the local military's brutal efforts to suppress them.[3]

In late 2009 and early 2010, Rio Tinto pushed Local 30 to the brink in contract renewal negotiations. The company had a long record of bitter fights with the union. A 132-day strike in 1974 was particularly violent, with dynamiting and gunplay as common occurrences.[4] Subsequent years were quieter, but during 2009–10, with labor unions generally on the defensive in the United States, Rio Tinto became especially aggressive. The company demanded the ability to eliminate certain jobs from the bargaining unit; to disregard seniority; to contract out numerous jobs; to hire temporary workers; to convert full-time jobs to part-time; to rearrange work shifts without warning; to cut holidays and sick leave; and to reduce pension payments.[5]

Reviewing these demands, the social historian Mike Davis wrote, "Rio Tinto, in essence, claims the right to rule by divine whim."[6] Peter Olney, the ILWU organizing director, concluded, "It was clear from the beginning that the company's objective was the complete evisceration of the labor contract."[7] The Local 30 members, with some coaching from the ILWU International, opted to resist all these concessions with short stop-work meetings and other forms of protest while remaining on the job. Rio Tinto locked them out on February 1, 2010 (see fig. 5.1).[8]

Local 30 mounted a spirited response. Chanting, "We want work," the miners and their families marched to the company gates on the first day of the lockout. Armed guards barred the company's doors while ushering in "scabs," as strikebreaking workers are labeled by unionists. Presenting the struggle to the public as a David-versus-Goliath narrative, over the next three months the ILWU enlisted the help of other unions, community individuals and organizations, and sympathetic politicians. It staged rallies and broadcast its message worldwide. The MUA demonstrated on the ILWU's behalf in Melbourne. The ILWU got inspiring aid from the Los Angeles County

Fig. 5.1. Union supporter Mike Shankin holding a *Los Angeles Times* front-page story forecasting Rio Tinto Corporation's 2010 lockout of ILWU Local 30 miners in Boron, California. Local 30 president Dave Liebengood, *right*, looks on. The company initially offered an extreme "take back" contract that the workers resisted. Courtesy of Anne Rand Library, ILWU.

Federation of Labor in the form of a support caravan that traveled from LA to Boron. Despite Rio Tinto's intimidating hired guards, reinforced by Kern County sheriff's deputies, and the powerful company's intransigence, the union's efforts eventually proved effective. By early May Rio Tinto was ready to settle the dispute.[9]

What remained was the resolution of a bargaining impasse. At this point, Bob stepped into the negotiations. Rob Remar provides the context for those discussions. Willie Adams reviews the Rio Tinto struggle and Bob's part in it. Bob then describes his entrance into the bargain process. In mid-May, Local 30 secured a contract from Rio Tinto that rolled back most of the company's drastic demands and included annual wage increases of 2.5 percent, although there were a few notable compromises. One was that new hires would get a 401(K) savings plan instead of a defined-benefit pension like older employees.[10] Such a compromise, which can divide union members, is not atypical for American unions struggling during a defensive era for organized labor. The company also got to retain some strikebreakers on its payroll.

ROB REMAR

At the time Bob got involved, Local 30 had been bargaining for many months on its own. It had used local attorneys as spokespeople, strategists, and people in charge of bargaining. They had this guy who was a young, relatively inexperienced attorney who was in charge. There was this complete breakdown in communication, rapport, and respect between him and the company negotiators. He was way in over his head. One indicator of that was when we went to find out what kind of legal claims does the local have against the employer, we learned that this attorney never took bargaining notes. So we had no documentation to establish bargaining history. What we ended up with was random note-taking from different members of the committee, none of it comprehensive, none of it very reliable. You cannot establish a legal claim of bad-faith bargaining or other types of illegal unfair labor practices unless you have bargaining notes.

That was very upsetting to us in addition to other problems. There were a lot of personality conflicts, political conflicts, and strategy conflicts within the local. They were also running out of money. They paid all of this money to their attorneys to run the show. It's a double whammy. First, they give up all of their power and all of their own responsibility—"they" meaning the local—to make decisions and to own the strategies. Then secondly, they lose their treasury in paying the attorneys to do this work for them. They went to the International seeking monies and help. Bob's decision was, "No, no, no. I'm not going to give you more heroin to get you all strung out even worse than you've already done. I won't give you money but I will give you our staff and our attorneys and in working with you guys we will help you."

Bob had Ray Familathe, the International vice president, provide support to try to improve things. Ray brought in the organizing staff of the International and had them all relocate to the desert to help build a united force internally among the members to fight the lockout. We had Peter Olney, the union's organizing director, out there. We had Craig Merrilees, the *ILWU Dispatcher* editor, out there. I was not there on any regular basis. I went there several times to deal with specific problems or to attend specific meetings where important decisions were going to be made and they needed the International's legal input. But I was not in the trenches on this one. Through the International we also began building an outside game of getting other unions, other community groups, and politicians to help, which the local had not done.

Bob was overseeing what Ray was doing and what I and other ILWU attorneys were doing. We would go back to him and report, "Okay, here's what's happening," or "Here's the problem." He was involved in helping to formulate what to do. We worked with the local attorneys and primarily with the partner who oversaw the young lawyer, not with him directly as much since he was difficult to deal with. We worked to develop an unfair-labor-practice strategy of National Labor Relations Board charges against the lockout. Eleanor Morton from Leonard Carder, our law firm, and I worked hard on developing the theories, doing the legal research, and collecting the evidence, but it was a team effort with the local attorneys.

We succeeded in convincing the Labor Board that the lockout was unlawful because the company did the lockout based on a last, best, and final proposal that contained provisions that were not mandatory subjects of bargaining. That is, the company wanted certain jobs removed from the bargaining unit. This is a subject matter which, under NLRB law, is nonmandatory. You can't force that in bargaining. The only mechanism for changing a bargaining unit when the parties disagree is filing a petition with the NLRB. The local office of the NLRB announced that they were going to go to court to undo the lockout and get all of these remedies, including monetary remedies, against the company. That changed everything. That was the catalyst for resolving the dispute and the catalyst for Bob getting directly involved.

Bob made a point—this was part of his strategy—of not coming in when the local first wanted the International involved and not getting into the weeds. Instead, he would keep his powder dry and his position distant from the ongoing fight. He would deal with things as an overseer and keep himself preserved for when the time would come for a new face, a new voice, and one much more powerful than there had been before. Then he would come in and try and get a deal and that is exactly what happened.

When the Labor Board announced their position that the lockout was unlawful, the company fired its attorneys and hired new ones. That's when Bob and the new company attorney said, "We want to see if we can settle this thing. We want to settle the NLRB problem and in settling the NLRB problem settle the contract at the same time." That's when Bob got directly involved. Accompanied by Eleanor Morton, who became the lead attorney towards the end, Bob went to downtown San Francisco to meet with Chris Robison, the Rio Tinto Northern Hemisphere CEO, and the company's attorneys.[11]

Later Bob negotiated a deal in a few days in conjunction with the people from the Boron local, but it was Bob's show. He took charge with the local's consent and desire to try and close the deal. Bob pushed back on certain things the company wanted and explained to them why their stance was not only bad for the workforce but also bad for the company. They listened and he got the lockout ended and the contract signed.

Next Willie Adams describes his working relationship with Bob and assesses the Boron struggle, Bob's role in it, and its resolution. Adams, from longshore Local 23 in Tacoma, Washington, was International secretary-treasurer from 2003 to 2018. In 2018 he won election as ILWU International president as Bob looked forward to retirement. Adams was the first African American elected to that office.

WILLIE ADAMS

Everything I seen about Bob, he's been front and center. He's a thinker, very patient. Bob does his best when he's under pressure. He's calm and lets things fester and play out. Bob does an analysis of the challenges in front of him. He's able to do a constant update in his mind and with people about where to go. Bob's also a strong, decisive leader. I mean, he's open-minded, he'll listen, but he'll make the final decision and he'll take the heat for it. People have called Bob a redneck, but Bob has always treated me well. We work very well together. A lot of people don't know Bob. His heart's always been in the right place. I think he sees a lot of injustices and that he has tried to do the best he could for all members in this union.

During Boron, I worked with Vice President Ray Familathe assisting the bargaining committee, getting international and community support, working with other unions, and encouraging the membership in the struggle. What Bob suggested when he first came out to Boron was to let the contract expire. His advice was to allow Rio Tinto to lock us out. Talking to the Local 30 Negotiating Committee, Bob said, "You don't want to find yourself in a strike." He knew they didn't have a strike fund and if they went on strike they wouldn't have an income. At least if they got locked out they would have unemployment coming in. If you got locked out, you would get unemployment benefits, whereas if you went on strike you wouldn't. Also, the sympathy of the public would be on the side of the workers if you were locked out instead of going on strike.[12]

Craig Merrilees and Peter Olney went to Boron after things were going on. They were hands-on when they saw that we weren't making any headway. Both of them worked lots of long hours. Peter had his staff out there. Craig was out there all the time. They knew we had to run a campaign to win the struggle and that's what we did.

We got help from friendly politicians. There was some federal legislation coming out of Arizona. Rio Tinto wanted a land-swap deal put forward by Arizona senator John McCain. It was a $60 billion deal for this copper mine. They weren't able to get that thing moved because California senator Barbara Boxer put a hold on the legislation for us. She talked to McCain. He went to Rio Tinto and said, "You've got to end the lockout. Otherwise, she's got enough senators, the bill is on hold, and we won't be able to move it."

The local had an attorney as their spokesperson. As International officers we felt that attorneys don't speak on behalf of you—that their job is to be there if you get in trouble. But they had an attorney representing them at the negotiating table. We felt that the negotiating committee members, with three hundred years of experience, were the best to speak on their own behalf on their own issues. They were paying a lot of money for this attorney. He had only been out of law school for a couple of years. His strategy, and what we thought and what our attorneys' strategies were, went counterclockwise to each other. He wanted to not negotiate very hard and just drag the process out. Maybe he thought he would wear the company down.

Bob came in as International president and interjected himself into the negotiations. He met with Rio Tinto vice president Chris Robison. Bob told him he wanted to get this thing done and assured him that the young attorney would no longer be negotiating. Bob said he would come in with his officers and he would be the spokesperson. The company vice president agreed. We were able to get an agreement. It was a good settlement. It was a six-year contract. The miners were able to stay in the game. They got their benefits, but more than anything they were able to live to fight another day. They might have not got back in there. Rio Tinto could have closed that place down and it would have been devastating to that community.

I think Boron was one of the great victories for the ILWU. Here was a local out in the middle of the desert, isolated by itself, and we brought people in to fight from all over on their behalf, to take on their struggle, and to show Rio Tinto true solidarity, that we had a united face and that the miners weren't alone. We raised over three hundred thousand dollars. People sent in money not only from our locals but from all over the world in support of the miners. For many contracts, the Boron workers had conceded to the company. For this contract, they took on Rio Tinto and won. They do have to set up a strike fund because within six years the company will be back. Every new contract Rio Tinto tries to get a little bit here and a little bit there.

In December 2015 the members of Local 30 voted to ratify a new five-year contract extension with Rio Tinto. It included a 2.5 percent pay raise in each of the five years and four medical plan options. Discussions broke down briefly in October 2015 when the company proposed changes in the contract's language and the Local 30 Negotiating Committee left the bargaining table. But the bargaining talks resumed after the company withdrew the proposals. Agreement was reached without a lockout or a strike.[13]

Finally, here are Bob's reflections on the 2010 Rio Tinto lockout. He begins with an account of working with the Local 30 Bargaining Committee. It shows that sometimes he had to employ as much negotiating ability dealing with the union's constituents as with difficult employers. He then describes his negotiations with Rio Tinto.

BOB MCELLRATH

You got to bargain with your union negotiating committee. I've watched so many of them. They develop a personality, if you can call it that. It takes twenty guys and everybody's an individual. You can't rush bargaining with a committee. The committee has to learn and develop. I'll sit there and after I learn how everybody's going to react, I can throw something on the table and almost to a guy I could figure out what he's going to say. Not exactly, but I could say, "He ain't going to like this." You have to understand your people and where they come from.

When I was in Boron, they'd already been bargaining for a long time. The guy that was doing the bargaining was an attorney. He was a young man, he never was a worker. Everything he was going to do was going to come straight out of a book. You can't bargain straight out of a book. Anyway, so I'm sitting there with our guys. The first day I'm trying to get things going. I'm trying to figure people out. The second day we got up in the morning to drive to the place to do the bargaining. We were having coffee. I told my officers, attorneys, and everybody, "Something just ain't right. I don't like the way this is going."

We get there. Our committee is very quiet. I was sitting there. They said, "Bob, we need to talk." I said, "Go ahead, talk." They said, "We don't like the way you're going." I said, "Tell me what you want. I'm here to be a mouthpiece. You guys have to tell me what you want. You guys ain't saying nothing." They said, "We didn't know. Maybe you wanted this." I said, "I don't want nothing. I just want you guys to get a contract. But, for Christ's sake, somebody say something to me, what do you want?" They said, "This is where we're at. Here's some of our demands for money." Well, they'd already given up their pension. They gave up all their sick days, gave up all their hours, gave up a lot shit. It was terrible.

So I said, "Now you guys are talking, it's about time." Their attorney, who I put off to the side, says, "You're done bargaining, I got this." He was making it hard on me when I wanted notes or previous minutes of something. He was making my life miserable. Finally we had this blowup. It was not a blowup, but it was getting the committee to own up to itself. I had to tell them, "This is you guys. This is your industry. Tell me what you got." They said, "This is what we want." And I got it all organized. I said, "Call them in." The employers came in and sat down. This is Rio Tinto. These are some big boys. They flew in the big guy, too.

So I threw the demands across the table and said, "This is what they want." He goes, "This ain't where we were last night." I said, "Dude, it sure ain't. To the man these guys said, 'No, no, and no.' So the answer is no. This is our position, these are the follow-up demands. That's where we're at." He grabs his stuff. He's shoving it in his briefcase and he stands up. He takes his committee, out the door he goes, and he slams the door. I never said a word. I just sat there. Everybody's looking at me. Someone says, "Well, Bob, what's going to happen?" I said, "Two things are going to happen. He's either halfway to his car heading for the airport or he's gonna knock on the door and want to talk to me."

I said, "This is how you do it. It's what you guys wanted and I totally agree with you. We're already locked out and in a fight. We don't give a shit, we'll fight some more." They sat there for about ten minutes. Pretty soon, knock, knock. The employer says, "Can we talk, Bob?" I said, "Sure we can talk." So he walks in there, goes in this little room and he shuts the door. It is just me and him. He said, "What the fuck is going on? I thought we were going somewhere yesterday." I said, "You were going somewhere, I thought we were going somewhere, but that committee in there says no and I work for that committee. You know that. Let me tell you where you're at. Have you ever heard the saying, 'Pigs get fat and hogs get slaughtered?' Man, you're at that trough and you're getting awful hoggish. You're taking shit from these guys."

I says, "I wouldn't go back to work. You took this, you took this, and you took this. What the hell else do you want? You ever heard of taking a few things, putting people back to work, and then coming back and trying to get a few more in the next contract? You're just trying to fucking destroy them all at once. I'm not going to put up with it." He said, "How can we fix this?" I said, "What do you got to have?" He says, "I got to have a six-year deal." I said, "Okay, you got a six-year deal. I'll go in there and get it for you but I got to have something." He said, "Yeah, what's that?" I said, "I want their sick-day pay back, I want their hundred dollars or two hundred dollars on their sick leave back, I want the holiday back, and I want a pay raise. That's a good contract and I'll bet you we can put this to bed." I went back in and said, "All right, guys, we got to have a six-year contract."

They said, "Oh, fuck that six-year contract." I said, "Wait a minute, whoa, whoa, whoa, a six-year deal, what's wrong with that? The longshoremen did that. You see how much pay raise you're gonna get? Give me the percentage of that pay raise." They figured it out. It's like two-point-three or two-point-five. They said, "We want a three-point pay raise." I said, "You know what longshore got? One-point-eight pay raise. Come on, guys." And we got a deal out of Boron.[14]

So your team has to take on a personality and you have to see them. Boron was a shock to me to do that within a couple of days or a week. Most of the time it takes a week or ten days just to make sure I know where all the guys are at. All of a sudden you see who's going to lunch with who every day. And with every committee you got one guy that will never be quiet. If you don't know everything there is on that contract, he's the guy that does, you know? So you start seeing where people are going.

Just as the Boron lockout was coming to a close, the union was trying to secure a first contract at Rite Aid Corporation's huge drug distribution center in Lancaster, California. The Rite Aid facility employed six hundred workers, so a win there would definitely strengthen the union's Warehouse Division and make an inroad into the drug industry supply chain. The company was located fifty-five miles by car or about an hour's drive from Boron in Antelope Valley at the western side of the Mojave Desert. With the two companies so close together, a loss at Boron would have threatened the union's Rite Aid organizing campaign. Willie Adams commented on that prospect.

WILLIE ADAMS

Everybody was watching to see what would happen, to see if the strength and the power of the ILWU still remained intact. When you get into a big struggle like Boron you can't afford to lose—it weakens you as a union and it makes you more susceptible to your enemies and those that think they can take you on. Losing at Boron might have made Lancaster that much tougher. But I think the win at Boron encouraged the workers out there in Lancaster.

The ILWU began organizing Rite Aid in spring 2006. With speed-ups, punishing production quotas, other unsafe working conditions, mandatory overtime on top of ten-hour shifts, employment "at will" with no job security, and labor in a desert facility lacking air conditioning in the summer or heating in the winter, Rite Aid warehouse employees had plenty of grievances. Still, for two years the company responded to the union's drive to organize its workers into Southern California ILWU warehouse Local 26 with intimidating threats, the firing of dozens of union supporters, and forty-nine documented violations of labor law. Functioning under Taft-Hartley guidelines, Rite Aid also had unlimited access to employees while activists could only discuss organizing with co-workers while off the clock. Undaunted, the ILWU won a closely contested union election in March 2008. The vote was 283 for the union and 261 against. The union had persevered, but by mid-2010, when the Boron lockout ended, the ILWU still had not convinced Rite Aid to sign a contract.[15]

The union battled Rite Aid by staging rallies and marches in multiple cities and enlisting the support of other unions and community organizations. The ILWU campaign included a dramatic worker delegation visit to a Rite Aid shareholders meeting in New York City to inform attendees of the company's union-busting tactics. It also mounted successful "pinpoint" boycotts of company pharmacies in San Pedro, California, where ILWU members spent thousands of dollars for prescription drugs. ILWU organizer Olney had Rite Aid stores picketed in Northern California as well. In early 2011, Rite Aid offered the union a contract that included extreme charges for employee healthcare and retention of the company's right to outsource jobs. The workers voted down the proposal by a 98 percent margin. Finally, in May 2011, Rite Aid agreed to a three-year contract with the union that featured guaranteed wages, protection against subcontracting, fair health insurance rates, and new tools to control the pace of work and promote safer conditions in the warehouse.[16]

During the Boron confrontation and the Lancaster campaign, Ray Familathe was ILWU International vice president for the US mainland. He was also responsible for the union's mainland organizing. A former ITF inspector and longshore Local 13 business agent, Familathe was International vice president between 2009 and 2018. In 2019 he was elected president of Los Angeles/Long Beach Harbor longshore Local 13. Here he recalls his role in the Rite Aid struggle.

RAY FAMILATHE

I was involved with Rite Aid for three years before I became vice president. In 2006 a call came to Local 13 when I was a business agent there. My buddy Richard Hansen, another business agent, fielded the call. It was a woman from Rite Aid. She said, "We'd like to join the ILWU. How do we do it?" Hansen and I passed the information along to the International Organizing Department in San Francisco. Peter Olney, the director of organizing, and the staff followed up. The organizing campaign went on, the election took place, and we were victorious in getting recognition. But that's just one step of the process. You still got to go win that first contract.

Negotiations went on for some time. I came on board in October of 2009 as International vice president. We went through the Rio Tinto struggle and once we finished that I shifted. I was in Boron so I just shifted to the other side of the Mojave over to Lancaster. We, including Peter Olney and the organizing department, had to get creative. We had some good strategies that were able to bring Rite Aid to conclude an agreement. Warehouse Local 26, ILWU, of Los Angeles still maintains it. That was a big victory for us but a huge battle.[17] You're miles from a port or a city where you might have community people that are union-friendly or union-oriented and activist. But we mobilized up there and were successful [see fig. 5.2].

Finally, Bob comments on the five-year Lancaster battle, which was the last major long-term, US mainland, nonmaritime organizing campaign concluded during his ILWU International presidency. The Rite Aid struggle, like the Blue Diamond loss in 2008, was costly, time-consuming, and stressful for the union and its staff. Despite his satisfaction with the Rite Aid win, Bob did not change his view, formed after

Fig. 5.2. ILWU Local 26 workers celebrating victory after a long Rite Aid warehouse organizing campaign at Lancaster, California, 2011. Five years of concerted union effort had passed before the company finally agreed to a contract. *Left to right*: Angel Warner, Jeanice Smiley, Lorena Ortiz. Courtesy of Anne Rand Library, ILWU.

the Blue Diamond experience, that expensive, multiyear organizing efforts beyond the waterfront would no longer be undertaken while he was the union's president.

It was a defensive era for labor with union density in decline, federal law stacked against organizing, and employers militant in their opposition to any new long-term worker representation campaigns. Facing this, Bob reasoned that the ILWU should only undertake eight-to-nine-month organizing efforts. He also noted that periodically, when longshore contract negotiating had to take priority over everything else, long-term organizing projects would suffer.[18] His reflections on these matters follow.

BOB MCELLRATH

When the time came to fight for the Rite Aid contract you seen what these guys did. They went to all them pharmacies, stopped everybody from buying drugs there, and the company capitulated. Ray Familathe did a hell of a job bargaining with that Rite Aid woman from back East. She came out. I said, "Did she call you? Then you got a contract coming. Otherwise she wouldn't be calling you and coming out. She wants a contract, so go get her while she's hot." He did and he got a contract.[19] That's how you do it. I told my guys, "If we got a site and we're going after 'em, you start carding within eight or nine months. We spent millions of dollars on that shit, tons. No more of this four-and-a-half-, five-and-a-half-year shit for me. Like I said, I'm not an organizer, but I can watch and see.

There remained one long-term project to conclude. But this was not an organizing campaign as such. It was the affiliation of an international maritime group, the Panama Canal pilots, with the ILWU during 2011–12. The Panama pilots numbered 250 at the time.[20] Three years later, 2,580 Panama dockworkers affiliated with the ILWU.[21] Bob, interviewed in 2013, comments on Panama. His statement puts the Panama affiliation into the broad context of his long-standing search for maritime friends and allies around the world.

BOB MCELLRATH

You might say that Panama was an organizing drive, but it wasn't. It was more of traveling the world and making friends. Through travels, going to the ITF meetings and all that, I made friends with these Panama guys. They came up to San Francisco in 2002 and were sitting in our bargaining. Ray Familathe was instrumental in that. As soon as I got to be president and Familathe was vice president, he come to me and said, "What do you think about Panama?" I said, "Now let's move." It took a year, year-and-a-half of just going and talking. I had Remar sit down along with Familathe. We drafted up a plan, drafted a contract between them and the ILWU. They're attached to us through a letter of recognition.[22] That just shows you how unions can work together.[23]

In 2012 events during a lockout of dockworkers in New Zealand highlighted Bob's policy of working with and supporting waterfront allies internationally. The port facilities at Auckland, New Zealand, are a public entity serviced by a private operator called the Ports of Auckland. During late 2011 and early 2012 negotiations between the Ports of Auckland and the Maritime Union of New Zealand (MUNZ), the operator pushed hard for the casualization of waterfront jobs. The Ports of Auckland demanded an end to regular shifts. The managers wanted the right to send workers home after three hours or at times to order them without notice to remain on the job for dangerous twelve-hour shifts. The company also tried to undermine the MUNZ by offering bonuses to workers willing to abandon the union. Finally, on March 7, 2012, the Ports of Auckland sent a letter to the MUNZ stating that it had decided to contract out stevedoring, making union workers superfluous. But current dockworkers were invited to apply for the new nonunion jobs![24]

International protests against the Ports of Auckland followed immediately. Leading the way, Bob called for an "emergency mobilization" of representatives from ILWU locals.[25] The ILWU sent a sixteen-member delegation of Longshore Division representatives to Auckland to meet with MUNZ dockers and join them in a March 10 rally and march to the port. The ILWU also coordinated a series of demonstrations on behalf of the MUNZ in ports along the US Pacific Coast. The Maritime Union of Australia (MUA), too, mounted protests in Australia. Then on March 21, bowing to pressure, the Ports of Auckland withdrew its firing order. The MUNZ, now on strike, voted to return to work. But the Ports of Auckland did not want peace. Instead, the managers issued a lockout notice. The Ports of Auckland ended the lockout on April 5, 2012, though, in the wake of an order to do so by New Zealand's Employment Court and in the face of the show of international solidarity mounted by the ILWU, the MUA, and others ITF-affiliated groups.[26]

The finalization of the MUNZ's 2011–12 negotiations with the Ports of Auckland took a long time. The union did not secure a contract until early 2015. Even then Joe Fleetwood, the general secretary of the MUNZ, had serious misgivings about the results, although the MUNZ had at least saved its jurisdiction with the Ports of Auckland.[27] Still, Fleetwood remembered the ILWU's help in 2012 and the value of Bob's emphasis on international solidarity. Here he recounts his memories of the Ports of Auckland struggle.

JOE FLEETWOOD

I worked directly with Bob through the Ports of Auckland campaign. This is probably 2011 into 2012. We're sitting in Sydney, Australia, for the MUA National Conference. I just mentioned to Bob, "I've got a mass rally happening. Apologies for the late notice but it's just been confirmed to me like the day before I arrived in Australia." It was about casualization. It was all about going to a monthly guarantee for only half of the workforce. It was about casualizing permanent work and turning it into precarious work to get rid of the union. Bob says, "When is it?" I says, "It's next week." So we

CHAPTER 5

Fig. 5.3. An ILWU delegation marching in support of locked-out Maritime Union of New Zealand (MUNZ) workers, Auckland, 2012. Bob McEllrath pressed hard to build international dockworker solidarity throughout his career as an ILWU officer. Courtesy of Anne Rand Library, ILWU.

sat there and have a good talk about it. We had a talk, say, 11:00 till about 3:00. Then Bob said, "I just had my guys make a telephone call." Inside of twenty-four hours all the ILWU presidents on the West Coast were on a plane and all converged on New Zealand.[28] Bob couldn't come over, but Vice President Familathe came over and headed the delegation.

We marched, nearly ten thousand strong, through the streets of Auckland, closed everything. People were coming out of the shops. By the time we got to the port, there was like nearly ten thousand people because people understood that if the longshoremen fall, everyone knows who is next. We had the meat workers, they were on strike at the time and they traveled down in their buses, buses full strong, and they attended our picket there [see fig. 5.3].

Three and a half years the Ports of Auckland dispute went. The ILWU stamped up a mess of donations for the workers. This was all passed at an ILWU Longshore Division Caucus.[29] I wasn't looking for donations but that was the caliber of Big Bob. He just talked to them and it just went, "bang." The thing that really I felt was heartening was what come off the floor. "Is it enough? Do we need to double it? Do they need more?" Bob was there and I said, "Please, please, it's fantastic as is." I won't say the figure but they says, "We don't care. This is a fight that needs to be funded and we've got to do it." Another man jumped up and put his hand up. He says, "I want to move we should double it. It needs to happen. These workers need to be protected, like we've done in the past." They didn't double it because I said, "Please, please, just leave it." It was a fantastic figure. That's another like a mark. It's another arrow in Bob's arsenal.

Finally it's about protecting the workers of the world. It gets back to the old saying, "Workers of the world must unite." That's what we should be doing.

In advocating for the workers of the world, the ILWU has generally supported fair trade policies over free trade arrangements. Free trade programs, with minimal or no trade restrictions, usually lead to the outsourcing of production jobs to the poorest developing countries with the lowest wages and fewest labor protections. Fair trade defenders hold that it is unethical to pay workers in developing countries wages that are too low to sustain humane existence. During the 1999 "Battle of Seattle," thousands demonstrated against a meeting of the World Trade Organization because of the WTO's free trade stance. ILWU president Brian McWilliams spoke at the demonstration and later condemned police abuse of those arrested.[30] Bob, for his part, later urged that the ILA and the ILWU should stand against free trade even though it could bring cargo to US waterfronts. He spoke against free trade, he said, "because it was the right thing to do for people."[31]

As part of their ongoing concern for workers everywhere and their continuing efforts to "travel the world and make friends," as Bob put it, shortly before June 2012 Bob and Wesley Furtado attended a convention of Zenkowan, the All-Japan Dockworkers' Union. On June 6, 2012, Akinobu Itoh, the president of Zenkowan, spoke at the ILWU International Convention meeting in San Diego, California. He said, "I am extremely honored to attend the ILWU convention and to sign the friendship and solidarity statement between the two unions."[32] An ILWU-Zenkowan statement of unity, that went back to Brian McWilliams's ILWU presidency, was renewed that day and signed by Bob, Furtado, and Itoh.[33]

The unity statement called for solidarity to improve working conditions, union rights, living standards, and the social welfare of union members in Japan and the United States. It also stated that the common objective of the two unions was to advance the living standards of workers everywhere in the world.[34] During his speech, Itoh noted that in February 2012, in a show of unity, Zenkowan had sent a delegation to Honolulu to participate in ILWU protests at the Pacific Beach Hotel, where the ILWU wanted a contract. Itoh also emphasized that Zenkowan was continuing to boycott the hotel.[35]

As serious as Bob and the union's bids for international docker unity were, on occasion there could be a lighter moment. Sometimes Bob used humor as part of his effort to build overseas friendship and solidarity. Furtado recalled one such incident during his and Bob's visit to the Zenkowan convention that took place before Itoh's trip to San Diego. He describes that occasion.

WESLEY FURTADO

We're at this conference that's like the International of the Japan dockers. They take us to have traditional Japanese food. We have to go in with kimonos on and sit on the floor. It was so funny because Bob put on his kimono and it looked like a miniskirt. The Japanese are really, what do you call that, they're all by status. The number one guy, like the president, lateral to Bob, sits right in the middle of a long table. Then there's rows and rows behind us all facing the same way.

The Zenkowan president sits down and we walk in. He goes, "Big Bob, Big Bob, sit next to me on the right." Then he goes, "Furtado-san, Furtado-san," and I sit next to his vice president. You have your food, and people would walk up, people from different areas like Yokohama and Osaka. It's like over here, you got an area delegation. They would come up and pour you a certain sake of their area. They pour it and toast, "Drink, drink." We're drinking, we're drinking. Bob started getting gassed up. He stands up, all the Japanese are looking at him. He gets down in a sumo stance and he slaps his leg and throws rice up in the air.[36] I said, "Bob, sit down, man, you're outnumbered." I mean you got five hundred Japanese and he's okay standing up slapping his leg like a sumo wrestler and throwing rice and everything.

Bob laughed and laughed and goes, "Oh, toast, toast." He sits down and he goes, "How was that, Wesley?" Then the Japanese president turns to me and goes, "Furtado-san, Furtado-san, we have to give Big Bob a Japanese name." My mom was Japanese. I know slang words I was brought up with. They know I know a little bit of Japanese. So I said, "I have a Japanese name for Big Bob." They go, "What is Big Bob's Japanese name?" I said, "Bakatare Bob." They laughed 'cause *bakatare* means crazy in Japanese, right? And then they go, "Bakatare Bob, Bakatare Bob." Bob's standing up, "Yeah," toasting. He goes "What the hell was that, Wesley?" I said, "That's Crazy Bob."[37]

You know, we travel, we work hard, but Bob has a good sense of humor. That's why a lot of people enjoy him.

Bob's humor in Japan helped to reinforce Zenkowan's relationship with the ILWU. Much later Bob remembered the mutual good feelings of that evening.[38] After Itoh attended the ILWU's 2012 convention in San Diego and spoke there, Zenkowan continued to boycott the Pacific Beach Hotel in Honolulu through December, when management finally agreed to a first contract with ILWU Local 142 after ten years of struggle. When the agreement was announced, *The Dispatcher*, the ILWU International newspaper, observed, "The solidarity of unions in Japan—led by Zenkowan, the All-Japan Dockworkers' Union—was especially critical because most of the hotel's guests were Japanese."[39] Here was a good example of Bob and Wesley Furtado's trips abroad to make international friends paying off directly.

The years 2011–12 also saw a major confrontation between the ILWU and Export Grain Terminal Development (EGT), a multinational grain exporter with a new facility in Longview, Washington. This was such a monumental battle that it requires a lengthy chapter of its own. But before we move on to EGT, there is one more story from 2012 that is worth telling. That year, Rob Remar's house was burglarized twice and his family traumatized. Rob, a humane labor lawyer with kindly instincts, considered buying a gun for protection. Bob counseled his counselor that this might not be a good idea. Bob McEllrath the labor leader was typically seen by unionists and others as a "man of action." But Rob's story, recounted here, reveals that there was also a thoughtful side to Bob.

ROB REMAR

The gun story takes place in July, August, of 2012. I was in Portland, Oregon, during that part of the year. While I was away doing trials and legal proceedings my home got broken into. We were living in the Oakland hills. We got robbed twice within a few weeks. Our cars got broken into and my wife and kids were really freaking out, as I was. We felt completely under attack and it was very difficult for me personally to be away. We did all sorts of security things. But we felt like we were under observation by some criminals or a criminal group that might come in at any time and rob us or do all sorts of other things.

I thought seriously about getting a gun for the protection of our home and for just peace of mind. I've never owned a gun, I had never held a gun, didn't know anything about them. That wasn't my background, but I know a lot of people whose background is different. They're hunters, their fathers taught them, whatever. It's part of their culture, part of their family. Most of them were saying, "Yeah, you should get a gun, definitely. Go out, get a gun, protect yourself, learn about it, shoot it."

I went to Bob because I know that Bob's a hunter and he knows a lot about guns. For many people who are in the Pacific Northwest and other parts of the country, that is part of their culture. I sat down with Bob and I said, "Bob, I want your advice on this. I'm thinking of getting a gun and I've gotten the advice from others to get a gun. What do you think of that?" He says, "Rob, I don't think you should be doing that. If it were me, I'd definitely have my guns out and ready to go, but you're not me. You don't know anything about guns, right?" I said, "Right." He says, "It's the worst thing you could do, where you're emotional and scared, to have a gun in your house or in your hands and you have no experience with it. You're going to end up killing somebody in your family. You're going to end up having that gun used against you and your family."

Bob said, "It's not just about having the gun and it's not just about the safety of working a gun, it's also about do you have the wherewithal, do you have it in your mind and heart to use the gun?" He says, "I know I do from my experiences hunting and my comfort level with growing up with a gun. But I don't think you do. And since you don't, you shouldn't have anything to do with guns." Then he gave me this long-term advice: "For the long-term, if you feel that it's important to you then don't get a gun, go to gun school, use their guns. Get trained, get familiar with a gun, build up your experience and your comfort level and only when you get to a certain point would you then have a gun in the house."

That completely turned me around. I was very close to getting a gun and I thought Bob's advice was very wise and helpful to me and very nuanced in many ways. It was sophisticated advice. It wasn't a "yes" or a "no." It was "no" certainly for the moment, but it was thought-out and long-term and I was very grateful for that. I think he saved me and my family from potential problems that would have been tragic.

As it turned out, the EGT challenge would demand a considerable amount of thought too. It would become such a momentous and complicated battle that it required both a man of thought and a man of action to deal with it on the picket line, in the courtroom, and finally in jail in the small Northwest town of Longview, Washington.

CHAPTER 5

6

"Trying to Win a Battle"

International President, 2011–2013

> It's not the longshoremen that are the bad guys, it was our cops in our town that were the bad people and that's not right.
>
> LADONNA CHAMBERLAIN

In June 2012 the ILWU met again in International Convention, this time in San Diego. Bob, now the veteran of many battles as International president, was nominated once more for the union's highest office. As in 2009, prominent delegates from the most influential locals in the union named and seconded him. Joe Cortez from Local 13 in the Los Angeles/Long Beach Harbor area emphasized how Bob had "prepared the union for new technology and mechanization." This was a clear reference to Bob's efforts to maintain the union's jurisdiction over the increasingly important waterfront mechanics as dockside automation loomed. Having known and respected Bob and his family for thirty years, Cortez also acknowledged Sally's role in backing Bob and the ILWU over time. He said, "As the saying goes, behind a great man stands a great woman. I would like to thank Sally McEllrath for her support and sacrifice for the union."[1]

Donna Domingo, the newly elected president of Hawaii's islands-wide Local 142, seconded Bob's nomination. So did Mark Gordienko from longshore Local 500 in Vancouver, British Columbia, Canada. Jeff Smith, who served several terms as president of longshore Local 8 in Portland, Oregon, also seconded the nomination. Finally, Sheldon Biga from Local 142 and Greg Mitre from Local 13 added their endorsements. In his nomination, Cortez said, "I hope my nomination is by acclamation." It was. There were no other nominations for International president. The assembled convention delegates then treated Bob to a standing ovation.[2]

In their statements, Cortez, Domingo, Gordienko, Smith, and Biga all referred in different ways to the issues surrounding the union's recent struggle in the Northwest with corporate behemoth Export Grain Terminal Development (EGT). The EGT fight had something in common with the existential threat to the ILWU of the 2002 West Coast longshore lockout since losing it had the potential to undermine one of the union's oldest and most important core jurisdictions, bulk grain handling on the waterfront. The company had signed a contract with the ILWU in early 2012. But months of intense battle going back well into 2011 had passed before the ILWU could find peace with EGT.

The issues in the long EGT battle were complex as well as important. Consequently, most of this chapter is devoted to the EGT confrontation. EGT was probably the most important battle of Bob's career as ILWU president because of its length and bitterness, the degree to which it threatened a core Longshore Division jurisdiction, and the implications of the agreement finally concluded. The EGT struggle was also central to the ILWU's decision to leave the AFL-CIO.

EGT is a multinational joint venture. In 2011 its members included the Japanese trading conglomerate Itochu Corporation, South Korea's STX Pan Ocean shipping company, and agribusiness giant Bunge North America, which alone operated in thirty countries. EGT's members made more than two billion dollars in 2010. The next year they opened a new $200 million grain terminal in Longview, Washington. Bulk-grain waterfront work in the Pacific Northwest had been within the ILWU's jurisdiction since at least 1938. By 2011 long-established area grain exporters had a contract with the ILWU known as the Northwest Grain Handlers Agreement. EGT, a newcomer, was not part of it. Still, anticipating good union jobs, Longview's ILWU longshore Local 21 members lobbied early on for EGT to come to town. But ILWU-EGT negotiations dragged on inconclusively from September 2009 through May 2011. The company demanded twelve-hour shifts without over-time and refused to recognize ILWU maintenance, repair, and master console jurisdiction. Twenty-five jobs were at issue. There was also cause for concern when EGT used nonunion construction contractors to build its new facility.[3]

On June 3, 2011, some 1,200 ILWU members from sixteen West Coast ports rallied in Portland in a show of solidarity. Things had initially seemed secure for the ILWU because the Port of Longview had a con-tract with EGT stating that the company must employ Local 21 mem-bers at the new plant. But EGT ignored the Port of Longview's obligation to the ILWU and hired nonunion workers when the grain terminal opened in July 2011. On July 11, about two hundred ILWU mem-bers entered the EGT facility to protest. Half were arrested for tres-passing. Two days later, the company tried to bring in 107 railcars loaded with grain. This time, six hundred Portland, Longview, and Van-couver, Washington, longshore workers successfully blocked the tracks leading to the EGT plant. Local 21 president Dan Coffman explained his union's stance: "We are fighting for our jobs in our juris-diction. To have a rich multinational corporation like EGT come in here and turn their backs on the local men and women who have worked these docks for seventy years so they can pocket a bigger profit is a problem."[4]

On July 16 EGT announced that it would hire union workers after all, but not from the ILWU. The next day the company said it planned to use a subcontractor to hire members of International Union of Operating Engineers Local 701 of Gladstone, Oregon, to handle its grain. Apparently EGT hoped to frame the conflict as union against union rather than union against company. For its part, Local 701 had a reputation as a rogue organization. The ILWU viewed it as an inter-loper and an opportunist that, in cooperation with EGT, threatened its traditional jurisdiction in the Northwest grain industry. On July 19 Local 701 reported that it would accept EGT's grain terminal jobs. Two days later, one hundred ILWU members picketed the plant, forcing it to shut down. But on July 25, EGT reopened its facility. The company's non-ILWU workers entered the terminal under police protection.[5]

For the next six weeks, the ILWU picketed EGT and held rallies and demonstrations. At the end of August the federal National Labor Relations Board filed a court complaint charging the ILWU with "aggressive picketing," which could be construed as an "unfair labor practice" under the Taft-Hartley Act. A few days later a federal district judge issued a ten-day restraining order against the ILWU that was later extended. Matters reached a boiling point on September 7. That morning Bob and others stopped a grain train in Vancouver that was headed for Longview. Later that day four hundred ILWU members, Bob among them, and community supporters stood in front of the train carrying grain toward EGT's Longview facility. Police attacked the demonstrators, including women and children, with pepper spray and batons. Cowlitz County Sheriff's Department deputies assaulted Bob and briefly detained him. On September 8, ILWU workers from several Northwest ports traveled to Longview, entered the EGT facility at 4:00 a.m., and dumped the grain out of seventy railcars.[6]

In the following days, the police began arresting ILWU members in Longview. Local 21 responded dramatically on September 16. That day, its entire membership of two hundred, escorted by spouses, children, and retirees, marched to the sheriff's department and offered to surrender en masse. The department refused. But later that day officers arrested Jacob Whiteside, Local 21's vice president, in a church parking lot and handcuffed him in front of his children. On September 21, Coffman and a dozen pro-ILWU women were charged with trespassing and blocking an EGT grain train. Bob was similarly charged five days later. By month's end, two hundred ILWU members had been arrested. On September 30, a federal judge imposed a $250,000 fine on the union. He said the ILWU should reimburse EGT, the NLRB, and the police for the actions of September 7–8. The union appealed. The *Dispatcher*, the ILWU newspaper, observed, "The September 30 court ruling against the ILWU by the Federal Court in Tacoma was not unexpected because federal labor laws generally favor business and commerce over workers and the community."[7] The union was ordered to obey the Taft-Hartley Act and not picket aggressively and block grain train movement.

During November and December, adherents of the Occupy protest movement that disrupted Wall Street and challenged American corporate power established encampments in ninety-five American cities in the fall of 2011, staged demonstrations, and briefly closed down West Coast ports in support of the Longview ILWU workers. An Occupy march that shut down the Port of Oakland was informally supported by some members of San Francisco Bay Area ILWU locals. ILWU people visited Occupy camps and donated supplies in Oakland, Portland, and Seattle. Unfortunately, in closing West Coast ports, the Occupiers acted without officially consulting the union. Initially sympathetic to the movement, ILWU officials, including Bob, said that Occupy's unilateral actions ignored the union's democratic decision-making process. Fearing big fines if they appeared to coordinate with the protesters, ILWU leaders from various Pacific Coast port locals subsequently distanced themselves from Occupy and its activities. Tensions reached the point where Seattle longshore workers disrupted a pro-Occupy panel on January 6, 2012, that included some ILWU members.[8]

In mid-January, a freighter entered the Columbia River intending to take on a load of EGT grain handled by Local 701. ILWU longshore workers and Occupy each separately considered blocking the ship, which was escorted by heavily armed Coast Guard members. It looked as if the federal government had enlisted the military on the side of a private corporation. Surprising to some, this was under the Democratic administration of President Barack Obama. A dangerous clash seemed imminent. Fearing violence and possible regionwide port shutdowns, on January 23 Washington State governor Christine Gregoire brokered a deal with Bob and the Local 21 Negotiating Committee that ended the long ILWU-EGT confrontation. The deal covered production and maintenance people, but it also set up a pool of employees who would work on incoming vessels and trains as needed for twelve-hour shifts. The pool enabled EGT to select workers outside of the union's traditional waterfront hiring hall. Some ILWU members saw this as a dangerous precedent. Still, the Local 701 workers were dismissed from the terminal and, most important, the ILWU gained jurisdiction at EGT and by implication potentially saved it within the whole Pacific Northwest grain industry.[9]

On February 10 the ILWU and EGT signed a five-year contract that officially acknowledged the Gregoire deal. Unfortunately, there were still one hundred cases against ILWU members and supporters filed by Cowlitz County and $300,000 in fines pending against the union sought by the National Labor Relations Board under the Taft-Hartley Act. Bob declared, "Individuals are still facing criminal charges related to our protest of EGT last summer. I won't consider this over until the last member and supporter who stood up and said 'no' to the loss of our historic work is cleared." Later Bob would be tried himself in Cowlitz County for train obstruction.[10]

In the weeks and months after the contract signing, police and court authorities in Longview continued their pursuit of ILWU supporters. Local 21 secretary-treasurer Byron Jacobs was jailed for a week during March 2012. He was isolated in a maximum security cell for no apparent reason. For four days, Jacobs was denied a cup and had to drink with his hands. In June, Bob stood trial for blocking the grain train headed for EGT on September 7, 2011. The jury failed to reach a verdict, but Bob was tried again in the Cowlitz County Court during September 2012. After a three-day trial witnessed by dozens of union supporters, Bob was found guilty of "obstructing a train." He was sentenced to ninety days in jail, which was commuted to two days of highway garbage pickup. Bob refused to pick up garbage. He was then sentenced to one day in jail, with the other eighty-nine days suspended. Bob also had to pay a fine of $543.[11]

During 2012–13, the ILWU resolved the legal issues still facing it in the wake of the EGT confrontation. As Bob had promised, all ILWU members charged with crimes while defending the union's jurisdiction received legal counsel. A number had their charges dismissed. A few with felony charges pled guilty to minor misdemeanors. The union's remaining contempt fines, now amounting to $300,000, were reduced to $200,000, payable to EGT and to the NLRB, but not to the police.[12]

One result of the EGT battle with long-term implications was the union's decision to leave the AFL-CIO. Bob was upset with the labor federation's failure to restrain Local 701 from what the ILWU saw as scabbing during the EGT fight. In his keynote speech to the Thirty-Fifth ILWU International Convention meeting at San Diego in June 2012, Bob pointed out that the AFL-CIO's national leadership asked the AFL-CIO state federations in Oregon and Washington not to pass resolutions supporting the ILWU in its EGT struggle. He emphasized that the national AFL-CIO also requested that the International Transport Workers' Federation (ITF) abstain from aiding his union during the EGT crisis. Bob concluded, "The leadership of the AFL-CIO actively worked to undermine our fight with EGT." Following a serious discussion, the 2012 ILWU convention delegates voted unanimously to authorize Bob to pull the union out of the AFL-CIO if and when he felt it was necessary. This he did in August 2013.[13]

This summary of the ILWU battle with EGT is based on the sources labor historians customarily rely on, such as newspaper reports, journal articles, and union convention proceedings. But a traditional overview cannot always convey the nuances of leadership decision-making or the "what it was like to be there" of history like oral history can. The EGT battle was arguably the greatest challenge of Bob's presidency. In this chapter we will hear about that challenge from Bob; Rob Remar; LaDonna Chamberlain, the wife of a Local 21 longshore worker; Dan Coffman, the president of Local 21 during 2011–12; Bob's wife, Sally; Norm Parks, a pensioner from longshore Local 8 in Portland; Helena Jones, a pensioner from marine clerks Local 63 of the Los Angeles/Long Beach waterfront; Willie Adams; and Wesley Furtado.

First, Bob recalls the ILWU's relationship with the operating engineers in the Northwest going back to the 1960s. He then explains why he was long convinced that his union had to aggressively protect the circumscribed dockside jurisdiction of its core entity, the ILWU Longshore Division.

BOB MCELLRATH

Back in the sixties we fought the operating engineers to get them off the cranes. It was a big deal. Can you imagine if the operating engineers were driving waterfront cranes today? They used to come in on these water cranes and hoist logs. I worked underneath them. We finally got rid of everybody. The mindset as of today, as we're taking this oral history [2013], is something that I tried to do even when I was a young man before I got into, I guess you call it, politics or union business. I could never understand why when we're on the dock it isn't all ILWU doing the work.

Because the only place the ILWU Longshore Division has to work is on the docks, we need to exercise our strength and put people off the docks. Let the Teamsters and the machinists and the ironworkers and the operating engineers do everything else across the United States, but leave us alone. That's always been my outlook.

Our life is connected for a few hundred feet or half of a mile of dock. After that, there's a fence and somebody else is out there doing it. Our employers are not downtown at Nordstrom's working. Our employers are on the dock. If Nordstrom needs a new building, the operating engineers, the electricians, and everybody else goes down there. They build and then the store moves in and then they go do something else, like build a bridge. I can't go nowhere. I have to stay with the ship, with the crane, and with what comes and goes.

I just want to be able to do the work on the dock. I told Richard Trumka, the AFL-CIO president, that when the operating engineers went into EGT. I called him and I said, "Look, this is wrong." He said, "It's the first contract, you got to file an Article 20 complaint."[14] I said, "This is bullshit, I ain't buying into it. Richard, what do you want me to do next? You want me to put a bid in on building the next overpass in Oakland or in Portland or Idaho? Shall I start building bridges and high-rises?" He didn't say anything. I said, "It's the same difference. I'm not doing that. But you got to leave me alone."

Rob Remar was intimately involved in the EGT campaign. He well recalls his and Bob's roles in the long EGT battle. It seems clear from Remar's comments that, in a defensive era for labor, Bob's concern with installing the union's grain jurisdiction at EGT was of prime importance to him as a key to preserving the ILWU itself. In reviewing this, Remar also describes the personal risk Bob was willing to take to make sure that EGT's workers were ILWU members.

ROB REMAR

I was the lead ILWU counselor for that case for all the litigation—and there was quite a bit of it—as well as advising and working with the leadership and developing strategies and tactics to win the thing. Bob was in charge. He was the one who made the ultimate decisions. He had Leal Sundet, the Northwest committeeman, there who was doing a lot of the groundwork and was involved in a lot of implementation of strategy and policy. But Bob was the one who called the shots. He also got more and more involved in the implementation of policy and strategy. It was his assessment that this was a question of long-term survival for the union, or what I would call an existential challenge to the union. He wouldn't use that term, but he would say it was a challenge to the continuation and longevity of the union.

Bob said, "If we can't secure this jurisdiction, it means we're going to lose all of the grain facilities. Then it's just a half step to starting to lose our jurisdiction in the ports." Also it pointed out that the ILWU was pretty much the last union bastion in the grain industry and Bob was not going to let that go down without pulling out all the stops. He wanted me to understand that I could give them all of the legal advice that I could muster and flag them as furiously as possible about all of the legal risks and consequences of things, but that they were going forward in a very informed and very considered manner. Well, ultimately Bob goes to jail. That's how it played out. That's how far he took it and that's how serious he was about it and committed. That's how true he was to his objective with putting his own body or life on the line. As it turned out, his jail time was very short, but he didn't know that. Nobody knew that in advance.

Early in the day on September 7, 2011, Bob was in his hometown of Vancouver, Washington, just forty miles south of Longview. The ILWU's relations with EGT had been strained for months. That morning Bob and members and supporters of longshore Local 4, Bob's home ILWU local, blocked a grain train that was headed north toward Longview and the EGT plant. As part of the Longview struggle, the Vancouver episode is a story in itself. Bob recalls what happened.

BOB MCELLRATH

We stopped that train at Vancouver in the morning, probably two and a half blocks from my Local 4 hall. There's a crossing there. We had intel where the train was at. So I got up and went down to the hall at about 6:00, 6:15 in the morning. The guys were monitoring things and they said, "Bob, the train is coming." We took off and walked down the street. There was about twenty or twenty-five of us. We got on the tracks and stopped the train [see fig. 6.1].

Well, here come all those black-booted cops and the railroad police. The railroad police have their own laws. They got their own system. It's completely diverted from the city police, state police, or any other kind of police. They go from one side of the tracks to the other. When you're on those tracks, you deal with the Burlington Northern Police. You step off, you're dealing with the city and the county and the state police. So you're screwed, right?

The city cops in Vancouver were there. When we got there we stopped them. They had a German shepherd, a police dog. This police guy said,

Fig. 6.1. Bob McEllrath leading members of ILWU Local 4 in Vancouver, Washington, on September 7, 2011. Activists blocked a grain train in Vancouver that morning as part of the union's hard-fought battle with Export Grain Terminal Development (EGT) of Longview, Washington, for recognition, a contract, and the preservation of ILWU jurisdiction in the Northwest grain industry. Courtesy of Dawn DesBrisay, photographer.

"I'm going to turn this dog loose." He started bringing the dog and the dog's going like this [demonstrating]. I said, "You can't." I started screaming at the cop, "You can't turn that dog loose. We're here, a peaceful protest. We have a right, we have our civil rights. We can protest and that's what we're going to do." The guy had a big canister with mace and he was going like this [demonstrating]. They can shoot it like thirty yards. I says, "You have no right to stop us from freedom of speech and stop us from peaceful protest. Don't you dare." So he pulled the dog back. I was worried. I would rather fight a guy than fight a dog, 'cause they train dogs to bite your nuts and every other thing. They're vicious things, and if you hurt a dog, it's like hurting a police officer. You shoot a dog, a police dog, it's like shooting a cop. They'll get you. You're done. Or kick it or knife it or something, you're done.

So they backed up. This whole time I'm doing this, I'm thinking to myself, "Okay, now what's your next move, Bob?" The next thing I know ten more people showed up. Then twenty more people showed up. Pretty soon we had about three hundred people. There was more comfort in numbers, but there was a lot of police, too. Pretty soon all kinds of police were talking to me. They were trying to cut a deal. One says, "We've got a warrant that says that you can't obstruct trains." I said, "Yeah. Read it." He did. I said, "It says you can't obstruct the trains in Cowlitz County. This is Clark County."[15] They were a little bit upset with me.

Then they were milling around there and it's a hot day. I think it got to 101 that day, hotter than heck. So it got into midday and now we got everything stopped. This cop came to me. He said, "Look, we've got other trains here, we've got passenger trains. We would like to bring them through." I said, "That's no problem, but that grain train ain't coming through." He said, "No problem. We just want these other trains to be able to pass." I said, "That's fine." I didn't want to make it any worse than it was and stop a passenger train or something. He said, "Okay, here's what I want you to do. Have all of your people muster over there across the tracks right over there."

Well, this is my backyard. I looked at it. What happens is the railroad tracks went like this [indicating] and then the road went like this [indicating]. There was a road and the railroad tracks was going like that [indicating]. There was a huge warehouse right here so he wanted us all to go right there. Now if everybody goes there and that train comes up and it stops then they got us boxed in. All's they got to do is line the cars up and you got no way out. They could have tear-gassed us, done anything they wanted. You're going to run into the building or have to run around the edge of the building. You were trapped.

So the cop said, "I want your people over there." I said, "Okay, I'll take care of that. You just worry about the train, you take care of that." Everybody in our group comes. They get around me. I said, "Okay, here's what I want. I need two guys to be captains." Two said, "Yeah, yeah." I said, "I want you to take half the people and stand here. I want you to take half the people and stand on the other side of the track." I split them in two so we'd be on both sides of the train. Then I said, "Keep your cell phones on 'cause I don't know what they're going to do. I don't trust them, but I agreed to let the passenger trains and other trains through." I said, "Okay, we're ready," and everybody starts splitting up. The cop comes to me and says, "No, no, no, no, I want you all over there." I said, "No, no, no, no, we're not going to all be over there. We stand over here and we stand over there." I didn't do the exact thing he wanted. So I knew I was pissing him off.

Toward noon it got to the point where the train backed up. It was gone and it stopped. Our people were getting hot and tired. I didn't want to lose them. They were starting to sit off way over there. So I got everybody together and said, "All right, everybody, we're done. Let's go to the hall." We all walked up there. I got in the back of a truck and gave a little speech. I said, "You guys did a good job. We stopped the train. Mission accomplished. I want everybody to keep their phones on. Let's see what happens." Everybody takes off and they go wherever they go. I got a beer and a sandwich or something. I'm sitting there and the phone rang. I said, "Yeah, what's up?" They said, "The train's on the move. It's going to Longview." When I got the phone call, I said, "All right. Start getting on the phone and tell 'em we'll meet you in Longview." Me and my son Pete jumped in his van and we headed up the road.

It was midday when Bob, his son Pete, who was the president of Portland's ILWU longshore walking bosses and foremen's Local 92, and many other ILWU activists departed hastily for Longview. There ILWU Local 21 members and their supporters blocked the grain train short of the EGT plant. The police response was belligerent and violent. Several ILWU demonstrators and their supporters were hurt. This confrontation was a central part of the entire EGT struggle. It also became the stuff of ILWU legend. Cowlitz County Sheriff's Department officers detained Bob briefly, but released him when the workers and their supporters rushed to his rescue. Dawn DesBrisay was then the president of Portland's ILWU marine clerks Local 40. She was also an accomplished photographer. DesBrisay took an iconic picture of Bob at the moment the police detained him. The photo went viral among labor adherents and contributed to making the day memorable. Below Bob describes his Longview experience on September 7, 2011, after he got there from Vancouver.

BOB MCELLRATH

The cops were fighting the hell out of us. They had me and they took me down. They had four or five cops. When our people seen them dragging me away, 350 men and women from under this railroad trestle came and rescued me. The cops let me go. They ran after this skirmish instead [see fig. 6.2].

People were getting maced and knocked down. Cops were falling down and 'rassling us. The cops claimed that we pepper-sprayed them. They were wrong because the wind was blowing in their face. As they sprayed pepper spray, they sprayed it back in their own eyes. They tried to blame us that we did it and we didn't do it.

Once the cops dropped my arms I ran back into the crowd. The cops got back and they all lined up. They stood on the side of the tracks. The captain called me over. He says, "I'll need to talk to you." I said, "Okay." He said, "You going to come over here?" I said, "Are you going to arrest me?" Everybody's listening. He says, "No, I won't touch you." So I walked through their police line. He kind of fumbled around a little bit. I said, "What's up?" He says to me, "We fucked up." I said, "Yeah, you did."

Then the captain said, "But I'm going to tell you something right now. We're not going to do that again. You see these guys lining up?" They were all lining up with their shotguns and loading them. He said, "We got it loaded with rubber bullets and we're going to empty all these shotguns on you and then we're going to throw tear gas and we're going to take as many people down as we can." I go, "Okay." He goes, "Now you know what?" I go, "What?" He said, "It's your move. Now go back over there."

So I walked back over there. There's a big crowd of longshoremen and other people. The guys are going, "What'd they say? What'd they say?"

Fig. 6.2. Bob McEllrath detained by law enforcement agents on September 7, 2011. The confrontation with Export Grain Terminal Development (EGT) had moved to Longview, Washington, by then. This picture became an iconic image of the union's struggle. Courtesy of Dawn DesBrisay, photographer.

My president at the time of longshore Local 4, Brad Clark, came up. He said, "Bob, what's going on?" I said, "Look at these guys." The cops were close on the tracks, lined up with all their gear on. Then I told Brad what was going on. He goes, "Oh shit!" We had little kids, we had women, we had supporters, it was a hot day and most of them had shorts on with a t-shirt or a tank top. It was about one hundred degrees. I had to make a decision [see fig. 6.3].

I stood there and watched the train back up. It backed all the way over to the freeway. It was almost two miles away and it disappeared. I knew then it was time.

Fig. 6.3. The melee in Longview, Washington, on September 7, 2011. That afternoon ILWU workers and their supporters were attacked by police using pepper spray and batons. Many unionists and their family members were injured, some seriously. Courtesy of Dawn DesBrisay, photographer.

They were going to start shooting and throwing tear gas. That's when I got up on the tracks and gave a speech. I said, "Look, guys, we're leaving. I want everybody to leave." But I also said, "I'm going to tell you cops something. The next time I come back there won't be three hundred of us, they'll be a thousand or there'll be three thousand of us." Then, of course, I had people there say, "Oh, we ain't leaving. You're backing down." I said, "No. We ain't backing down. Did we come here to fight the police? Where's the train? The train is gone. The train backed up and parked clear over there by the freeway. We've accomplished our mission. We're done. Everybody go home." So everybody headed out.

The only trouble was with a few dissidents. There were sixteen people that stayed and got arrested, which cost us about four grand a person. They were arrested for trespass. Later the charges were dropped on them but we still had to bail them out and pay everything. They were a mishmash of guys from longshore Locals 4, 8, and 21. To this day [2013] I still chew these people out and say, "You didn't listen to me." I almost didn't pay their bail, but it would have looked like I left my troops to flounder. So politically I just said, "Okay, we'll pay it," and we did.

That whole day was like 6:00 in the morning till 11:00 a.m. in Vancouver and then from about 2:30, 3:00 p.m. we got to Longview and then it lasted till about 5:00 or 6:00. I was wore out. It was just draining because of the strain trying to take care of the people that you represent and having to reply to the cops. Back in Vancouver I walked in the house. My wife looked at me. She said, "You look terrible." I said, "I'm going to bed." She said, "What happened?" I told her a little bit of what happened. She said, "What are you doing?" I says, "Get me up at 3:30 a.m." She said, "Why?" I said, "We're going back to Longview," and then that's the next day. It's history, too.[16]

LaDonna Chamberlain, a Longview native and a stalwart ILWU supporter, well recalls the EGT struggle. Chamberlain's family has deep roots in Longview and in Local 21. Her testimony echoes some things Bob said about Longview and the events of September 7, 2011.

LADONNA CHAMBERLAIN

I was born in 1968 in Longview, Washington, a little town. Lived there all my life. I married my husband, Stewart, in 1992. He was a casual longshoreman. He's twenty-five years in now [2018]. My family is fourth generation. We have three boys. Two of them are longshoremen. My husband's father was a longshoreman and so was his grandfather. We have a huge family in Local 21 that are all related, all from the Chamberlain and Tow side of the family. The first one would be Roy Tow. His son-in-law is eighty-eight years old, so Roy had to be one of the first ones down there.

My husband cooked breakfast and made soup for everybody during the 2002 lockout. He used to own a restaurant and I used to run it. We're the Chamberlain family that fed everybody. I hear Bob's name a lot. I've seen him a couple of times. We had a longshoreman pass away in our port. He was a very young man. He died falling. It was devastating. Big Bob came down for the funeral service. That was huge.

During EGT they sent a group of women down there to sit on the railroad tracks. The cops were so mean to them that they caused a lot of damage to some of the women. The Longview police force came in their riot gear. Even though nobody caused a scene, they were the first ones to be brutal to anybody. One woman broke her wrist because of the way the cops twisted her arm in order to have handcuffs on her. One of the gals sprained her ankle. The cops were trying to drag her. They picked up women that were sitting on the railroad tracks and dragged them off. Some were elderly or retired women. The cops didn't care, they still dragged them off those tracks. I wasn't allowed to participate in a lot of the activities where the brutality was because my husband was worried about me. So he kept me away on the brutality part. It's not the long-shoremen that are the bad guys, it was our cops in our town that were the bad people and that's not right.

Dan Coffman, the president of Local 21 in 2011–12, was detained by the police more than once during the EGT campaign. His testimony confirms the impressions of police brutality in Longview that Chamberlain remembered.

DAN COFFMAN

I was born in 1956 at Longview and started casualing in 1974. You lashed a lot of log ships as a casual then. I got in as a B-man in '81. My dad was a longshoreman and I have three kids in Local 21. During EGT I was arrested a couple different times. One time was when me and the gals went to block a train. The Ladies Auxiliary was very active in our local. I'd put them up to any of them on the West Coast. They wanted to help. We came up with the idea that we take myself and these women and go sit on the tracks. Our feeling was that a lot of people respect children and women. As it turned out, it didn't work out very well. We had one of the grandmothers got her rotator cuff ripped out of its socket. She had surgeries and stuff after that. A couple of the gals were roughed up pretty good.

Then when some of our men seen what was happening, a couple of them come to the rescue. Two of them, Kelly Mueller, who was very active in the union, and Byron Jacobs, a younger kid that was our treasurer at the time, were assaulted terribly. They were shot with mace by the Burlington Northern cops, and this is the military-type mace. Those people are ruthless. Not only did they give them mouthfuls of that stuff and eyefuls, they'd wait a little bit and then give them another shot of it.[17]

The guy that had me in the beginning whispered in my ear. He says, "I support you 100 percent. I don't want to be here." He treated me great. But then walking to the police vans they had waiting for us another cop grabbed me by the back in handcuffs, by the thumb. He pulled my hand and my thumb in an upwards motion with my hand behind me. I mean it hurt. I said, "What are you doing this for? This is uncalled for. I'm not fighting, I'm not resisting." He just kept doing it a few more times. Me and him got into a little verbal altercation after that. All of us ended up down at the police station. I stayed in a holding cell for four or five hours. I remember them handing me a sack lunch. It was pretty pathetic, a piece of baloney and a hard roll that I think you could have broke a window with. The only thing I ate was an orange. Everything else I threw in the garbage.

In the aftermath of September 7–8, while the police in Longview hunted, harassed, and jailed Local 21 activists and their supporters, a warrant was issued for Bob's arrest as well. He recalls his response.

BOB MCELLRATH

I came down to San Francisco, spent a week, and then had to go back up home to Vancouver. I was driving down the road. My neighbor stepped out and stopped me. We live very close. He's a cop, a police officer for

Camas, a little town just a bit further east.[18] He says, "Bob, I got to tell you something. They been sitting on your house. They're watching you." They were the FBI or whoever the hell it was, the marshals of something-something. He said, "They been here two or three days. They keep coming back. They came to my house. This guy flashed his badge so I flashed my badge." They told him, "Do you know this neighbor guy?" He goes, "Yeah, I know Bob." They asked, "You know he's the president?" He said, "Yeah, I know he's president, he's all that stuff. He's a good guy, he's a friend of mine."

They gave him a card and says, "You call us when he shows up at his house." He said, "I'm not going to call you. You call me. I'll tell you the truth if he's here or not but I'm not calling you." He told me, "They're not here right how. If they call me, I'm going to tell them you're here." I said, "No problem, I don't want you to get in trouble. You got a family to raise." He says, "They got a warrant out for your arrest." At that time we had sent guys to the Longview police station to turn themselves in. They wouldn't take them.[19] Instead, we had a couple of fellows in Longview drive into school or church to pick up their kids in daycare and the cop cars came in there. The cops would throw the guy on the ground in front of his kids, handcuff him, and throw him in the back of the car. The cops were following people to do it.

So my neighbor cop told me, "They got this one big guy. They use him and they're waiting for you. They want to take you down and they're going to take you down hard. I suggest that that you don't stick around here. Go turn yourself in or do something. They won't be here today, but tomorrow is Friday. They want to take you in on Friday because the court shuts down Friday afternoon. You'll sit in the hoosegow Friday, Saturday, Sunday, and maybe Monday afternoon you'll go in front of the judge." I said, "Oh, shit."

I called the attorneys. I said, "What can they do if they knock on the door and I don't answer?" My attorney says, "They can come in the house if they want." My grandkids wanted to come over. I told them, "Nobody comes to the house." I got my wife there. We set up a camera to make sure that if they do come, she's going to start videoing it. I got in the car, went up the road, and rented a hotel room. I stayed in the hotel room on the Friday and Saturday nights. My wife would go out to dinner and then she'd go home. That way she wouldn't get in trouble.

On Monday I got the attorney and we drove to Longview. I walked into the police station. Everybody's with me.[20] The police said, "Who are you?" I said, "I'm Robert McEllrath. They've got a warrant out for my arrest. I'm here to give myself up." They just looked at me 'cause I've got attorneys there, I've got everybody there. But they had a list, they knew who they wanted. Pretty soon this guy comes out and says, "Come with me." So I went in the back and they booked me and they signed everything. I had hearings, stays and hearings, and this and this and this. I must have went up there three or four times before we ever got to trial.

Bob's wife, Sally, also recalls Bob's arrest during the EGT campaign.

SALLY MCELLRATH

Bob's been in trouble before and he's been arrested before. The last time was when he stopped the train. We were having our house worked on and then the police came. So he had to tell the contractor young men, well, "just in case," what was going on. It's just always worrisome. It doesn't stick very long on him, I don't know. It seems like we get through it.

Rob Remar, too, reflected upon Bob's arrest in the days following the September 7 grain train protest in Longview.

ROB REMAR

The police were targeting Bob because he was not only the president, he also made a point that day on the tracks as being visibly the guy responsible for the demonstration. He stepped out in front of everybody and made sure that people let him do that. He told me this before, when he was preparing for that day, and afterwards. He wanted to make sure that any consequences and responsibility for the civil disobedience fell directly on his shoulders first, that he fully owned it and that he didn't want to have others go out and be the pawns or the sacrifices for the cause. That's who he is. Once he makes a decision on something, he owns it, makes sure that everybody understands that he owns it, and will face the consequences good or bad. I've seen him do that on decisions that he wasn't too happy about making. I think on this one he didn't have any second thoughts about it.

Remar dealt with many legal problems during the EGT campaign. Here he recalls those issues, which suggest how difficult it is for organized workers to maneuver in a defensive era for labor when federal law is not favorable to unions.

ROB REMAR

The National Labor Relations Board was seeking to impose injunctions on the ILWU's collective protest actions. We succeeded in defeating a total ban on activity but there were still injunctions issued by the federal court sitting in Tacoma, Washington, that restricted things like mass gatherings that served as sort of a human barricade. Civil disobedience was prohibited such as blocking trains and entrances to the EGT facility.

Other legal work that I did personally was defending against contempt charges against the union and individuals for violations of the federal injunction. We had two different trials, two different groupings of alleged violations of the injunction. We lost, but we didn't lose as badly as the government wanted us to. The penalties weren't as severe as the government hoped for. We appealed to the Ninth Circuit Court of Appeals. Those were sitting in front of the Ninth Circuit at the time we settled.

The early 2012 EGT settlement provided the ILWU with jurisdiction at the plant. But it conceded to the employers the right to have a pool of select workers who did not have to go through the union's traditional hiring hall to get jobs. Since 1934, the ILWU-controlled hall dispatch system had shielded members against exploitation. The settlement also mandated twelve-hour shifts in certain cases. Most Local 21 members were happy that the long EGT campaign was over and that ILWU jurisdiction was secured. Yet the settlement had its critics. In March longtime ILWU critic Jack Heyman and Portland longshore Local 8 member Jack Mulcahy criticized the settlement in a coauthored article. They wrote, "We kept our jurisdiction but got shackled with the worst concessionary contract ever."[21]

Norm Parks, a pensioner from longshore Local 8, also questioned the EGT settlement. Over a forty-three-year career spanning 1960 to 2003, Parks worked on grain committees and held many posts in his local, including secretary-treasurer. His record of twenty-eight years on the ILWU International Executive Board and service on seven coastwide longshore contract negotiating committees was remarkable.[22] Parks sometimes took minority positions critical of the union's leadership. His comments on the EGT agreement follow.

NORM PARKS

I think we could have done much better than we did. Absolutely I am opposed to doing away with the hiring hall and allowing the employers to pick the people that work. We should have took a more militant stance with EGT.

Now Bob reviews the end of the EGT struggle. He describes the severe challenges the ILWU faced, including a rogue union entrenched in the plant and a grain ship approaching EGT that was protected by Coast

Guard personnel ready to shoot and kill ILWU protesters.[23] Along the way Bob accounts for the contract's shortcomings. He also explains his view that the ILWU's most critical challenge during the EGT campaign was the operating engineers' decision to take jobs that traditionally fell within ILWU jurisdiction.

It was of grave concern to Bob that the AFL-CIO would not help the ILWU against Local 701's raiding. Historically, jurisdictional raiding has been a problem for the American labor movement. Big unions like the United Brotherhood of Carpenters and Joiners of America (UBCJA) and the Teamsters raided smaller unions for years. Sometimes umbrella labor groups set up to arbitrate jurisdiction seemed powerless to stop raiding or just honored the wishes of the biggest member unions. The International Union of Operating Engineers had a membership of four hundred thousand and was the tenth-largest union in the AFL-CIO in 2010. It was far bigger than the ILWU at the time of the EGT struggle.[24]

BOB MCELLRATH

There was a lot of people that said I sold out the contract. Well, not a lot. But it's awful hard to beat a huge grain company while you're also trying to fight another organization, another union while they're in there working and you're standing out here trying to win a battle. That was just atrocious what happened there. The predicament we were in was that the grain ship was coming and the operating engineers were going to load the ship. We have never had operating engineers loading grain in the Pacific Northwest. No other union has ever done it in my entire career. That was the pressure I was under.

I'll tell you what I wouldn't have liked. I wouldn't have liked the operating engineers loading a vessel, loading the grain, because today they would be loading grain in Vancouver, Washington, at Columbia Grain in Portland, and at all those other grain elevators. We'd have been out. Members would have looked at me and says, "Why didn't you take the deal that they offered you?" You know, you talk about legacy, whoo, my God!

We wound up with Christine Gregoire, the governor of Washington. She mediated between me and the employers and we finally put things to bed. EGT got some employer rights, how they can hire you, which sticks in my craw. But, hopefully, on the next go-around we'll get rid of that stuff.

We were fighting about every agency that you can fight—the Coast Guard, the state police, the county police, the city police. It was like we're the enemy, the union's the enemy. The head of the Coast Guard emailed to the county sheriff congratulating him on arresting the president of the ILWU, McEllrath. It said, "Congratulations and good luck in court against him." What kind of shit is this? You're fighting for community jobs, for good-paying union jobs, and you got every agency in the government against you.

But the problem wasn't the EGT itself; it wasn't the law; it wasn't even the government; the one I was really concerned with was the operating engineers. That's just a hell of a place to be. That, if you ask me, was why we got out of the AFL-CIO, because I screamed and hollered and said, "Tell these guys to back off." They wouldn't, and the AFL-CIO wouldn't do anything. I was super upset with AFL-CIO president Richard Trumka. He never did anything. I think we could have done a lot better had the unions worked together, if they would have come up to me and said, "Tell you what, Bob, we'll push these guys. We're not going to go against the ILWU." We could have solved this thing, it would have been great for everybody, and we would have been close friends with the operating engineers. It would have been fantastic for the labor movement.

Instead, I just said, "That's it. That's it." I threw my hands up. I said, "I don't know what kind of principles we're going to stand on here if I go to the AFL-CIO and they just look at me and say, 'That doesn't mean nothing.'" That was bad. People say, "Oh, you're running, you're scared of the government. Oh, you're scared of this." No. It was our own people, our own union brothers that made this whole thing bastardized.

Helena Jones is a retired ILWU marine clerks Local 63 worker. She and her longtime friend Christine Gordon are active in the union's

Southern California retiree group, which is part of the Pacific Coast Pensioners Association (PCPA). Gordon has served as the PCPA coast-wide treasurer. Jones, a former ironworker and longshore Local 13 member, overcame harassment from male workers in the building trades and on the waterfront while caring for her disabled sister and four children, most of the time as a single parent. She was a pioneer woman worker in both industries. In her oral history, she talked about her family background in San Pedro and, as a former member of an AFL-CIO skilled-trade union, recalled her response to Bob's decision to leave the AFL-CIO.

HELENA JONES

My uncles, Victor and Vincent McManus, were there in 1934, the night that Knudsen and Parker got shot on the LA docks. My mom was born in 1922. She remembers that night. Her brothers come piling into the house. They were all beat up. They were merchant marines. They went down there that night helping the union. I think that's really cool because then I ended up being down there. They were there that night where the first blood was shed on the West Coast.[25] They didn't know what they did for their little niece in my life. Through the union I kept my house, I was able to make my mortgage. If it wasn't for the ILWU we wouldn't have had a roof over our heads. We'd have been in the gutter big time.

I just can't believe the AFL-CIO. I mean, we're all supposed to be solidarity, solid and organized together. They just weren't being a team player. Big Bob made that decision and I think it was a good decision.

Rob Remar reviewed the issues involved in the EGT settlement of early 2012. His exploration reveals both the power of the courts in influencing labor-management affairs and the tenacity of the ILWU in facing both legal challenges and corporate intransigence. It also demonstrates how complex both labor negotiations and union democracy can sometimes be in practice.

ROB REMAR

The company came to us after the second trial for contempt. They wanted to discuss possible settlement. We spent many hours in the EGT attorneys' law firm developing language. Bob was the chair of our bargaining settlement committee. With him was Leal Sundet, me, Brad Clark, and Jason Lundquist of Local 21, then a new labor relations committee member. It was a hard challenge for the union. We knew we weren't going to be able to get everything. The question was how much do we compromise for the purpose of securing the jurisdiction and getting a foothold in the EGT facility as a legal collective bargaining representative? That would allow the union to do the things you're allowed to do in the next round of contract negotiations without being on the outside and without having the government and the courts telling us that the whole thing was legally invalid from the start and that the union had no business trying to even talk to EGT about bargaining a contract.

The settlement was a good thing. It was necessary under the circumstances. Those of us who were on the front lines were intimately aware of all the government and economic business forces against us. Once we settled, I asked the company attorneys, "Why did you even initiate settlement? Here you had criminal charges against most of the members and all of the local officers and our International president. You had the union subject to orders of contempt of court twice by a federal judge. You were winning on every legal front. You were keeping the union out. The injunctions were slowing things down in terms of protest activity. Why did you settle?"

They said, "Well, frankly, we didn't count on the kind of tenacity and determination and militancy of the ILWU. Our whole game plan and strategy was that we would shut you down with the first injunction and that didn't work; and then we would shut you down with the second injunction and that didn't work; and then we would certainly shut you down with the first contempt rulings and that didn't work; and then we would shut you down with the second contempt rulings and that didn't work."

At that point, the union was developing a series of protest activities and civil disobedience against EGT that was going to involve picket boats. The ILWU was going to come at EGT from the water as well as the land. The water approach was a new innovation. That was publicized purposefully to galvanize support and build power. The other factor was that the company knew that the Occupy movement was getting involved in the EGT fight and that Occupy saw this as a way to promote their objectives or their protest concerning the huge economic inequities in our country. So there was a lot of people and energy being directed towards EGT.

At length the attorneys for EGT told me they thought we were just going to keep on coming and nothing was going to stop us short of blood. With regard to blood, they told me that the Coast Guard and the Department of Homeland Security had a meeting with them to help them organize their plan for the defense or the response against the planned ILWU actions. The Coast Guard told the company executives and their attorneys that they should expect blood to be spilled if the ILWU disobeyed their orders on the water or on the docks. They were going to shoot. That freaked out the company. The company attorneys said, "We didn't want to see people die and we certainly didn't want that on our heads. We didn't want that on the company's reputation and its PR. We didn't want a type of martyrdom in which we're the bad guy and we generate all of this anger against us." So the company went to us to settle.

We had a legal problem with the settlement. The company wasn't going to settle unless they knew what the collective bargaining agreement was going to include in its basic parameters. They weren't going to settle with the union only to have to bargain a contract and face union demands they knew nothing about. They wanted peace, but the federal labor law does not allow for that kind of a resolution because where there is no collective bargaining relationship, then the law prohibits an employer and a union from negotiating terms before the union establishes its lawful representation of the workforce and its lawful bargaining relationship with the employer.

Now about a year before this dispute, the National Labor Relations Board came out with a decision that softened the prohibition on bargaining before there's proper recognition and proper establishment of the bargaining relationship. This softening provided that the union and the employer in these situations are allowed to discuss basic parameters or concepts. Using that as our legal basis, we listened regarding all the things the company said it needed. It took us forever to get them to back off on most of what they wanted and to compromise on other things. We ended up with a document that set out basic parameters using the law's changing. We told the company up front, "Whatever we do here, we're not making a deal with you without a vote of the membership. Everything we do is subject to review, scrutiny, vote, and rejection if they want by the Local 21 membership in Longview." They were nervous about that. They wanted certainty and peace. But they said, "Okay."

We had the local organize an all-hands-on-deck meeting of the membership so we could go through the document. Bob was there, I was there, Leal Sundet, and all the officers of Local 21. It was unanimously recommended. I was asked to explain the legal situation and the terms of the settlement point by point. There were questions asked and we answered them. We said, "We're not allowed to have a collective bargaining agreement with the company right now. We can't do that. All we can do is have these basic parameters and they're not going to settle this thing and give you the jobs unless we do it this way. The final terms of the collective bargaining agreement are going to have to be concluded later. You have to understand that what you're voting on is not just these terms but some other things that we ourselves don't necessarily know that are going to be in the final contract. We think you should vote yes to end the fight, get the jurisdiction, and avoid further risk and harm to the union."

The place was packed. One guy raised his hand and talked against the arrangement. He says, "This is bullshit. It's a sellout. It doesn't have standard PCLCD [Pacific Coast Longshore Contract Document] terms and there are some substandard provisions." We had explained that there were some substandard provisions. The guy also objected to the notion of the membership voting for some basic parameters without having a complete document of agreement. And he objected to the membership not being able to vote on the final collective bargaining agreement later on. We explained to him what we had said before about what the risks were and that ultimately it was left to the membership to decide what they want to do. They took a vote right there. I think there were less than five votes against. It was nearly unanimous in favor of our approach. So that's how we got the settlement. When the contract was finalized, it was done so without another vote because that was part of what the membership had voted for.

We had the settlement done in January, early February of 2012. We had to eat shit on part of it, like the pool. The company had to eat shit on other parts. They didn't want to pay into the benefit plan's pension and health and welfare, but finally they did. That's a big one. That was a huge, huge issue for us. They had their issues, we had ours.

During the EGT campaign, members of the Occupy movement protested the company's behavior and picketed some ports without consulting the union. Bob was sympathetic to the Occupy idea, but he was concerned with the organization's loose structure and the dangers he felt it presented. So he did not bid for a tight alliance with the Occupy movement on the West Coast. Below he reviews his thinking then.

BOB MCELLRATH

The Occupiers wanted to get involved. It's good to have community support. The idea of the 1 percent and what they started back in New York City on Wall Street was on the right track.[26] But what happened is there were too many undercover agencies involved in the Occupy—FBI, CIA, cops, undercover cops, or whatever they are. They're agitating and coming to our town hall meetings and listening to us about whatever strategy the union officers may have. It's really dangerous. Do I want public support? Absolutely. But it's turned around and it's dangerous. I don't know that the Occupiers were helpful in the EGT thing because we never really did put together the great big huge couple thousand mass of people.

Tensions were so great over Occupy and the general pressure of the EGT battle that near the end of the campaign Dan Coffman was called on the carpet by the International at the point when the grain ship was heading up the Columbia River toward Longview. He describes that unhappy experience and then recalls the toll the EGT campaign took on him and on other Local 21 activists and supporters.

DAN COFFMAN

Let's go to when the Coast Guard brought the ship in. A few days previous to that the International called for a presidents-only meeting. Basically that was to take me and my officers to San Francisco and chew our ass. We had a Judas in our local organization that wasn't an officer at that time that was making phone calls to people in the International behind our backs and telling them stuff that wasn't true. We were having a meeting in the back room to organize our boat patrols in case of boat pickets. This individual walked in, seen this meeting going on, and thought we were having some secret meeting. We got called to San Francisco to get an ass-chewing because they had heard rumors, I think, that we were involved with Occupy.

I remember in the conference room that they kicked everybody out and left me in there with eighteen other presidents and the International officers. It was one of the worst days of my life. Here I am a president of a two-hundred-man local trying to fight a multinational corporation and everybody took potshots at me. They said, "Who are you working with?" I told them the only Occupier I knew in Longview was a retired schoolteacher that you would see on the corner of the Walmart Store waving a sign because he absolutely hated the place.

EGT took a big toll on me. At one point I stayed in the office of our local hall for one week when the police were rounding up our officers. They were looking for me and were going to arrest me. After six days my parents came and traded me cars so I could go home and see my wife and daughter. My mom and dad hadn't gone three blocks and there was two cop cars on each side of them. They knew my car. My parents are in their eighties. The cops looked in there. My dad was driving and my mom was sitting in the passenger seat. My dad said it was hilarious because the cops were expecting to see me driving the car. At least I spent one day at home, but I'd spent a whole week at the hall like a prisoner.

The sacrifice some of my members made during the EGT struggle also needs to be noted. We had three individuals that spent a long period of time in jail for blocking trains and fighting the good fight. Those guys put their necks on the line and need to be thanked. Ron Stavas, Sonny Holiday, and Connor McCloud spend thirty days in jail. I'm proud of those guys plus all the other people that had to endure police brutality. We had union officers that were tracked down and roughed up in front of their kids. Jake Whiteside, our vice president, was tracked down in a church parking lot. They came right to Shelly Porter's house and drug her out. Yes, we had a lot of people that did a lot of things and weren't afraid. I was proud of our local and of our membership. Our local is also grateful to ILWU Local 10 in San Francisco. They were the first union to give us ten thousand dollars to work with. They knew what we were up against.

Rob Remar coordinated the defense of the many Local 21 people and their supporters arrested and charged in connection with the EGT campaign. Below he recounts that service.

ROB REMAR

I was involved in the coordination of the defense of the people. Bob and Leal Sundet organized the hiring of local defense attorneys for all the people that got arrested, including nonmembers who got arrested in support of the union cause. There must have been fifteen to twenty criminal defense attorneys that were paid for by the union for everybody's defense. We needed multiple attorneys because under criminal law there's a lot of strict rules about conflict of interest when you're representing multiple people accused of the same incident. We listened to the lawyers as to what their limits were concerning how many individuals a single defense attorney could represent.

I did not serve as a defense attorney for any of the individuals. We had a lot more things to be doing related to EGT. As to the criminal attorneys, some were politically progressive and some were not. We had to sit down and organize them and say, "Look, this is a cause that you're part of and that you are defending. We expect you to do your duty to your client as being the primary obligation, but we want this thing coordinated and we want it understood and dealt with in the context of a political labor dispute."

In the weeks and months after the EGT settlement, the police and the prosecuting attorney in Longview continued to pursue Bob. He was brought to trial twice in 2012 for blocking the grain train on September 7, 2011. He recalls those experiences.

BOB MCELLRATH

We went to trial. They charged me with obstruction and trespass. They dropped the trespass but got me for obstruction of a train. We were tried for two days. It became a hung jury. They couldn't come to a decision. We spent two days and they couldn't get me. So they had another trial a month later. They got a whole new jury and they started it over again. That time we spent three days of trial. The place was pretty well packed with ILWU supporters. The judge had called in police officers to stand at the sides and back. He warned everybody, "I don't want no outbursts or nothing or I'll arrest you and find you in contempt. I want it quiet in here." Now we've got five days of trial and a lot of expense for everybody. And they found me guilty.[27]

Several of the people who attended Bob's trials were representatives from overseas maritime unions that Bob and Wesley Furtado had cultivated through the years. In commenting on the turn of events in Longview, Bob touches again on why he prioritized connecting with international waterfront worker organizations.

BOB MCELLRATH

I've told you and I'm telling you again. The only friends we got in this world are other dockers. I've flown all over this world trying to build docker unity. I know it's been here since Harry Bridges and Jimmy Herman and everybody, but I don't think anybody pushed it as hard as I've pushed it. When I got arrested there was people from all over the world that came with their flags waiting to see what they were going to do with the president of the ILWU. They offered great support. What those guys rallied around wasn't just for Bob McEllrath, it was for the president of the ILWU, who could have been anybody. That's what they rallied around and it just happened to be me in that position.

Willie Adams, then ILWU International secretary-treasurer, attended the court proceedings. His reflections confirm Bob's comments about the overseas support he got in Longview.

WILLIE ADAMS

I was at the trial. It was really good to see the outpouring because there were people that came from all over the world. They came from Australia, New Zealand, and Europe to support Bob. The grain problem was in his backyard, so I know he took that personally. He took it upon himself by blocking the train. He knew what was required of him as a leader and he had the support of the membership.

At his second trial, Bob was sentenced to a day in jail and eighty-nine days of suspended time. He recalls what transpired in court next.

BOB MCELLRATH

The judge said, "Before we pass sentence on you, do you have anything to say?" I stood up and said, "Yes, I do." The judge was ornery. He said, "What do you have to say for yourself?" I said, "I don't have any regrets for what I did to stand up for my men and women that I represent." He didn't like that at all. He persisted to chew my ass out and, I thought, scold me. Then he turned to the prosecutor and said, "What do you recommend?"

They gave me ninety days in jail. They suspended eighty-nine days and said, "You got to pick up garbage for a couple days." I turned to my attorney. He was a good criminal attorney out of Vancouver, Washington. And then I had another guy out of Seattle, another criminal attorney. Anyway, I turned to my attorney and said, "I ain't picking up no garbage." He said, "What?" I said, "Tell them I'm not picking up garbage." My attorney didn't even want to say anything. But he stood up and said, "Your Honor, my client refuses to pick up garbage." The prosecuting attorney opened his mouth quickly and said, "Just pick up garbage for two days. If you refuse, for every two days you have to spend one day in jail." I said, "Then I'll spend one day in jail. I'm not picking up any garbage."

The judge was mad. I was sitting there looking and I thought, "Oh." I was waiting for him 'cause he wanted to give me thirty or forty or sixty days, but that prosecuting attorney opened his mouth too fast. I think they got to the prosecuting attorney and said, "You can't put this president in for thirty days. We don't know what's going to happen up and down the coast. You may have yourself a all-out war, nobody's going to work, and you're going to get some government people involved then." So they stuck me in jail for one day. I spent one day in jail after five days plus all the other hearings I had to go to. And to put a guy in jail for one night it cost the county and everybody hundreds of thousands of dollars. I thought, "This is crazy."

Wesley Furtado, the ILWU International vice president for Hawaii, also attended Bob's trials. His impressions appear here.

WESLEY FURTADO

I went to Longview and I went to the court hearings five days. We had to go back twice. First it was a hung jury. They retried him. This time they set it up so damn good. At lunch I said to Bob, "They going to find you guilty." He goes, "I agree." But I think that was a highlight of his career. As soon as he got sentenced people were calling us from around the world. Okay, they gave him ninety days in prison and then the prosecuting attorney says, "I want to suspend eighty-nine days to just have him do one." They were smart because it would have created chaos, right? We got in our van and we're driving on the freeway. Everybody's calling. I think it went viral when Bob was found guilty. People around the world says, "We'll shut it down one week or whatever as long as Bob's in prison." Bob goes, "No, you don't have to."[28]

Below Bob recounts what it was like to serve his one day in the Longview jail.

BOB MCELLRATH

The judge said to me, "When do you want to sit it out?" I said, "How about Monday?" He said, "No, you can't do it Monday." I said, "Can you do it like on Tuesday?" He said, "No, the only time you can go in is a Thursday or a Saturday." I said, "Well, I'll do it Thursday then." He said, "Okay. On this date you report at 6:00 at night to the jailhouse across the street." That day came and I went and parked the car, got out, and went over there. There was a lot of old-timers, a lot of Longview guys there to support me. I said, "Okay, thank you." I went in there and told them what my name was. They said "Come with us." They undressed me. I was naked. They check your orifices for drugs, the whole nine yards.

They give you a pair of overalls, some slippers, a bedroll and a blanket. No pillow, just a blanket and maybe a toothbrush. Then I went in—it's like a bunkhouse. One floor had five bunks for ten guys. There was probably twenty to twenty-five guys in there. They had these fixed tables. I went in there, sat down, and tried to organize myself. The cops told me what bunk I had. The cops left and I walked around. Then all the guys came and talked. They asked, "Who are you?" Most of the guys were pretty good. I listened to their stories and felt sorry for them. The guy next to me had been in there for quite some time waiting for his trial. They were ramrodding him. His grandfather was a longshoreman who I knew very well.

There was one guy in there that I think was probably a skinhead or something. He had tattoos, a bald head, and was a husky guy. Right away he didn't like me. I was a pretty large guy and he was very large. He kept walking by me. Some of the guys said, "Ah, just ignore him, don't worry about it." Well, I thought maybe they had planted him or went to him to get me into a fight so I would spend the other eighty-nine days. I said to myself, "I've seen this play before. I'm not going to get involved in this shit." I just kept quiet, nodded my head, didn't say anything.

They'd come in with food. It was horrible. These guys were just loving it. I think I ate the carrots, anything that was vegetable. About the rest I'd say, "Do you want this?" The guys would grab it and just wolf it down 'cause they had been in there for thirty or sixty days and that's all you get. They had one thing they called "sweaty meat." It was for lunch. It was a round piece of baloney. It was very thin but it was slippery and gooey. It was kind of like if you leave a piece of baloney or something in the fridge and it starts to decay and it gets a slime on it. I didn't eat it. If they had Jell-O or carrots I ate that. That was it. Then I drank a milk or a juice.

The showers were terrible. The guys said, "Don't use this shower, it's plugged up, it'll leak and go all over the floor." The floor is where you sit to eat 'cause it's right there. I didn't take a shower. I would not have enjoyed spending even a week in that jail. Thirty days? I probably would have been nuts by then. I'm certain I would have been in a fight, just knowing myself.

I went from 7:00 at night for twenty-four hours. At five minutes to 7:00 the following day—twenty-three hours and fifty-five minutes—they come and got me. They walked me down from the bunkhouse and gave me back my clothes. I got undressed, put all my clothes on, and walked out. All the guys were there, greeting me again. I shook their hands and said, "Thank you very much for the support," got into my car and drove all the way from Longview back to Vancouver. I stopped and got me something good to eat and drink and drove home.

The last of the ILWU's EGT-related court defense cases were finalized by mid-2013, and, as noted, Bob led the ILWU out of the AFL-CIO in August of that year.[29] In his interview in 2018, Willie Adams recalled that decision: "I was around Bob the day he decided to pull out of the AFL-CIO, which was a very hard decision weighing heavy on his heart." The ILWU battle with EGT for jurisdiction was over, although there were repercussions of it as other grain company negotiators looked to EGT contract concessions for inspiration. One result was a multicompany lockout of ILWU grain workers in the Pacific Northwest during 2013–14. That, though, is a story for another chapter.

7

"Up Against Some Difficult Times"

International President, 2013–2015

> This was not a lockout to exert leverage on us. This was a lockout to get rid of us.
>
> BRAD CLARK

The ILWU met again in International Convention from June 8 to June 12, 2015. This time, the elected delegates convened in Honolulu, the center of the union's largest regional body, Hawaii's islands-wide ILWU Local 142. Bob had survived the EGT grain confrontation, an eighteen-month 2013–14 lockout by powerful Northwest grain companies, and a long and exhausting Longshore Division negotiating campaign covering 2014–15 that ultimately secured a five-year contract with the waterfront employers' Pacific Maritime Association. Bob was sixty-four. People wondered if he would retire at that point. Prior to the convention he did not publicly announce his intentions. Partly this was to keep the employers guessing. He opted to run for International president again.

As had become customary, prominent leaders from notable ILWU locals rose to nominate Bob for the union's most important position. Joe Cortez of Los Angeles/Long Beach longshore Local 13 initially echoed what he had said at the union's convention in 2012. First he thanked Sally McEllrath again for her support of Bob and her sacrifice for the ILWU. In a reference to the recent EGT struggle, Cortez also pointed out how Bob had stood tall in the face of "many battles against the government and other trade unions that have sought not only to destroy us, but to split our united front." He expressed his admiration for Bob's "steadfast loyalty to the union, even at the price of going to jail."[1] Then he nominated Bob for a fourth term as president.

Rainiero Salas, secretary general of the Panama Canal Pilots Union, and Willie Adams, ILWU International secretary-treasurer and Tacoma, Washington, longshore Local 23 delegate, seconded Bob's nomination. Adams emphasized how he had watched Bob grow in office and exercise calm and courage under fire. "The guy has the guts of a gun slinger," Adams declared.[2] Brad Clark of longshore Local 4, Bob's home local, provided an extraordinary second as well. Covering six pages in the union's convention proceedings, Clark's speech highlighted Bob's leadership during the EGT fight and the 2013–14 Northwest grain lockout, which disrupted waterfront operations in Portland, Oregon, and Vancouver, Washington. There were no other nominations. Bolstered by a standing ovation, Hawaiian music, and a great vote of confidence, Bob would now serve as ILWU International president for another three years.[3]

As the union's latest major economic battle, the 2013–14 grain lockout was still on the minds of all those assembled. The union's contractual relationship with the employers' Pacific Northwest Grain Handlers Association (PNGHA) dated back to the 1930s. By 2011 Pacific Northwest ports processed close to a third of all US grain exports. With profits amounting to billions of dollars a year, PNGHA employer groups were among the world's most powerful multinational corporations. PNGHA membership included two Japanese-owned companies, Mitsui-United Grain of Vancouver, Washington, and Marubeni-Columbia Grain of Portland, Oregon. A third company,

French-owned and Netherlands-based Louis Dreyfus Commodities, had grain export facilities in Seattle and Portland. The only US-based PNGHA unit was TEMCO, owned by Midwest agricultural processing giant Cargill, Inc. TEMCO operated grain terminals in Kalama and Tacoma, Washington, and Portland.[4]

Negotiations for a renewed grain contract began in late August 2012. In this round of talks, the PNGHA's adherents were emboldened by the resistance that nonmember EGT had mustered against the ILWU in Longview, Washington, before conceding recognition and agreeing to a contract the prior February. During late 2012 negotiations, the PNGHA asked for concessions, including the right to sub-contract jobs in the event that three work stoppages were declared illegal under the union contract. Work stoppages did sometimes occur over issues like safety. The employers also insisted that if a work stoppage should be deemed illegal, the union would have to pay them a million dollars and damages. ILWU negotiators saw these demands as unreasonable. By a 94 percent "no" vote, the membership of the ILWU Northwest grain locals agreed with their negotiators. There would be no quick and easy contract agreement.[5]

Mitsui-United Grain locked out ILWU longshore Local 4 in Vancouver on February 27, 2013. On May 4, Marubeni-Columbia Grain locked out ILWU longshore Local 8 in Portland. Louis Dreyfus Commodities declared a "maintenance" closure. But US-based TEMCO broke ranks with the PNGHA. It negotiated an agreement with the ILWU to stay open pending whatever final contract stipulations emerged after the dispute ended. United Grain and Columbia Grain both imported strike-breakers in an effort to run their facilities. The union responded with round-the-clock picketing in Vancouver and Portland and the strategic deployment of recreational-style boats on the Columbia River to slow grain deliveries. The ILWU-affiliated Inlandboatmen's Union (IBU) aided the longshoremen as much as possible. So did the Masters, Mates, and Pilots (MMP). But members of the International Brotherhood of Electrical Workers (IBEW) crossed the ILWU picket lines and local police and the Coast Guard sided with the employers during the confrontation.[6]

After months of struggle, in August 2014 members of the ILWU locals that handled Pacific Northwest grain ratified a new contract with the PNGHA. The vote was 88.4 percent to accept. Locals voting included 4 of Vancouver, 8 of Portland, 19 of Seattle, 21 of Longview, and 23 of Tacoma. Mitsui-United Grain's lockout in Vancouver had lasted for eighteen months, Marubeni-Columbia Grain's in Portland for fifteen. The agreement terms would apply to Louis Dreyfus Commodities and to TEMCO. Perhaps the most positive outcome for the union was that it maintained the majority of its jurisdiction in the region's grain terminals. The ILWU also won some annual wage increases and the continuation of 100 percent employer contributions to the union's pension and health and welfare plans.[7]

Union concessions were also part of the settlement. The contract let managers perform bargaining unit tasks if there was a work stoppage, although the union employees would be paid for lost wages if the stoppage should be deemed legal. For example, this might be the case where employees stopped work over a valid safety concern. The agreement gave management the right to operate the control room console, which directed the flow of products in grain elevators. Further, the contract did not require the use of a union "supercargo" clerk, a ship clerk who, in working bulk cargo longshore operations, frequently passes information along to other clerks, tracks cargo tonnage, and keeps an hourly log of work.[8] The loss of console operations and supercargo clerk responsibilities meant that the union had relinquished some jurisdiction. The new agreement also echoed previous ILWU grain contracts that permitted twelve-hour shifts with overtime compensation after eight hours.[9]

A few perennial ILWU critics complained that the PNGHA got grain console and supercargo control and allowed the employers to use non-ILWU labor when work was stopped. Longshore Local 10's Jack Heyman called the agreement "a mockery of our hard-won rights to honor picket lines [and] standby on safety."[10] Nonetheless, the ILWU was back on the Northwest grain docks after eighteen months of battle.

In this chapter, we will hear from Brad Clark of ILWU Local 4 in Vancouver, Washington; Bob McEllrath; Willie Adams; Melvin Mackay of

ILWU Local 10 in Northern California; Rich Austin, former president of the ILWU Pacific Coast Pensioners Association; Rob Remar; Ed Ferris of Local 10; John Castanho, the ILWU Pacific Coast benefits specialist; and Paddy Crumlin from the MUA. All were active participants in the 2013–14 Northwest grain lockout and/or the 2014–15 ILWU Longshore Division master contract negotiations, except for Crumlin, who nonetheless followed these events closely. In June 2015 Crumlin came over from Australia to attend the ILWU International Convention in Honolulu, where he dramatically highlighted his steadfast unity with Bob and the ILWU.

Local 4's Brad Clark was there for the EGT battle in Longview as well as the 2013–14 grain lockout. Clark, who was born in 1965, got his first taste of waterfront labor in 1988. He began working consistently on the Vancouver waterfront in the early 1990s. In talking about longshoring, Clark said, "I always felt good after a hard day's work but, in all honesty, I really didn't enjoy the work. I enjoyed the people." He has been ILWU small-ports representative, Oregon/Columbia region, the same post Bob once held. Clark won election as Local 4 president in 2000 and served several terms in that capacity. He became Oregon area arbitrator after the 2015 signing of the Pacific Coast longshore industry's new master contract. Here Clark recalls the EGT and the PNGHA struggles and Bob's role in negotiating settlements for both confrontations.

BRAD CLARK

Up in Longview at EGT, we had to man two gates. Local 4 and Local 8 from Portland made sure that we had our people up there for twelve hours a day. Then Local 21 of Longview covered the twelve hours at night. Every member in Local 4 was assigned to a team. I think it was every ten days they had to go up and take a day off work and drive an hour up there, serve six hours on picket duty, and drive an hour back. That's the price of membership in Local 4.

Longview, Local 21, did a tremendous job with EGT. In EGT there were no concessions made because we never had a contract! I remember having a discussion with Bob. He said, "Tell me what you think." At that point, we were losing our army. They were really coming after our people and we were facing jail time. So I said, "Bob, I think if you can get one job in there, you got to do it."

We bargained with Larry Clarke, the head of EGT, and with Christine Gregoire, the governor of Washington. I was there. After about four days we got the deal done. I want to say it was one in the morning maybe. In negotiating, I'm impressed by how Bob can come from being removed from the situation except by phone or by the periodic meeting with somebody who's there all the time and can take the information he's given, show up at bargaining, and have a grasp of the situation. Good leaders have that ability. Bob's one of the best I've seen. He has that ability to multitask. There's a lot of issues going on at the coast level at any one time. He can compartmentalize all those other issues and set them aside and deal with this one and really understand what the fight's about. He does that not just because he has an innate ability to problem-solve. He does it through listening to everybody else. He listens to people and really tries to hear what they're saying.

With EGT, we didn't get as far as we wanted to get, but as I was saying we really didn't make any concessions because we started with nothing. The work was being done by operating engineers, people other than longshoremen. When we got in there, we captured whatever we could capture. And if we would have taken the EGT agreement without the pension and the health and welfare benefits that longshoremen have, we would have really been climbing uphill in the 2014 grain agreement. That was the mastery of Bob being our lead spokesman in those EGT negotiations.

I think Bob realized if we don't secure what we have to secure at EGT, we're going to jeopardize it all. You saw how hard that grain struggle was even after we got what we got at EGT. But when we did finally get back into Northwest grain, we took away some of the ammunition those employers had against us. They couldn't say, "We can't pay your pensions anymore, we can't pay your benefits anymore," because we just showed that EGT was able to do it. It at least allowed us to sit up a little higher at the table in that year and a half of grain bargaining.

BRAD CLARK

When the 2013 lockout happened, one of the good things from prior struggle was that Local 4 had developed good strike and lockout rules. We knew how to form our picket committees. We had to picket not just down at the grain elevator but at their corporate offices in downtown Vancouver as well. The Local 4 president at the time, Cager Clabaugh, and the officers, Troy Olson and others, got the picket teams together. We got help from the pensioners and the Ladies Auxiliary.

The only days we took off in Vancouver in that year and a half were Thanksgiving, Christmas, and New Year's. We picketed twenty-four hours a day, seven days a week at the facility other than those three days. We did 6:00 a.m. to 6:00 p.m. at the corporate offices five days a week.

We also had twenty-four-hour boat pickets out on the Columbia River. Because it gets dangerous in the winter at night out there, we would pull the pickets when the winds came up and you couldn't see anything. But we had Local 4 or Portland Local 8 guys out there at 6:00 a.m. at least, rain or shine, snow, or whatever. Anytime a tug was bringing a barge down or a ship in, whoever was on the picket boat would get ahold of another boat picket and we'd get two boats out there to heckle the guys making the moves. We'd slow down or stop barges from coming in. We worked with the Inlandboatmen's Union and in some ways with the Masters, Mates, and Pilots because they're the ones that knew when everything was moving. They let us know and we'd let our guys know.

And on land all these scabs were coming from all over the country to work for Gettier, a Delaware-based company that was a strikebreaking outfit. They came in a bus or vans twice a day. There'd be about fifteen to eighteen of them. They were the guards of the plant. For a couple of months we had Local 4 guys staying in a room in the hotel next door to the hotel where the scabs were staying. We'd shift guys in and out,

Fig. 7.1. ILWU demonstrators in Vancouver, Washington, during the 2013–14 Northwest grain lockout. The employers imported strikebreakers, called "scabs" by the workers, in an effort to dislodge the union during what became a year-and-a-half-long struggle. Courtesy of Dawn DesBrisay, photographer.

watching Gettier's operations. We learned their schedules, when they were shifting people in and out. The scabs did three-month shifts and then they'd send them home and bring in new guys. We'd go up to their hotel at maybe six in the morning. It'd be pretty much Local 4 members. We might have a hundred people there with bullhorns, making noise. Then we'd leave [see fig. 7.1].

One time we decided to have a rally in the evening at the scabs' hotel. The police met with our local officers. Our officers told them we were going to have a rally. Our guys said, "No big deal, we're just going to march up there." Well, what did the police do? They notified the employers about the scabs' hotel. What did the employers do? They didn't pick the scabs up there as usual, they did it at the mall. So we never saw them. We felt very slighted by the police. We still decided to have a rally. It wasn't a big one, maybe fifty of us. We went out there and did our thing.

We also printed up a flyer, one flyer. It was basically like a plan for the Local 4 membership. It said, "We are going to meet at six o'clock and we're going to make noise till 6:30 p.m. At 6:30 on the dot, everybody leave. But we're going to come back at 7:30 and do the same thing for a short amount of time. Then everybody leave again." Then the flyer said, "At 11:00, our friends from California and Puget Sound are bringing their buses in, and at 11:00 we're going to have a big rally." It went on, "Don't bring family, don't bring friends, it's ILWU longshore members only. Dress in black."

At our second rally that evening, we crumpled up the flyer and threw it in the bushes. We threw it where the police would find it. Then everybody left. The police called our officers and asked, "What's going on?" Our officers said, "We don't know. Last time we talked to you, you went and told the employers, and now our own membership isn't talking to us. So we have no idea what this letter's about." We just played stupid. Well, at 11:00 that night the police had the SWAT team, they had dogs, and our guys in the hotel were calling me, "You wouldn't believe this! There's got to be fifty cops out there. It sounds like a kennel, they all got their dogs." So the police had mobilized and brought everybody in that was off-duty. But nobody showed up. About 11:30 they realized the big rally wasn't going to happen. There were a lot of fun ways to agitate. No harm's done in anything like that either.

Occasionally, as can be the case during any dispute, there was an incident that was not quite so innocent and fun. Bob recalled taking action during the 2013–14 grain lockout to block some counterproductive catcalls aimed at the strikebreakers.

BOB MCELLRATH

In grain we were up there locked out. They were bringing in this Louisiana, Tennessee, strikebreaking outfit. Well, you know what 95 percent of them were? Black guys. Now all of a sudden there's been some racial slurs thrown in. I went up there; I had an executive board meeting. I told the guys to knock it off. I says, "The employers are winning that way, you're not. The employers are getting what they want. They want you to do that and the public's going to see it. We got no public support if you start using racial slurs. You can call them an asshole, a scab, a no-good, rotten bastard, but you keep the racial slurs out."

In the long run, it took the ILWU Pacific Northwest grain locals more than seventy negotiating meetings over eighteen months to finally secure a new contract with the PNGHA.[11] Brad Clark and Bob were involved in the process. Clark reviews that experience.

BRAD CLARK

There was an extended break in negotiations when we were locked out. We went a long time without meeting. The employers definitely had it in their minds that we were done. In my opinion, this was not a lockout to exert leverage on us. This was a lockout to get rid of us. When they made that move to lock us out, it was their intention to never let us back in there again. I don't think we could say that about the 2002 struggle. This one they had put fencing up. I think they finally realized that the expertise of guys that had been working there for thirty years just isn't replaced in a year—especially the maintenance part of it. When our guys came back in, they said that place wasn't going to last much longer. Things didn't get greased, you know? I think after a while the employers realized, "Well, maybe we do need those guys."

I know Bob was directly involved in the negotiations at the end. I think Bob trusts the people that he's got in place. When we went into bargaining, most of the guys in there had been through at least a couple of grain bargaining cycles. It wasn't a rookie committee. Rich Austin Jr. and Cameron Williams were there. Cam was there because he was president of Local 19 in Seattle at the time. Bob lets negotiations go and, hopefully, it gets settled. When it doesn't get settled, then he's really good at picking the right time of stepping in. There's no sense in him stepping in when there's no settlement to be had. Everybody could see the fight's going to go on a while. You don't send in your knight in shining armor when the end of the war is months away. In this regard, Bob acted as a closer.

We had a mediator there for maybe the last twenty grain bargaining sessions. He was high up, like second or third in the Federal Mediation and Conciliation Service. I think he was the deputy to the director.[12] But those of us that had been in bargaining for a year didn't want the mediator. A mediator doesn't do any good. The only reason we accommodated one was for how it looked politically, how it looked in public relations. I think our dissatisfaction with having a mediator there was apparent. We all kind of bad-mouthed this guy.

When Bob came in, he treated that man with respect. He listened to what the mediator said, he engaged with that mediator, and he formed a relationship with him. I know the mediator knew that none of us wanted him there. Bob didn't give him that impression. Then when the 2014 longshore master contract negotiations came up, guess who the feds sent? And guess who had a great relationship with him? The president of the ILWU. I never heard Bob say it, but what he taught us then is don't ever burn a bridge. You never know when you're going to need that guy. When that guy came in during the longshore negotiations, he had a relationship with Bob. Jim McKenna of the PMA [Pacific Maritime Association] didn't. Again, I don't think he really helped in bargaining, but it sure as hell didn't hurt us.

Bob came in and started from scratch with the mediator and formed a great relationship. That's what a statesman does. I think between 2012 and 2018 Bob went from a leader to a statesman. He's been through so much bargaining he knows just how far he can push. He's very patient. And he doesn't like late-night bargaining sessions. I can only think of twice that we went really late into the night bargaining with Bob. He always told us, "If you've been bargaining all day, you make mistakes at 10:00 at night. If it's a good deal at 10:00 at night, it's going to be a good deal at 9:00 a.m. the next morning." That's how we bargained.

In the end, there wasn't anybody in the ILWU who liked the grain agreement. You probably won't find a lot of longshoremen today that wouldn't tell you, "We would have stayed out there for five years, if it took five years." But after a year and a half, people wanted off the line. It was very disruptive to families. When guys are having to take that time for no pay twice a week to go down there in the middle of the night, they have to work vacations around it or find somebody to cover them and switch. If you're picketing from noon to six today, you can't come into the hall and get a job at a place that was not locked out because you've got to be on picket duty. So you're missing wages.

If the agreement we eventually agreed to was put in front of us even a month before it was signed, it would have been rejected. Management got rights in that contract they didn't previously have. If anybody on our committee of twelve would have said, "No, we're going to keep going," we might not have brought the agreement back to the membership. But I think everybody on that committee knew, "This is as good as we're going to get in this round." I mean, you fought as hard as you could fight, you pushed as far as you could push, but at some point you got to end the war, make it work, and get it back down the road. Still, we maintained what we had to maintain, which was the maintenance and repair and the actual loading and unloading of the grain elevator.

Bob also commented on the bargaining issues of the 2013–14 Northwest grain lockout. His recollections follow.

BOB MCELLRATH

I was helping out behind the scenes and eventually got involved in the bargaining with the committee toward the end. We called in Scot Beckenbaugh, who works for the federal mediation program. He later was called in for 2014 Longshore Division bargaining. But, yeah, I got involved in it toward the end and we finally put the grain contract to bed. There is a few things that we surrendered. We wound up having to go to a twelve-hour workday. The supercargo was taken off the vessel. What the grain elevators did was then start stevedoring the vessels themselves, so they weren't using a PMA stevedore. But they wound up paying them through the PMA as a nonparticipant member, so they're still paying into the pension plan and the welfare plan. We had started to lose the supercargo back in the late eighties, early nineties at Peavey Elevator. It's now called KEX. That's one we're still fighting with.[13]

In May 2014, even before the Northwest grain agreement was in place, Bob and a sixteen-member ILWU Longshore Division bargaining committee met for the first time with PMA representatives to discuss renewal of the union's Pacific Coast waterfront master contract. Dozens of elected delegates from the union's waterfront locals had met in caucus in San Francisco the prior month to establish the union's demands. Once concluded, the master longshore agreement would cover twenty thousand registered and casual workers at twenty-nine West Coast ports. It took ten months of talks in San Francisco to produce a tentative five-year contract in February 2015. This was the longest set of coastwide longshore negotiations in years. In April the union's Longshore Division membership voted by 82 percent to accept the new agreement. The ILWU Coast Balloting Committee certified the vote on May 22, 2015. Employer outsourcing of container chassis inspection, maintenance, and repair jobs previously done by longshore workers, and PMA initial refusal to improve safety conditions, contributed to the long delay in reaching agreement. So did employer mini-lockouts during the negotiations.[14]

The new contract maintained good longshore health and pension benefits and boosted wages. It called for limiting the outsourcing of chassis jobs and addressed safety concerns. There was also a new arbitration system that replaced individual arbitrators in four port areas with a three-member panel. The PMA and the ILWU would each nominate one arbitrator. The third arbitrator would be a neutral person from the Federal Mediation and Conciliation Service or the American Arbitration Association. The new contract did not address automation directly. Before the union membership had voted in

April 2015, some members had argued for a no vote. They emphasized that the new agreement allowed for automation without providing for concessions to union members like shorter shifts tied to wage increases. But the employers already had the right to introduce new cargo-handling equipment going back to the 2008 coastwide longshore master agreement. They had made jurisdictional commitments to the union then in exchange for a free hand in automation.[15]

ILWU International secretary-treasurer Willie Adams remembered the tone of the 2014–15 negotiations. Here he describes some of the problems Bob had to deal with and what his own role entailed in visiting Washington, DC, to keep federal government officials informed about the progress of negotiations and resistant to rhetoric that might harm the union's cause. His main task was to try to keep the federal government from interfering with the negotiations to the union's disadvantage.

WILLIE ADAMS

It was tough negotiations. Unlike some previous negotiations, there were a lot of local issues. Bob stopped the negotiations to deal with local issues the locals couldn't seem to deal with. He said, "We got to get these done first before we can get the rest of the contract done," and he did that. Local 10 had some issues. Ship clerks Local 34 had some issues. Normally those issues don't come up to the big table.[16] Bob had the Northwest grain lockout going on. He had to stop for that to finish up.

Bob sent myself and International vice president Wesley Furtado of Hawaii to Washington, DC. We went to the White House and gave President Obama's aides an update on what was going on in negotiations. We said, "The president of the ILWU sent us back here so you won't be listening to rumors. He doesn't want you reading things in the paper or looking at things from social media. We're here to tell you what the issues are." We met with Democratic House leader Nancy Pelosi and with Democrats and Republicans. We updated them how we were working very hard to get issues done, although they were some very tough issues.

Melvin Mackay, who served multiple terms as president of Northern California ILWU Local 10 and was on the 2014–15 longshore negotiating committee, spoke about Bob's handling of regional issues during the talks.

MELVIN MACKAY

I can tell Bob the problems I have in Local 10. If that brings about coast-wide significance, okay. If it's in detriment, he'll tell me no. But if it's something good, he'll say, "Let's go for it." During negotiations in 2008 as well as 2014 there were a lot of things that Local 10 needed to get straightened out. We had to do this at the big table because locally we weren't getting any movement. So naturally I would go to Bob and/or Leal Sundet, who was a coast committeeman at the time.

Bob was very instrumental, as was Leal, with the PMA at the International level. They would assist with those issues we had. We've had our run-ins, as every man does, but for the most part Bob's genuine. I respect him to the utmost. The things I don't like really doesn't make a difference. Bob has done a lot for the ILWU. He is a very conscious person about the structure of the union. His tenure has been to assist. He'll try to bring it to where, "This is best for all. It's for the masses." Bob wants to help you as well as the little man. He's a person of means, you know?

Rich Austin Sr. has had a long career in the ILWU. He was a coast committeeman and has held other important union posts. In retirement in the Northwest, Austin served several terms as president of the Pacific Coast Pensioners' Association (PCPA). During 2014–15, he was the PCPA representative on the coastwide longshore contract negotiating committee. He recalls challenges from the 2014–15 negotiations and Bob's response.

RICH AUSTIN SR.

These people at the PCPA feel this love and gratitude about our ILWU. I don't know of another union in the United States that treats its pensioners the way the ILWU does. We get to voice our opinions at caucuses and at conventions. We're asked to sit on the negotiating committee. We're asked to participate in legislative conferences, going back to Washington, DC. In 2014 I was the pensioner designee on the negotiating committee. That means I was in San Francisco for ten months. What we do for the union is a labor of love. We don't get paid. Well, I should say, we get paid every day. It's called a longshore pension!

One of the things about Bob was that he got the negotiating committee all amongst ourselves, and we got to blow off steam. It's very important because everybody on the committee is representing their constituency, and they're representing the whole coast. So they have to feel like they got to say what they needed to say and were listened to, and that what they had to say got some discussion. That happened with Bob.

The negotiating committee is schooled. We do all the research we need to do. So when we sit across the table and hear employers say things that we know aren't true, when they put on PowerPoint presentations identifying issues that have been disproved three years ago, we know this is not good-faith negotiations. When you call them on it—"Christ no, three years ago we disproved that"—they'd say, "Oh well, you got us." That's basically their attitude. It became frustrating. I felt like going across the table on them a couple of times. I'd be the person to do it, too, because they can't deregister me![17] No, that would break up the decorum of the negotiations. You have to sit there with a poker face. The ILWU International president did call them. They'd just say, "We hear you."

What we would do is make sure we were right. Bob is very mindful of that. You don't want to throw crap across the table that you can't prove. So we would re-research and find out what the truth was. Bob would throw papers back at them. He was the spokesperson. We had one spokesperson, not everybody chipping away. Bob would throw back the facts across the table and point them out, one, two, three, four, five, six, seven. They would say, "Yeah, well, we hear you."

I'm sure it was frustrating for Bob. He did a good job. He was up against some difficult times. They were trying to stall us. One of the things they did during the negotiations is lock us out. The employers wanted to create a scenario that we would get the blame for slowdowns. They would hire two gangs of workers on a vessel when normally they would have four. Then they would complain to the press that productivity was down 50 percent. But the press doesn't know how to ask, "Were you hiring the same amount of people?" So the employers would get away with that. They created this thing to get the farmers and so on against the union. They created it to put the union in a bad light. The secretary of labor, Tom Perez, came out and said President Obama wanted a settlement. Bob made it very clear: "We want a settlement, too, but we're not going to sell our soul in order to get a settlement. If you call us back to Washington, DC, that's the way it's going to be, but we're not going to give up on this." So it turned out okay.[18]

Brad Clark from Local 4, Bob's home local, was also on the negotiating committee in 2014–15. He remembers Bob's negotiating style at the time.

BRAD CLARK

Bob had the patience to figure things out. It might not be when the employers pass a document to us. It might be the next day or the day after that. Or maybe it was when he talked to somebody over a beer the night before. He had the ability to say, "Okay, they're throwing this out, but that ain't what they want. They're using this to draw our attention. It's over here that they want. So let's walk them down that path because sooner or later they've got to tip their hand over here." This is the ability to think of bargaining as a chess match. You saw the same thing from Jim McKenna of the PMA. They're playing at a different level than I am, that's for sure. They're playing grand master chess and someone like me is playing beginner's.

There is something else in the 2014 agreement I believe shows how Bob thinks. In this contract, everybody got the same wage money. I take that back, mechanics did get a little bit more. But some clerks, maybe some supercargoes, were upset. They thought, "Wait, a basic guy got a dollar and that's all I get? How come I don't get 30 percent more?" I think Bob's mentality is, "In order to give you a dollar thirty I can't give him a dollar. I can only give him seventy cents." That was a struggle on our negotiating committee, but Bob was right. He negotiated for everybody and nobody can say he showed favoritism. We have all these skill wage rates, and I think Bob said, "Enough, a flat rate for everybody. A crane operator doesn't get more pension than a basic guy, why should he get more of a wage hike?" I think that's an old-school labor belief. And Bob's able to get people to understand that.

Rob Remar also has clear memories of the 2014–15 negotiations. Below he recalls those impressions.

ROB REMAR

I remember how freaking long the thing was. It was the longest bargaining of longshore anyway in the longshore industry that I have ever seen. It went a good ten months. There were a lot of issues in which both sides had institutional security at stake that were in conflict. In terms of time, the longest issue was health and welfare. It usually is.

We also had a problem with the employers having run out on us with respect to chassis maintenance and repair. They have always owned the chassis that are used in the yards in the container terminals. At most of the terminals we have always done the work related to this. By the time the contract came around in 2014 to be renegotiated, the employers had quietly and without notice to us transferred all of their chassis to third-party owners and contractors that had no bargaining obligations to the ILWU. That was a real conundrum. The employers claimed, and maybe they were correct under the law anyway, that they no longer had control over the chassis. Therefore, they couldn't bargain with us about those issues. It's like, "The horse is already out of the barn. The train has left the station. There's nothing we can do now."

The union position was that this is an existential, institutional security issue. If the employers could get away with transferring the equipment we work on, then there's no end to it. Today it's the chassis they transfer. Tomorrow it's the containers. The next week it's the machines, it's the lifts and cranes, the transtainers.[19] We ended up agreeing to certain what were called "road ability inspection protocols" assigned to the longshore workforce at those terminals where longshoremen have traditionally done the work. There are some terminals where other unions have performed the mechanical work, the maintenance work, and for those terminals we gave up a claim to those tasks. But for the ones that we have traditionally done M and R work, we maintained our position and got some good resolutions out of it.

Bob had negotiated comprehensive provisions for that in 2008. The basic grand bargain there was employers get to institute or implement robotics in exchange for giving the ILWU all of the maintenance and repair work that goes with robotics as well as the existing maintenance and repair work the employers control. Then by law we had to have exceptions for those facilities where other unions were performing the work. Well, we had problems with compliance with the 2008 provisions in 2014. There were different things we wanted to do to secure that. We got some protection, but ultimately it comes down to being able to enforce the contract on the ground during the administration of it, chasing the employers and catching them when they violate the deal. You can have the best language in the world on paper, but if the employers want to renege on it, you still got to catch them. You still got to enforce it.

It might be recalled that the employers actually had the right "to intro-duce labor-saving devices" going back to the first Pacific Coast long-shore master contract installed after the Big Strike of 1934.[20] The clauses in that contract were handed down by a federal arbitration board. They were not negotiated for directly by Harry Bridges. In 1934 the members of that arbitration board could not envision the kind of potential destruction to waterfront workers, their families, and their communities that the elimination of jobs by automation and robotics might pose in the twenty-first century. Consequently, at least in part, resisting the impact of "the machine" has been an uphill battle for the ILWU ever since. The conclusion of the Mechanization and Moderniza-tion Agreement with the PMA in 1960 that allowed the employers to introduce containerization on the waterfront without a big struggle is just one example. In 2019 the union was still trying to deal with the worst implications of automation in places like the Ports of Long Beach and Los Angeles.[21]

In addition to automation, safety has long been of concern on the waterfront. Ed Ferris from Local 10 in Northern California was on the negotiating committee during 2014–15. Because of his special interest in safety, he was on a safety subcommittee during bargaining sessions. He has served as Local 10 business agent, secretary-treasurer, vice president, and president. In 2016 he was appointed to the federal government's Maritime Advisory Committee for Occupational Safety and Health, in part because Bob was impressed with his safety record. Ferris was elected ILWU International secretary-treasurer in 2018. Here he describes Bob and the 2014–15 negotiations.

ED FERRIS

I am very proud that I consider Bob a good friend. Got to spend a lot of time with him, especially over the 2014 bargaining. The fact that he's been able to be an International officer for the ILWU coming from a small local is truly amazing. Our International presidents typically come from the larger locals, but Bob's a special guy. I think his personality and charisma have a lot to do with where he's ended up. He doesn't push his position on anybody, he's very patient, and he is willing to listen. We don't always agree on everything, but we do have a lot of common interests. I remember the first time I talked to Bob. It was at the San Diego International Convention in 2012. I was so impressed that this guy would talk to a nobody like myself. He has a gift of making people feel important. That's a strong trait of a leader and it's something I've appreciated about Bob for many years.

At the time of the 2014 bargaining, I was vice president of Local 10 and I was a caucus delegate. I went to the caucus and was hoping to get on the safety committee. That happened. Working as a crane mechanic as I did, there's a lot of inherent dangers. There are electrical hazards, fall hazards, crushing hazards. I've always been interested in improving safety. Then the group I worked with elected me chairman of the safety committee. Bob was very supportive along with the coast committee, making sure we had everything we needed. That's where I really got to know Bob a lot better.

Bargaining in 2014 was a long, drawn-out experience. I don't know that we'll ever see that length of bargaining again based on the amount of outcry from all the lobbyists and corporations that were unhappy. They did an excellent job of lobbying in Washington, DC, to get more of a spotlight on the ILWU and the PMA. Outfits like the National Retail Federation were claiming all these economic damages that had nothing to do with the ILWU. The problem was decisions made by the PMA. But by using high-paid PR firms, the lobbyists got it out that labor unrest was preventing ships from getting in and out quickly. Yet we had no control over shutting down night or weekend longshore operations. That's something the employers did, but we got blamed for it.[22] Now [in 2017], because of all this outside influence and pressure, we are talking about a contract extension and that is very unusual for us. That's a result of the 2014 bargaining and the election of President Donald Trump.

The problem with negotiations wasn't because of the union not trying to get it done. Three months was dedicated just to securing maintenance of benefits. It's ridiculous that it took that long, but we were doing our best. I can speak personally from our negotiations in safety.[23] There were times when we would give a proposal and not hear back from the employers for several hours or maybe not until the end of the day. And it was something rather simple that was going to prevent injuries and be a cost savings to the employers. But they were dug in just to be difficult. Looking back on it, I think this was an orchestrated move. The PMA ultimately offset a lot of their costs to the consumers. When you have the other side of the table not motivated to have bargaining completed in a short effective time, you're going to have problems.

In 2014 there were also problems with our arbitration system, specifically here in Northern California. We needed relief. Thank God we got it. Now we have a fair system where in each of four regions there's three arbitrators: A union pick, an employer pick, and a neutral. That has really helped Local 10.

During 2014 I was involved directly with the safety negotiations until the last few weeks. Then I saw Bob at the big bargaining table. He's immovable. When he speaks, the other side listens. Bob's very sharp with numbers. He's able to calculate stuff in his head, like a calculator, and be spot-on with his figures. And in internal meetings with our negotiating committee, where he might have been getting heated or whatever, he allowed the process of democracy to continue. He didn't stifle debate. I've always appreciated that.

I can remember in 2014 the PMA not being agreeable to a reasonable proposal. It was near the end of negotiations. We had a few proposals left on the table. The secretary of labor, Tom Perez, was in the building. Things were getting very pressurized. But when Bob said, "Let's go," everybody went. Everybody got up and left and rallied right behind him. That makes a point.

Bob, too, retains sharp memories of the 2014–15 Longshore Division negotiations. Among other issues, he was quite tuned into the need for reform in the arbitration system that Ed Ferris referred to.

The first thing that we bargain is always the benefits. We don't get off the benefits until we get them sewed up. The Longshore Caucus wants you to do that and I've done it. Ever since I've been on the negotiating committee we've always gone after welfare. You get welfare and then you get into the guts of the whole thing. When you start talking about jurisdiction, like we got in 2008 and then 2014, there was some things we wanted. We wanted a change in who was being the arbitrators. That was the sticking point. We couldn't live the way we were living with the system the way it was because I believe that it got abused.

In the old arbitration system you had two employers and two union guys in four regions. Southern California had a union, Northern Cal had an employer, Columbia River had an employer, and Puget Sound had a union guy. We had a problem with a couple of them, one even being a union guy. We fought it and fought it. The PMA came to us with the proposal to have three arbitrators on each area panel. That would be an employer, a union, and a neutral.[24] So the negotiating committee decided on it, we took it to a Longshore Caucus, and the caucus voted for it.

I had a knot in my stomach because here I am now going to change the arbitration system that's been in place since 1948, or whatever year that came in. Sam Kagel helped devise all this stuff. He used to be the long-time coast arbitrator you'd appeal an area decision to.[25] I don't think it was a bad system but I think some people became jaded bad. Now [2018] if you ask me, probably one of the best things I was ever associated with was changing the system because it's fair right down the middle. The employers hate it. Now they're careful about what they arbitrate because they know they don't have it in the bag. It has changed the waterfront.

John Castanho, the union's Pacific Coast benefits coordinator, was at the 2014–15 bargaining sessions as well. He remembers the pressures on Bob toward the end of negotiations and how Bob handled them.

Negotiations in 2014 dragged and dragged and dragged. A lot of it had to do with addressing issues in the healthcare plan. The third-party administrator we had for claims paying was doing a very poor job at the time. We spent a lot of time trying to get that administrator replaced and trying to get other improvements in the welfare plan enacted so we could streamline the claims-paying process. We spent I would say four and a half to five months just on healthcare. So if the entire bargaining went ten or eleven months, almost half of it was dedicated just to the problems we were having in the welfare plan.

We got toward the end of negotiations and Bob was notified by the Obama administration that President Obama was going to send the secretary of labor and the secretary of commerce out here to San Francisco. Secretary of Labor Tom Perez met with the employers and met with us. He actually took the time to read *The ILWU Story*, which he found online.[26] Perez told us he admired the social justice issues our union stands up for.

Having said that, Perez warned us that we had a week to get the contract done or Bob and Jim McKenna of the PMA were going to board a plane for Washington, DC, and the negotiations were going to be done with the direct oversight of the White House. There was a letter signed by people in Congress that was sent to Bob and Jim McKenna urging both sides to get this contract done. There was also pressure internally from our members to get the contract wrapped up. So there was an enormous amount of pressure at the time and Bob handled that very well. When there was frustration on the negotiating committee, he would say, "Everyone came here because you wanted to. This is just part of it. Sometimes it's easier and sometimes it's harder."

When we had the last draft of bargaining done, Bob went around the entire table and asked every negotiator, "Do you say 'yes' or do you say 'no' to this?" He wanted to make sure we had a unanimous "yes" vote so there was no second-guessing. Everybody was on record as supporting that memorandum of understanding. I thought that was brilliant because then everyone was expected to go back to their respective locals and to the caucus and say, "I voted 'yes' and here's why." This helps with the ratification process. If you're in a local and the negotiator you selected is telling you, "I'm saying 'yes' and here's why, and I reported that to the caucus and I'm reporting that to my rank and file," it gives a rank and filer cause to believe, "This must be a good contract so I'm going to listen to what they have to say. I'll weigh it for myself, but the fact that my negotiator is saying 'yes' is going to add some weight to my decision."

The ILWU Balloting Committee certified the rank-and-file vote to accept the new 2015 Longshore Division master contract in May, just in time for the ILWU International Convention in Hawaii the following month. Despite all of the struggles the union had been through, and all of the serious debates and democratic votes on resolutions that transpired in Honolulu, there did remain a little time for fun, although even that had a symbolic meaning.

Paddy Crumlin, the national secretary of the MUA, came to the convention from Australia as a guest and a featured speaker.[27] He also challenged Bob to a surf-off contest. No matter who won the friendly competition, the symbolic gesture of unity across the seas was clear. The surfing contest put a capstone on Bob's long efforts as an ILWU officer to emphasize international longshore union solidarity.

Crumlin, it turned out, was on solid ground, so to speak. He had been an accomplished surfer as a young man. Crumlin even knew the waters around Hawaii because he had surfed there many years ago. He recalled his early days in Hawaii and described the great 2015 presidential surfing contest he participated in with Bob.

PADDY CRUMLIN

I was always a surfer. I worked for a few surfboard makers on the North Shore and have fond memories of the 1970s.[28] I went to sea, traveled the world, and used to say, "If you can play football [soccer] and make a surf-board, you can fit into any community in the world." I had a special love for Hawaii. I hadn't been back since that period of time because your life gets caught up. To come back to Hawaii as part of this wonderful family of the ILWU, much more aware of the role that the ILWU played with the agricultural workers and the transition from agricultural to resort workers there, and with this rich and wonderful contribution the union has made in Hawaii over such a period of time in mind, I thought, "What can we do that's special?"

A very good friend of mine makes surfboards. I met some of the family that's actually related to longshoremen in Honolulu. My old mate Barry Bennett is eighty-seven now [in 2018] and in the Shapers Hall of Fame. In 1962 he shaped a balsa board for a famous Australian surfer named Midget Farrelly. I said to Bennett's son, Greg, "Do you think Barry would shape a board for me along the same classic lines?" He said, "Yeah, sure." Barry made the board. We got all of these photos on there of Australians surfing Hawaii and in the middle were photos of Harry Bridges in Honolulu Harbor and some of the protest marches.

I said to Bob, "We'll do a contest." Bob said, "I've never surfed in me life." So I got onto Wesley Furtado and said, "You better teach him how to surf. If he doesn't win, I'm taking the board home. This is the presidential surf-off." But secretly I'd had another board made exactly the same. There was a young Hawaiian shaper working for Barry. He made another more modern one. I gave it to the Hawaii local.

Then, of course, I won the contest and Bob looked a bit down in the mouth. Well, I had the extra classic board behind the bushes. It was for him. I said, "Gee, it's just as well I brought two, Bob!" It did encapsulate everything about Hawaii and Australia and the ILWU and the MUA, just that community of interest, the sharing in the quality of our lives. So it was a very special moment for everyone there.

Bob remembered the surfboard contest as well.

BOB MCELLRATH

Paddy is a hell of a labor leader, one of the best I have ever seen who I have had the chance to meet or call my friend. He's a fantastic guy. He used to hang out in Hawaii when he was a kid. He made surfboards and was one of these surf bum guys. I don't know, they just chase the waves. He was a hell of a great surfer in his day. He hadn't been back to Hawaii for a long time. Then when we had our convention there, he just got all excited. He had a couple of surfboards made and presented me with one. He came up with this surf-off contest idea. I said, "That's great, let's do it." Why? Because we're friends. But I'm not a surfer and I was trying to surf on one of these little boards. I'd call it a small jet surfboard. Paddy had this big standup paddleboard. That's what I needed. I think I would have done better then [chuckles].

"Live to Fight Another Day"

International President, 2016–2018

Above all else, all the great minds the ILWU has had, the one thing that will continue is the life and the heart and the soul of this union.

BOBBY OLVERA JR.

Between June 4 and June 8, 2018, the ILWU met again in convention, this time in Portland, Oregon. After twelve years in office, Bob would not run for president again. He was sixty-seven. The union's constitution said that after reaching sixty-five no one could run for International president.[1] Instead of renominating Bob, convention delegates introduced a resolution recognizing his dedication and service to the union and urging that he receive the title of "President Emeritus." Cager Clabaugh, president of Local 4, Bob's home local in Vancouver, introduced the resolution to a standing ovation. It highlighted Bob's career in the union and was passed unanimously.[2]

Thirty-five delegates rose to speak on behalf of the resolution. The testimonies covered forty-two pages in the 2018 convention proceedings.[3] This was the kind of tribute not often seen at ILWU conventions. It was comparable to the union convention resolution passed in 1977

Fig. 8.1. ILWU leaders with Paddy Crumlin of the Maritime Union of Australia (MUA) at the 2018 ILWU International Convention in Portland, Oregon. As the retiring ILWU International president, Bob McEllrath was given the title "President Emeritus" at the gathering. *Left to right*: ILWU secretary-treasurer Willie Adams; ILWU vice president (mainland) Ray Familathe; MUA national secretary Paddy Crumlin; ILWU International president Robert McEllrath; ILWU International vice president (Hawaii) Wesley Furtado. Courtesy of Dawn DesBrisay, photographer.

that conferred emeritus status on retiring ILWU notables Harry Bridges, president; Bill Chester, vice president; and Louis Goldblatt, secretary-treasurer. The testimonies that year featured thirty speakers.[4] When another esteemed officer, President Jimmy Herman, retired in 1991 after fourteen years in office, sixteen delegates spoke in support of a resolution naming him president emeritus.[5] Clearly, Bob was in rare company (see fig. 8.1).

At the 2018 Portland convention, Bob received a number of retirement gifts from delegates representing various ILWU locals. Joe Cortez and Mark Mendoza from Los Angeles/Long Beach Local 13 presented him with a check and a jacket. Dennis Young from the ILWU Alaska Longshore Division gave Bob a carving from Juneau that featured a raven and a beaver. Delegate Antonio Pantuse from ILWU

Canada longshore Local 500 honored Bob with the gift of an artistic thunderbird, which he described as "a legendary creature in certain North American Indigenous people's history and culture."[6]

The Local 500 present seemed appropriately symbolic. From its beginning, the ILWU had championed the causes of marginalized peoples, including African Americans and Native Americans. ILWU membership in Alaska and Canada had long included several Indigenous workers. The union's convention resolutions over the decades were filled with examples of outreach to disadvantaged communities. Social justice action was a hallmark of ILWU identity.[7]

When Native Americans occupied Alcatraz Island in San Francisco Bay for nineteen months during 1969–71, ILWU longshore Local 10 sent a support delegation to the island led by International secretary-treasurer Louis Goldblatt.[8] A Native American member of longshore Local 10 secured the pier that allowed Alcatraz occupiers access to freshwater and other provisions. In 1973 the union's International convention approved resolutions against racism, in favor of freedom for fifty indicted Indigenous Wounded Knee protesters, and in opposition to all "discrimination against Native Indians."[9]

At the 2018 ILWU convention, delegates passed another resolution in support of the struggles of Native Americans. The impetus this time was the protest begun in April 2016 by Standing Rock Reservation Lakota, thousands of other Native Americans, and many non-Indigenous supporters against the Dakota Access Pipeline, a project of the Energy Transfer Partners Company. The North Dakota project investors sought completion of a pipeline intended to transfer thousands of tons of crude oil to Illinois for refining. Their project threatened to contaminate tribal water from the Missouri River and to disrupt Native American burial sites and archeological resources. In response, the insurgents set up camps in an effort to block the project. The protest, which lasted for months, attracted the largest gathering of Native Americans and sympathetic supporters seen in decades. Security guards and police attacked the insurgents with pepper spray, tear gas, rubber bullets, and Tasers. By November, authorities had arrested four hundred Native Americans and their allies.[10]

Previous chapters have largely highlighted the ILWU's focus on trade union survival in a defensive era. But the union's longtime commitment to social justice endured despite existential challenges. During 2016 representatives from ILWU Locals 4, 10, 13, 23, and ILWU Canada visited North Dakota, joined the protesters, and brought supplies with them as donations. The ILWU Pacific Coast Pensioners Association was the first ILWU affiliate to act. In September 2016 it passed a resolution in support of the Standing Rock protesters. The next month Steve Hunt, Jamison Roberts, and Josh Goodwin of Local 4 drove to North Dakota with provisions. Ed Ferris of Local 10 and Bobby Olvera Jr. of Local 13 soon went to North Dakota as well. In December the ILWU International Executive Board voted unanimously to oppose the Dakota Access Pipeline and to send ten thousand dollars to help the Standing Rock Lakota. The union's Coast Longshore Committee added five thousand dollars. Bob backed his union's response to the Native American insurgency by emphasizing, "The ILWU has never been afraid to take a stand on important political issues."[11]

In this chapter we hear how the union continued to support social justice issues even as it fended off threats in an increasingly hostile political environment that helped prompt it to extend its key Longshore Division contract. Commenting on this dangerous era are Bob McEllrath; Ed Ferris from longshore Local 10; Bobby Olvera Jr. from longshore Local 13 in Los Angeles/Long Beach; Troy Olson and Brad Clark from longshore Local 4 in Vancouver, Washington; Mike Jagielski from longshore Local 23 in Tacoma, Washington; Willie Adams; Fred Pecker from warehouse Local 6 in Northern California; and Sally McEllrath.

The 2018 International convention was just a few weeks away in mid-May 2018 when Bob sat for a recording session. He commented that the Standing Rock crisis had moved him to consider how ILWU International officers might more effectively continue the union's social justice tradition.

Oh yeah, yeah, yeah, we're still social justice, absolutely. We're always trying to help, especially, you might say, the underdog. What I am going to introduce at the convention is a resolution. It's like with Standing Rock, the officers wanted to give them twenty-five thousand dollars, but we always have to wait to ask the executive board. I think we're going backwards. People need the resources immediately. I'm making a resolution I forwarded to the executive board. They passed it already. We're taking it to the convention. It says the officers have the right to one hundred thousand dollars and to immediately write a check for social issues and causes up to twenty-five thousand dollars per cause. Then we report it to the e-board. This is because if something happens and you got to wait two and a half months before an e-board meets, it's gone.

Bob was pointing to the requirement that the union's International officers had to get approval from the union's executive board before making substantial donations. But the executive board meets only once every three months. The resolution Bob introduced at the June 2018 convention characterized the problem as the need for immediate disaster relief. It held that "the membership of the ILWU has always been generous and compassionate" and advocated creating a "Disaster Relief Fund" of one hundred thousand dollars. The union's International officers would be authorized to make donations from the fund over a three-year period, that is, during the time between International conventions. Bob invoked the Standing Rock case when he testified in favor of the resolution. It passed unanimously.[12]

Speaking in support of the fund resolution that June, Dean McGrath, president of Tacoma longshore Local 23, reminded convention delegates that in addition to checks, "boots on the ground" were important in aiding people in crisis.[13] ILWU activists, of course, had gone to North Dakota to join the Standing Rock Lakota and their allies, Ed Ferris among them. Ferris was president of San Francisco Bay Area longshore Local 10 in December 2016 when he and other ILWU members, including Local 13's Bobby Olvera Jr., went to North Dakota. In January 2017 Ferris described what it was like to join other ILWU stalwarts who put their boots on the ground to help the Native American cause. Ferris's testimony illustrates the kind of ILWU commitment to social justice that Bob referred to in May 2018.

ED FERRIS

That was an amazing experience. Local 13, Local 10, and ILWU Canada on this particular trip sent a delegation to go up and help. Local 23 had been up there previously and made contacts along with Local 4. It was terribly cold, but it was important work. We built structures to protect people from the elements. We provided gear and tools they can use to help themselves. The International Executive Board and the Coast Committee made a donation of fifteen thousand dollars, which really was helpful for the people.

The struggle's not over. The pipeline sponsors have already resorted to violence. I fully expect these private security firms to resort to those tactics again. The courage the people are showing is amazing. They not only have to deal with the tough elements, but they're dealing with fire hoses being turned on them in subzero weather, rubber bullets, and concussion grenades. It's some scary stuff that is taking place on their territory that they've had since the 1800s and they're being told that they're trespassing on their own land. It's disgusting.

Ours was a rank-and-file effort. And the International got behind it and supported it. I'm very proud of what we've done. We need to continue to do those kinds of things. It's right in line with our tradition.

Bobby Olvera Jr. also recalled the North Dakota effort of December 2016 to support the Native Americans. Like Ed Ferris, he viewed the union's Standing Rock participation in the context of the ILWU's long history of outreach.

Olvera comes from an extended Mexican American family of long-shore workers dating back to 1906–7 on the San Pedro waterfront. His grandfather and great uncle were both active in the Big Strike of 1934. Olvera's father was a longshore Local 13 business agent in the 1970s and an ILWU coast committeeman in the 1980s. Of his father's time in office when he was a teenager, Olvera said, "I got a dose of union history at that time. It was when I started falling in love with the culture of the ILWU."

Bobby Olvera Jr. began working on the waterfront in 1989, did a stint in the Marine Corps, and received his class-A ILWU Longshore Division registration through San Francisco's Local 10 in 1993. Returning to Southern California, Olvera served three terms as Local 13 vice president and three as president. He was elected ILWU International vice president (mainland) in 2018. Considering the union's history of social justice protest, Olvera said, "If you want to play it safe, that's fine, that's great, you can be vanilla your whole life. But the ILWU is the opposite of vanilla." He has vivid memories of Standing Rock. His testimony has a little to say about how things sometimes work in the ILWU and a lot to say about the union's patented social justice heritage.

BOBBY OLVERA JR.

It was one of these moments in history. The guys in Tacoma had gone back to Standing Rock. Dean McGrath from Local 23 had been calling me. I was president of Local 13 down in LA. We're talking, "How are we going to get the Coast Longshore Committee to do something?" Tacoma sends some people anyways. So I got my local executive board. As Local 13 president I had gained a lot of support because there was open debate. We could talk about things and disagree, but we were going to do whatever the majority decided. We decided to do it as a local, just like Tacoma. I talked to Local 10 and said, "Hey, let's get together," which is nice because there was a time when Local 10 and 13 worked closely and then there'd been a gap. But Ed Ferris of Local 10 and I, over the course of our relationship, we've been able to find common issues where we could do things. So we decided, "Hey, we're going."

Julie Brady was our Local 13 International Executive Board member. We were like, "You need to go to the IEB and tell them, 'We're going whether the IEB's going to go or not.'" Then the coast committee called us and said, "We're going to donate some money." They gave us five grand, plus we had another ten grand from the International. So we fly to North Dakota and we drive out. About ten miles outside the airport we started getting a tail. Friends had told us, "Anybody that's walking in with the union, they're going to follow you." We got followed to our first stop and our second stop, all the way out these barren roads to Standing Rock. People were creeped out a bit.

Then we get there. In the middle of all this white vastness there's this encampment with flags and banners and color in contrast against the snow. There were tents and lean-tos and Quonsets, shacks that were hastily put together. There was so much visual stimulation that it was, "Whoa, okay, this is a little bit different!" Local 23 had established a relationship with some Indians from Oregon. They had set up a Quonset hut that slept about thirty people with cots right next to each other. They had set up a community. We thought, "I'm here to support the Standing Rock tribe," but Standing Rock became an outcry to all tribes within the continental United States of it's about us, it's about our culture, and here's where we're going to take a stand. It became more than just, "We're here to stop this pipeline."

In this Quonset hut where we were it was fifteen below zero. It was so cold you slept in your clothes. We asked, "What do you need to survive?" We ended up going to like a Home Depot and we bought tools for them to build semipermanent structures with furnaces. We bought things that would have long-lasting benefit. When we left to shop, this kid was with his mom. She's helping in the kitchen and she's like, "Oh, we could use other things like tubs and stuff." Somebody had talked to the kid. He was maybe seven or eight years old. He wanted a bike. We made sure to put a bike on the list. We came back with our rent-a-cars full of stuff and we had a bike. The kid got to ride it around on the hard ice. It was another very human moment, right?

The first night we were there we walked up to where the river is. Up on the hill were all these lights and water cannons and military vehicles.

In the middle of the night in freezing weather we're looking across and they're looking at us. Then a couple of older tribal leaders started doing their chant and I had to look across the river and see my tax dollars staring back at me with big powered lights and water cannons.[14]

Despite the best efforts of thousands of Native Americans and their allies, in early February 2017, shortly after taking office, US president Donald Trump told the Army Corps of Engineers to proceed with construction of the pipeline. The protesters began to disperse. The National Guard and police forces evicted the last group of protesters at the end of the month. The pipeline was finished by April. Oil deliveries using the pipeline began in May. But the story did not end there. In 2020, a federal judge ordered a new environmental review of the pipeline.[15] Then, in January 2021, the new president, Joseph Biden, signed an executive order revoking the permit of another crude oil project, the XL Pipeline, which had been issued by the Trump administration in 2019 without tribal consultation or attention to Native American treaty rights or environmental concerns.[16]

Speaking in 2019, at a point when the Dakota Access Pipeline battle seemed irretrievably lost, Bobby Olvera Jr. presented his view of that campaign in thoughtful and spiritual terms.

BOBBY OLVERA JR.

We did everything we could. We built a wall. Ed Ferris was instrumental because he's great with hammer and nails. We got lumber and built a shelter around the Spirit Fire that's never supposed to go out. Seeing a bunch of longshoremen heavily dressed head-to-toe and with big gloves on trying to hammer and use saws was a very small gesture, but a very big moment. There was a cultural story there, a moral story. There's no happy ending to it, but it was a special moment in time. We were on the right side of history. Even in defeat there's victory because it's a victory of the mind and the heart and the soul. Above all else, all the great minds the

Fig. 8.2. ILWU members supporting Native Americans during their struggle against the completion of the Dakota Access Pipeline, North Dakota, 2016. The pipeline project seriously threatened Indigenous people's natural and cultural resources. *Left to right*: Isaiah Barnes, Sioux Nation; Jason Roberts, ILWU Local 4; Steve Hunt, ILWU Local 4. Courtesy of Anne Rand Library, ILWU.

ILWU has had, the one thing that will continue is the life and the heart and the soul of this union [see fig. 8.2].

Even while continuing its commitment to social justice during Bob's last term in office as president, the union was debating a highly contested internal issue. In spring 2016, the PMA offered to extend the Longshore Division's coastwide contract. The employer proposal was limited to three categories: wages, pensions, and the length of the extension. Many membership discussions followed in meetings and union halls. In April 2017, the Longshore Division Caucus voted to submit a tentative agreement to the division's membership for ratification.

The proposed deal included a 3.1 percent annual wage raise, a five-dollar-per-service-year pension increase, and a three-year contract extension. The Longshore Division rank and file ratified the arrangement by a 67 percent yes vote. The five-year coastwide contract, originally scheduled to expire on July 1, 2019, was extended to July 1, 2022.[17]

Ed Ferris addressed the idea of a contract extension in early January 2017, just as President-elect Donald Trump was about to take office. Trump would have the backing of many conservative members of Congress, too. Ferris's statement succinctly outlined how he assumed the ILWU would deal with the issue at hand.

ED FERRIS

I believe we're not in a good climate with the current Congress and we're not in a good climate with the president-elect. We've had some good discussions that extension may be a good idea. We're going to end up ultimately having to talk about it as a caucus. We're a democratic union; we'll take it to our memberships and they'll ultimately decide.

Speaking in May 2018, several months after the ratification vote on the extension, Bob reviewed how the extension came about, whether he felt ratification had been good for the union, and what benefits had been gained. His testimony and testimonies that follow illustrate how union democracy works in the ILWU.

BOB MCELLRATH

The employers wanted it. They had me in front of the shippers' Trans Pacific Maritime Conference down in Los Angeles. I was asked the question, would I do a contract extension? They asked Jim McKenna of the PMA [Pacific Maritime Association]. McKenna said, "yes," he would. They asked me and I said, "Well, if he presented me one, I'd take it to my officers and then take it to the rank and file." That's what I said in front of about 2,500 businessmen from around the world. McKenna brought me an offer and we banged it out for a few days, pro and con, whatever. He had what he wanted and I argued for more and more and more, as you should, and we came up with it.

Then the question for us was, "Do you want it or don't you want it?" At the caucus my only point was, "You're not going to vote it up and you're not going to vote it down, it's going to go to the membership and they'll decide." Because if I say go ahead and vote it up or down and you vote it down, it never gets to the membership and I don't think that's fair. We fought that thing at the caucus for a week. Finally it went to the membership. Some locals got together and en masse tried to block it. But the only one that really blocked it was Local 10 and it still passed coastwide by 67 percent. Some locals passed it in the nineties. Tacoma, Seattle, LA passed it. Most all the other locals passed it overwhelmingly.[18]

I'm glad we passed it because now I'm looking back. I'm going to be leaving here as president in about three months. Had it not passed, the new president would have been bargaining within the next five months, and with the current US president [Donald Trump] and with the way things are going, I think it would be a very rough go for the ILWU Longshore Division. At the time, I would say either way, it didn't matter to me. Now if you ask me, I'll say I think it was a good thing.

We did get some survivor pension benefit gains. All the surviving spouses, husband or wife, went to 75 percent. Before, some of them were at 60 to 65. The newer ones were already at 75, so we brought all of them up to 75. That was a huge increase. That was also offered to the watchmen and to Hawaii, because when I sat down with McKenna I said, "I have no trouble sitting here, Jim, talking about an extension, but this extension has to apply to Hawaii and it has to apply to the watchmen in Southern Cal and Northern Cal." They're not part of the Pacific Coast longshore contract, but they go off of our contract. They got the same employers we got. It's different contract, same employers.

I said, "So you have to give those people the same percentages and the same increases. If we agree, they get offered the same thing." Jim said, "I'll have to get back to you." I said, "Okay, then this meeting's over," and our whole committee that was with me left. Jim came back a couple of weeks later and said, "We'll give those contracts the same, exactly the same." Wesley Furtado, our vice president from Hawaii, went home, bargained the thing, and got everything laid out perfect. Built up his pension, everything. The watchmen in the Bay Area went from 55 percent in some of their pensions to 75 percent, a 20 percent increase. Plus they got a 3.1 percent raise on their wages.[19]

Troy Olson from Local 4 also evaluated the contract extension. Born in 1969, the same year that Bob came into the local, Olson began work on the Vancouver, Washington, waterfront as a casual in 1995. He worked break-bulk cargo, got registered, and served on the Local 4 Executive Board for four years. He then ran for dispatcher, which was Bob's old post in the local, and won. In April 2018, when he was interviewed, he had been the dispatcher for twelve years. Olson's overview of the extension reveals why some members voted against ratification or considered doing so.

TROY OLSON

I'm a caucus delegate, so we sat there and we talked about it before we brought it back to our rank and file. Delegates are there to make good arguments, like, "We've never done it before, why should we do it?" Some people were worried about the new federal administration coming in. Other people were staunch enough to say, "We're not worried about the new administration. We're the ILWU, we'll power through it. We've powered through other bad administrations."

The way it was talked about, there were three items. The proposal by the employers was for wages, pensions, and duration, that is, the length of the extension. But as far as the caucus was concerned, we had issues that we wanted to talk about, too. We didn't want to be painted into a corner for an extension with only three issues. We have technology issues, we have jurisdiction issues, and we have different issues that we were not going to be able to bring to the table. The one thing was that if we're going to talk about a contract extension, should we open the whole thing up, or should we just talk about these three items?

It was a pretty heavy-duty week. Then you had to come back and report to your rank and file, educate the rank and file, and inform them. The rank and file were worried about the same issues, had the same concerns. That's what I remember about the extension. Was I for it or against? I'm sure I changed my mind three or four times before I checked that box. Finally I voted against it. Our local was about 73 percent for. I voted against it just with the staunch idea that we are the ILWU and the ILWU doesn't worry about the administration. But as of today [2018], I'm glad we have an extension, because I don't agree with the way this federal administration is running the United States. I don't agree with the way President Trump treats American workers. If we were in contract negotiations and he was our president, I think that we would be in a battle.

Brad Clark was interviewed with Troy Olson in April 2018. Like Olson, Clark reflected on the status of the extension at that time. His comments, like those of others, suggest how seriously union democracy and the direction of the union are taken in the ILWU.

BRAD CLARK

Me and Troy talked a lot about it and I was like him. I went back and forth. I ended up voting in favor of it. I wasn't comfortable with that vote by any means. My reservation was about long agreements. We had a six-year agreement in 2002, we had a six-year agreement in 2008, we have a five-year agreement in 2015, and now we're going to make it an eight-year agreement. There are problems, like Troy mentioned, that the longshoremen needed fixed. Did we want to wait?

We got the extension last year, so five years left. What's our pension funding going to look like in 2022? What's the political landscape going to look like in 2022? What's the legal landscape going to look like? There are so many unknowns and we're putting it off for a long time. Those are the questions, well, maybe it's not a good idea. But on the flip side are those same issues, what's the political landscape going to look like, what's our pension funding going to be if we don't agree to it? If we get in a struggle like we did in 2002, is the membership prepared for that? You walk a membership into a big struggle like 2002 or grain and they're not ready for it, you're in trouble. When you've gone from struggle to struggle to struggle, sometimes the membership needs a break. They get war weary, battle fatigue kind of.

We won't know if we did the right thing until 2019, when that contract would have expired. If we turned it down and that was the wrong choice, I think it could have been disastrous. If we turned it down and we went into contract bargaining and the stock market had crumbled like it did in '08 after we got that '08 agreement, bargaining in 2019 could pose a problem. On the flip side, maybe the stock market keeps going up and we want to be back in bargaining. But, like Troy said, we got a guy in the White House [President Donald Trump] that we're afraid of—not afraid of, but we don't know where he is going.

The main reason I voted for the extension, or one of the main reasons, is that going into bargaining in 2019, a question was, who was going to be sitting in our president's chair bargaining for us? Nobody knows yet. It could be a handful of guys. That is, who is taking Bob's spot? What if it turns out that it is the wrong guy for the job? We won't know if that's the right fit until 2019 or 2020 and we're going to dump that guy on the most important contract in the union. By dragging it out to 2022, we're going to elect a guy in 2018. We're going to decide by 2021 if he's the right guy or not.[20] If he's the right guy, he's going to be there for 2022. If he's the wrong guy, hopefully the next guy will know what needs to be changed and we'll have him in place.

What's important about the extension is what Troy said now. Troy was a caucus delegate, one of two from our local that came back to this membership and explained what was going on and what the pros and cons were. He voted no, but the membership voted 75 percent in favor. He came back and gave them the facts and the membership made the decision. He didn't come back and try to sell that extension to people. Matter of fact, we both kind of knew how the vote would come out of our membership. A lot of that was war fatigue, I think. I don't think anybody wanted to get back in another fight.

But that's how Bob was in our local, that's how the elected officials in this local were before. Give the guys the facts. We'll go to the job and we'll argue about it, but at the end of the day you vote the way you want. In 2017, I think both Local 4 caucus delegates voted against it but the membership didn't. That's the way it should be. And as Troy told you, he's not sure if he voted the right way, either. In some ways, it's who knows?

In 2019 Bobby Olvera Jr. discussed the extension as well. He emphasized the case for opposition.

BOBBY OLVERA JR.

I was opposed to it. Opposition to it came from multiple people and I think for a multitude of reasons. Some were just, "Hey, we should be negotiating twenty-four seven; it keeps us strong, it keeps us on our toes." Some were against it because anything Bob brought to them they thought was wrong. But I think that was a very small minority. Some were against it because we saw providing the employers with an extended period of stability is a dangerous thing in these times.

My reference is to automation at Pier 400 in LA, right? Back when I was president of Local 13, we were working at one point with no contract in place yet. My ability to shut TraPac Terminal down for forty-five days and cost them $25 million and jam them up when they brought automation to LA was predicated on we didn't have a contract, therefore there was no legal work stoppage because there was no arbitrator. When we have the grievance machinery in place, there's very little that we can do. That allows the employer to say, "Hey, I got peace. I can maybe do some investment, I can look at some things."

I had a guy tell me when I spoke against the contract in LA, "Why are you against this extension?" It was outside the membership meeting one night. I told him, "Because we need to have our ability to sit at the table and negotiate." There was a part of me that knew Bob was going to be leaving and if there was not a seamless transition of leadership we would be put in a position where we'd be walking into negotiations in a very weak spot. But I believe no matter how bad it is, when we work together all of us will be all right. That was what I championed in moving towards voting against the extension.

This guy also said, "Man, I'm working seven days a week right now, I made more money last week than I've ever made in a week. Hey, every other union does these extensions, this is how the world is." I says, "I understand all that, but I want you to remember this conversation because in a couple years I may be wrong or you may be wrong and maybe we'll sit and have this conversation again." Sure enough, about eighteen months passed after the extension, and this guy sees me at the membership meeting one night. By this time I'm not in office, I'm just a rank and filer, a Local 13 Executive Board member, and a caucus delegate.

The guy comes over and goes, "This is bullshit. We're trying to get two men per machine for the container yards. Our president is trying to negotiate. How come they're not giving it to us, Bobby? Man, this machine tears me up, I'm sore all the time. We need two men per machine." I'm like, "Well, that's a big table thing. We have to negotiate that. Remember, we talked about this last year. You gave up your rights to negotiate until 2022, so what you got is what you got unless the employers are willing to sit and talk and they're not willing to sit and talk to us unless we got something for them or unless they want something." He looked at me. I said, "I'm not going to tell you, 'I told you so,'" and I gave him my little look. There was nothing he could say.

Mike Jagielski, who retired from Tacoma longshore Local 23, was president of his pensioners' club when he was interviewed in 2017 and 2018. His father was a member of Portland longshore Local 8. Mike began work on the Portland waterfront as a casual in 1967 when he was twenty, served as an Army medic, got work out of Coos Bay, Oregon, longshore Local 12, and finally settled in Tacoma in the mid-1980s. He echoed some of Olvera's remarks in questioning the 2017 longshore contract extension.

MIKE JAGIELSKI

I liked loading lumber. We did a lot of that in Tacoma. In traditional break-bulk longshoring, you have to have certain skills, certain techniques, a certain touch, good depth perception. That was right up my alley. There're little tricks you learn about coming in at a little bit of an angle so you can get around a corner. And you're part of a team. There's like six people bringing big paper rolls to the barge or stacking lumber in the warehouse for the next whatever. It was just fun.

About Bob, he herds cats so well. You've been to how many caucuses? You've seen everybody's got an opinion, there's lots of finger-pointing, and Bob looks like he's asleep sometimes. Then he wakes up and says, "Okay, so you've all had your say and this is what I say we're going to do. What do you think about that?" It's great to have that much patience, to let it all run its course. He's a master at it.

With the extension, the employers bought votes, basically. They offered an increase in the pension, they offered money. This is a good thing, I'm not against this. But I think we could have got these same things at the bargaining table. They also offered increases in the pension rates for pensioners who had retired before 2002 and for all of the surviving spouses. So there was a lot of sweetener there to encourage people to vote yes. But Ed Ferris posted on Facebook a list of seven reasons to vote no. The downside, according to Ed, was it'll be eight years between negotiations and there are issues that need to be addressed now, not in 2022. Automation was one of them, certainly. That's the changing face of our industry. This is not the industry we all knew thirty years ago, it's not the industry we knew ten years ago. Issues like this have to be addressed now and we're not going to.

Willie Adams was elected ILWU International president in late 2018. In May of that year, while he was still the ILWU International secretary-treasurer, he too evaluated the contract extension. Like Jagielski, he came from Tacoma longshore Local 23. But unlike Jagielski, Adams supported ratification of the extension in 2017. It was generally a defensive era for labor, there was an unfriendly administration in the White House, and the union was in a period of leadership transition. Adams considered the extension strategically advantageous.

WILLIE ADAMS

It was a very heated discussion. I come from Tacoma longshore Local 23. My delegation was split, four for it, six against. I spoke for it in my local in Tacoma and it passed 537 to 40, something like that.[21] I think a lot of the younger people didn't want it. They maybe saw it as a sign of weakness. But I think it was probably the best thing that happened. The ILA on the East Coast just signed a six-year contract extension to 2025. They don't want to lose any cargo to the West Coast. You got to live to fight another day and with this president [Donald Trump] that we have in office, we have to be careful. With Bridges and the old-timers, they knew when to fight and when not to fight, and when they fought, they fought on their own ground. People got to remember this is not 1934 and nobody here is Harry Bridges.

Adams's comment, "This is not 1934 and nobody here is Harry Bridges," holds symbolic significance. In an era when labor law and national political power are arrayed against you, discretion can seem the better part of valor.

WILLIE ADAMS

So you got to be able to fight in these days' times. There's a lot of legislation that's hanging in DC I think they would have put on us. The employers could have come in because they knew they had Trump in the White House. They got the Congress, they got the Senate, and they got the

Supreme Court.[22] Sometimes it's about time, and you're going to have new officers. I think it's a lot to throw at somebody. It's no need to be in a hurry. Let's get ready, take our time. Why would we want to be the target of this president? To show what kind of balls we got and not show any brains? Then you go in there and you get a shit sandwich. It might not be very good when you showed them how much balls you had but you didn't show them that you had much brains. And we got this big hundred-million-dollar lawsuit with International Container Terminal Services, Inc. [ICTSI] where we've been found guilty.[23]

The "big hundred-million-dollar lawsuit" by ICTSI that Adams referred to in mid-2018 was a serious challenge to the ILWU that continued beyond Bob's presidency. The company's suit was of such proportions that it threatened the union's solvency.

ICTSI is a powerful Philippines-based cargo-handling company with a global reach. In 2019 it had thirty-one marine terminals in nineteen countries and an annual income of $2.5 billion. Much of ICTSI's business is concentrated in countries with weak labor rights. Enrique Razon, the company's owner, has personal assets exceeding four billion dollars and benefits from close ties to Rodrigo Duterte, the authoritarian president of the Philippines. Razon once declared, "The countries with the best infrastructure in the world are dictatorships."[24]

In 2010 ICTSI Oregon leased Terminal 6 from the Port of Portland. The company began operations at Terminal 6 the following year. Shortly after signing a lease with the Port of Portland, ICTSI joined the PMA and provided written assurance that it was not bound by any labor agreement beyond the one between the PMA and ILWU. However, the Port of Portland and ICTSI in their lease agreement had reserved the work of plugging, unplugging, and monitoring refrigerated shipping containers, or "reefers," for other port workers. Under the terms of the contract ICTSI signed onto with the PMA, the ILWU claimed jurisdiction over this reefer work, consistent with the practice under the contract up and down the West Coast. In a labor-management agreement at the coast labor relations level, the ILWU-PMA agreed that the contract required the assignment of reefer work to the ILWU. But ICTSI said it could do nothing because reefer work was reserved for another workforce under its lease with the Port of Portland. In 2012 the National Labor Relations Board awarded the reefer work to Port of Portland workers. Relations between the ILWU and ICTSI deteriorated as both the ILWU and the PMA sued ICTSI for enforcement of the contract. ICTSI countersued both the ILWU and the PMA, and, according to the ILWU and court records, ICTSI took retaliatory action against ILWU dockworkers at Terminal 6 in Portland.[25]

Another NLRB proceeding found the union guilty of a secondary boycott for engaging in a work slowdown against ICTSI. The company contended that the reefer jobs were being managed directly by the Port of Portland, so any ILWU slowdowns over those positions improperly punished it for a dispute that should have been between the port and the ILWU. Recall that secondary boycotts have been illegal under labor law since the 1947 passage of the Taft-Hartley Act.[26]

In 2017 ICTSI terminated its lease with the Port of Portland and closed its operations at Terminal 6. The company, as part of its countersuit against the ILWU, sought $101 million in damages for lost business between 2012 and 2017. Section 303 of the Taft-Hartley Act allows an employer to sue a union in US District Court for losses due to a secondary boycott violation. In early November 2019, after a tense and emotion-filled two-week trial before US District Judge Michael H. Simon in Portland, an eight-member jury held the union liable for $93.6 million. The jury assigned 55 percent of the charges to the ILWU International and 45 percent to longshore Local 8 of Portland.[27]

The labor historian and public intellectual Nelson Lichtenstein called the decision and the size of the penalty "an extremely dangerous precedent" for the struggling American labor movement.[28] James Gregory, a labor historian at the University of Washington, put the case into historical perspective: "It harkens back to the Gilded Age when corporations used employer-friendly courts to bankrupt and destroy unions. More important, it threatens the existence of a union that has long been a model of progressive politics and democratic governance, a union that fights for labor rights worldwide, a union that has beaten back every challenge since 1934. And if the courts are again going to issue rulings bankrupting unions, no union is safe."[29]

Assessing the jury decision, Judge Simon declared, "The amount of damages found by the jury is quite high and may result in the bankruptcy of a union that traces its beginnings to at least 1933 and arguably into the nineteenth century."[30] In early March 2020, Simon exercised his prerogative as a federal judge to reduce the $93.6 million in damages to $19 million. In his written opinion, Simon concluded, "The evidence does not support a damage award of $93.6 million."[31] ICTSI could accept the judge's decision or ask for a new trial limited to determining the award amount.[32] Two weeks later, ICTSI rejected the $19 million. The ILWU was then granted interlocutory appeal with the Ninth Circuit Court of Appeals to hear its claims regarding errors at the trial court level. The case promised to drag on well into the future.[33]

Some have suggested that the union got into a great deal of trouble over a few reefer jobs. But, discussing the case in November 2019, Bob explained that there was much more at stake in the ICTSI dispute than a few jobs. In so doing, Bob referenced his and the ILWU's perennial concern during a defensive era for labor with preserving the jurisdictional integrity of the union's core unit, the ILWU Longshore Division.

BOB MCELLRATH

It started out with the way ICTSI signed the lease. They went and signed a lease with the Port of Portland. Through discovery we found out that Bill Wyatt, who had been the director of the Port of Portland, had written the lease to go around the ILWU-PMA contract so that they wouldn't have to give the plugging and unplugging and the inspection of the reefers to longshore, which is in our ILWU-PMA contract. ICTSI made that agreement with the Port of Portland. Then, right after signing the lease, they joined the PMA and then we said, "You can't do it." We went through the agreements machinery and everything and they had to assign us the work, but they wouldn't do it because they said they had a lease with the Port of Portland.[34] Leal Sundet was the Northwest Coast committeeman. Portland's his backyard and I let him run with it.[35] People said, "It's only two jobs." It wasn't. If we hadn't fought them there, they could have done the same thing with another port such as Seattle, Tacoma, Long Beach, LA, San Francisco. It was completely against our contract, so we had to fight them.

Teamster raiding was another problem that confronted the ILWU toward the end of Bob's career as International president. The ILWU Warehouse Division, once a powerful sector of the union, had declined in membership numbers since its height just after World War II. Northern California warehouse Local 6 had 19,000 members in 1946–47, although that figure had been inflated by war production. Shortly before the war, Local 6 had boasted 8,500 members.[36] Los Angeles/Southern California warehouse Local 26, while it was usually not as large as Local 6, had 6,000 members in 1941, reached 10,000 in the 1960s, then declined. Teamster redbaiting and raiding during the Cold War in 1950 weakened Local 6 economically. Still, in 1973 Local 6 had 10,000 members.[37] In 1981, the combined membership of Local 6 and warehouse Local 17 of Sacramento, California, remained more than 6,000.[38]

But during the 1980s and after, "runaway shops" that left Northern California's Bay Area as well as structural changes like corporate consolidations in the warehouse, distribution, and production industries reduced the Warehouse Division's numbers dramatically. Fred Pecker, who started work at Local 6's Guittard Chocolate factory in 1983, became the local's chief steward in 1986 and a business agent in 1991. A few years later he was elected Local 6 secretary-treasurer. He served in that capacity until 2017. Over time, Pecker observed the decline in Local 6's numbers to a low of 1,800 in 2012.[39] In July 2018 he reviewed what he had seen.

I lived through it. It was in full swing by the time I was there, but it continued and it goes on. Hiram Walker, the coffee houses, Folgers in San Francisco. Some of these losses happened not in the eighties but in the nineties. Hills brothers Coffee, S&W Coffee, all of the paper houses, all of the industries are gone now. I negotiated a lot of severances. They were not situations where the company was looking for a way to stay in business. The company had made a business decision and was trying to put some lipstick on a pig and make the workers feel like it wasn't the end. They were trying to keep things calm until they shut. There were a bunch of corporate takeovers that preceded a lot of this stuff. Companies that were making money got consolidated. The whole corporate raider kind of thing has been in place for a really long time. It may have gone through different faces, but no matter what face, the result is the same.

With such challenges ongoing, in 2012 the Teamsters raided warehouse Local 17 in Sacramento. Local 17 traced its roots back to the West Coast longshore union's beginnings in 1934, when the indomitable Frank Thompson organized it.[40] But in 2012 the Teamsters took over the local. At the June 2012 ILWU International Convention, Bob reviewed what happened.

BOB MCELLRATH

Local 17 in Sacramento, California, was struggling financially, trying to keep their heads above water and trying to survive. The International fought for this local, just like we fight for all of the ILWU locals. We serviced Local 17 just like we service all locals. Unfortunately, the self-serving leadership of Local 17 convinced their membership it was in their best interest to leave the International and join the Teamsters. The leadership of Local 17 was looking out for themselves. They sold out their members and the rest of the union using pension and welfare benefits as a tool to go against the ILWU.[41]

A year later Bob reflected on the Local 17 situation in an oral history interview. There he put things in even stronger terms.

BOB MCELLRATH

The Teamsters were a pain in the ass. You know what they did to us at Local 17? They went around the bush and used the business agents and the officers in ILWU Local 17 and chummed them with jobs and money to convince their people to vote the other way. That's going to come back. The Teamsters promised in there to take care of their medical problems, saying they'll take care of everything. I don't believe it.

Even as the ILWU was losing ground to Teamster raiders, it continued to recruit warehouse workers where it could. During 2011–13, Fred Pecker organized waste management and recycling workers into Local 6 in the hope of lifting them out of poverty while strengthening the local's undercapitalized pension fund. When Teamster officials ordered their drivers to pass through Local 6 picket lines at the recycler Alameda County Industries, Pecker and those supporting him still persevered.[42]

Pecker had grown up in New York in a strong union family. Of his mother he said, "She was the person who told us if we ever crossed a picket line we were going to have some broken legs—and she was a nonviolent person!" For years Pecker worked closely with his uncle, longtime ILWU Local 6 icon LeRoy King. Pecker occasionally felt that the International under Bob seemed too focused on the union's Longshore Division. But he also offered this assessment of the Local 6 recycling drive, which achieved success in raising people's wages and getting them medical coverage and other benefits.

FRED PECKER

Under Bob's leadership the International provided the resources to make change with the recycling workers. The International Organizing Department came in, saw what was going on, and worked with us. The people that moved it were the membership, but the International Organizing Department staff, Peter Olney, Augustin Ramirez, and Amy Willis, along with Joe Nunez of Local 6, were certainly a big part of it.

The gains made, though, were not sufficient to overcome the threat to Local 6's master contract pension fund, which had a ratio of eight retirees to each active worker in 2018. Pecker urged his members to stay militant, to find a way to solve the pension problem themselves, and to resist any Teamster offer of help that might erode Local 6's cohesion and independence. But the Teamsters convinced Local 6's membership to vote to join the better-funded Western Conference of Teamsters Pension Trust. In exchange, Local 6 had to transfer control of its master contract to the Teamsters. Pecker was profoundly disturbed about this turn of events.[43] In his oral history in July 2018, he evaluated what happened.

FRED PECKER

What my organization just did, Local 6 now, is they gave away a contract to another organization. People were scared about losing their pension, which is perfectly reasonable, I'm scared about it, too, because it is my pension also. But they cut a deal with the Teamsters. The contract says in it now that the sole collective bargaining agent for this contract is Teamsters Local 853. So we were raided, even if it was a willing raid.[44]

Bob was undoubtedly disturbed by this turn of events as well. But since the ILWU is a democratic organization, there was little he could do about it. The Local 6 vote stood. In a new development, toward the end of Bob's era as ILWU International president, Local 6 began organizing in new industries such as animal care and craft beer production. These efforts offered renewed hope for strengthening the local.[45]

Teamster raiding of the ILWU actually predated both Bob and Fred Pecker. This behavior seems endemic to the transportation, distribution, and warehouse industry. There were significant Teamster raids on Local 6 in 1938 and, as noted, in 1950. Both occurred under Teamster leader Dave Beck, when Harry Bridges was president of the ILWU. The 1938 raid was largely ineffective. The 1950 raid did more damage.[46] Regardless, it seems that no ILWU leader has ever been able to prevent Teamster raids.

Teamster incursions are just a few of the many problems confronting ILWU presidents. In the face of employer attacks, threats of automation, and antilabor legislation, clearly the position is stressful. As recorded in 2013, five years before retiring, Bob reflects on the demands as well as the rewards of the job.

BOB MCELLRATH

I've made a good life, me and my wife, and I'm happy. But this job will kill you. My wife worries about me 'cause there's some stress on this thing. I sit here talking to you guys, I got to worry about what's going on in Longview and in Vancouver and Portland locked out. I got to worry about what's going on in the Labor Board. I got another lawsuit down in LA, they're attacking us there. You know what I'm saying? You try to juggle all this stuff. It does take its toll. I'm not trying to whine here or nothing. I took the job, I love the job, and I'm going to do the job to the best of my ability. You know, you got some pride.

I go see a doctor. He says, "Well, you're staying reasonably fit. You're not overweight too much. You don't smoke, that's good. You drink a little too much, that's normal. Everything seems to be working. There's only one thing I can't help you with. You got to control your stress. It'll cause things in your body to react that'll kill you as much as drinking or eating too much will kill you. You got to watch that." I said, "Wow." He said, "Just try to tell yourself to calm down and make sure you do something relaxing." I do go exercise, which is a release. I do love to hunt and fish. I'll go in the woods and sit by myself all day. It gives you time to think. You see animals and birds and kind of ground yourself.

But in this game there's home runs and then there's strikeouts. There are times when I shake my head and ask myself, "God, what am I doing?" You really get beat up sometimes. But I'll tell you, the rewards are so rewarding when you can deliver a contract or you can help people. I always try to go back to when I was working in the hold of a ship. I say, "If I make this decision today, what would I think of a guy that did the same decision and I was down in the hold slinging up loads or something? How would I feel? Would I feel good about it or would I be angry?" I always try to make myself the working guy looking back and saying, "Why did you do that? Why did you make that decision?" It's pretty tough sometimes, I can tell you that.

Even for Sally, Bob's wife, stress and sacrifice were part of the cost of Bob's being on the road. She long maintained the family home in Vancouver, Washington, while Bob was at the ILWU International office in San Francisco. Joe Cortez acknowledged her sacrifice at several International conventions. Sally discussed it herself at her 2016 interview.

SALLY MCELLRATH

It works out. I'm pretty independent. Whenever he has something he has to do I just accept it. I don't like it when he has to leave after he's been home because you get used to him being home again and then it's kind of hard when he has to leave. I used to travel down to San Francisco a lot more. It was always a big adventure. Then we got dogs again and it was kind of hard.

For Bob's part, he discussed retirement in May 2018, when he had just a few months to go in office.

BOB MCELLRATH

I just want to be home. Somebody said, "You're going to get bored." I said, "Well, let me get bored first and then I'll decide." This is a pretty intense job. My doctor said, "I want you to make sure you're prepared to retire because you're going to go from one hundred miles per hour to zero." I've walked up here in these halls [at the ILWU International office in San Francisco] for twenty-one straight years. That's a long time. It has been fifty years "on the docks," this being my forty-ninth qualifying year. I've enjoyed it, loved it, great challenges. But I like the outdoors, deer and elk everywhere, trout fishing. I'm looking forward to all that.

When he looked toward retirement in mid-2018, Bob had led the ILWU as president for twelve years. Although the union was now independent of the AFL-CIO, the problems it had faced during Bob's service at the International level as coast committeeman, vice president (mainland), and president were similar to those challenging all of organized labor since the ascendency of the Reagan administration in 1980, indeed since the passage of the Taft-Hartley Act in 1947. Bob had dealt with many such difficulties, some even existential threats, with both wins and compromises.

Labor law reform might have helped Bob but never made it through Congress during his years in office. The Employee Free Choice Act of the early Obama years was the last attempt to reform Taft-Hartley while Bob was an ILWU official. It would have helped American workers organize but unfortunately failed to become law, leaving the need for change painfully obvious.[47] Ultimately, Bob sought ILWU survival in a defensive era for labor by prioritizing the union's core waterfront jurisdiction and by cultivating longshore allies overseas. Problems remained—the ICTSI lawsuit was still an issue—yet Bob would retire from his watch in 2018 with the ILWU intact.

In the end, Bobby Olvera Jr. captured something essential about Bob's leadership in his 2019 oral history. As a young ILWU longshore Local 13 leader in Los Angeles, Olvera was not always in Bob's best graces. As he put it, "When I first came in as Local 13 vice president in 2010 I wanted to do everything and I wanted to do it overnight." Olvera was forty at the time; Bob was close to sixty. Things improved during the 2014 longshore contract negotiations, though Olvera said that when he advocated against the 2017 contract extension, "Bob and I went head-to-head again." Regardless, Olvera said that his watchword, borrowed from Local 10's Leo Robinson, was always, "You attack the policy, you don't attack the person." He testified eloquently about Bob's role during the 2011 EGT (Export Grain Terminal) battle, about Bob's legacy, and ultimately about the ILWU itself.

BOBBY OLVERA JR.

One thing that could be built upon for an entire generation until we find that next great moment is the optics of Bob being walked down the railroad tracks at EGT. It shows an International officer being assaulted by authority and standing abreast, whether you like Bob or not. There's a lion's share that love Bob and respect the man and there's always the minority that is going to hate great sourdough bread with some nice jam on it. It's not about the politics, it's about the optics and that's great optics. Bob's the one that stood in front of the tank just like in Tiananmen Square with no regard for his life or his safety because he knows his brothers and sisters will take care of his family. He knows there's the pension and the welfare and that regardless of what happened to him physically on this earth he's better for it and everybody would be better for it. It's not just about EGT, not just the grain, not just Big Bob. There's a story there about militancy and an International officer that personified that in that moment.

Bob's leadership came from a lot of things. His stature was one, right? He's a big dude. He had all of the ingredients, but just having the ingredients in the kitchen doesn't mean you know how to make soup. He had some intangibles that were key to what he's accomplished. The guy can drink a frigging camel under the table. That helps because this is who we are. We sit at a bar and we drink some beers and we talk about each other and our families and the guys on the dock and about the damn employer. And Bob has a way and a manner that says, "I'll throw some logs with you, I'll lash with you, I'll sit here and sock a guy in the jaw with you," but the man can sit down and talk to you about the pension plan and the welfare plan like he was an actuary. For a big White boy from the Northwest to be able to come to Los Angeles full of Mexicans and Slavs—and an Irishman at that—it's amazing.

Bob's a leader for good and bad. EGT is a perfect example, right? Bob's always going to take a lot of heat for that, for the twelve-hour shifts. But he made a decision he had to make to protect this union knowing full well that once one domino falls, it's only a matter of time. He felt, "We'll do what we can to hold on." He made tough decisions that nobody will ever understand because nobody else will be in the shoes that he was in at that time with all the things that were happening around him. Nobody will know the conversations he had with people in the government that were telling him what could possibly happen or what would happen. In the end he guarded this union, took care of it like somebody takes care of beautiful champion roses. God bless the man. He deserves every day of his retirement and I hope he collects pension benefits until he's 150. There're a lot of people living good and stable lives that didn't go to union meetings, that didn't vote, that are living with what they have because of Bob and people like him.

ACKNOWLEDGMENTS

Writing a book often seems like a lonely endeavor. But the production of any book actually depends on the contributions of generous people. We owe numerous debts of gratitude and wish to acknowledge them here. First, we want to thank the forty-one individuals who sat for oral history interviews for this book, in some cases for multiple sessions over several days. Most are quoted here. Their patience and willingness to teach us about the events they witnessed or helped shape was indispensable to the making of this text.

The ILWU International officers, Longshore Division Coast Committeemen, International Executive Board members, and Convention and Longshore Caucus delegates all generously supported our work while we conducted interviews, did archival research, and wrote this book. We benefited greatly in being invited to ILWU International Conventions and Longshore Division Caucuses where we could record people from different places gathered at one location. We are also obliged to the officers and members of the ILWU Pacific Coast Pensioners Association. PCPA officials, including Greg Mitre, Rich Austin Sr., and Dave Arian, and many volunteers facilitated our attending PCPA annual conventions between 2013 and 2019, enabling us to interview PCPA delegates there. Conor Casey, the director of the Labor Archives of Washington, aided us significantly at those conventions with his recording skill and intellectual contributions.

After freely giving us time for multiple interviews while still in office, ILWU International president Bob McEllrath read chapter drafts. He corrected errors and misunderstandings without imposing constraints on our coverage of major issues. We appreciate his forthright answers to our many inquiries. Bob and Sally McEllrath welcomed Ron Magden into their home during a field trip in addition to their sitting for interviews.

Robin Walker, ILWU director of educational services, librarian, and archivist, was crucial to the success of this project. She aided our work unstintingly from arranging funding for transcriptions of recordings to carefully reading and commenting perceptively on chapter drafts. We are extremely grateful for her encouragement, counsel, and moral support. Ed Ferris, ILWU International secretary-treasurer, and Kirsten Donovan, ILWU director of contract administration and arbitration, also read chapter drafts and made valuable suggestions for improvement. Russ Bargmann, ILWU research director, answered our inquiries and provided helpful advice.

Alexa Jurczak, ILWU senior policy advisor and former ILWU executive assistant to the International president, helped our cause consistently with guidance and good cheer. The same can be said of Linda Kuhn, who preceded Jurczak as executive assistant to the International president. We had many instructive discussions, too, with Craig Merrilees, former ILWU communications director and *ILWU Dispatcher* managing editor, and with Roy San Filippo, current ILWU communications director and *ILWU Dispatcher* editor. Both always answered our many questions patiently and insightfully.

San Filippo helped greatly as well with our photo search. So did ILWU Local 4 dispatcher Troy Olson. Retired ILWU member and photographer Frank Silva and former marine clerks Local 40 president and photographer Dawn DesBrisay graciously donated their advice and their superb pictures for our use.

We benefited as well from speaking at various times with ILWU coast committeeman Cameron Williams and ILWU marine clerks Local 34 relief dispatcher Russell K. Miyashiro. Gene Vrana, retired ILWU director of educational services, librarian, and archivist and longtime supporter of our work, always provided thoughtful responses to inquiries. Early on

Vrana prompted us to pay special attention to Bob McEllrath's focus on international maritime solidarity. PCPA activist Mike Jagielski facilitated the preservation of many of Ron Magden's recorded interviews. Thanks also to Claudette Allison, our persevering transcriber over many years.

Many other people have helped us in various ways, including ILWU administrative assistant Angelica Ayala, ILWU Coast Communications director Jennifer Sargent Bokaie, ILWU custodian Claude Capute, ILWU Accounting Department manager Rebecca Contreras, ILWU building engineers Victor and Mauricio Duran, American historian Ken Gleason, ILWU coast administrator Diana Gomez, ILWU administrative assistant Debra Keith, ILWU bookkeeper Sue Lew, ILWU coast accounting manager Haydee Lind, Bay Area Longshoremen's Memorial Association Office coordinator Angelique V. Mayer, Beth Magden, David Magden, Kim Magden, ILWU walking bosses Local 92 president Pete McEllrath, former ILWU International president Brian McWilliams, ILWU bookkeeper Heidi Merriman, former California Federation of Teachers secretary-treasurer Michael Nye, ILWU longshore Local 10 administrative secretary Mercedes Perez, former ILWU director of organizing Peter Olney, and former ILWU longshore Local 10 president Mike Villeggiante.

We very much appreciate the contributions of the two University of Washington Press peer reviewers who read this book in manuscript form. Peter Cole's insight and constructive criticism improved this volume immensely; Erik Loomis's interest in the project and his suggestions for improvement were also extremely helpful. We benefited greatly as well from the help of UWP acquisitions editor Mike Baccam, UWP Mellon University Press Diversity Fellow Chad M. Attenborough, and senior project editor Joeth F. Zucco. Copyeditor Karen H. Brown, proofreader Judy Loeven, and indexer Chris Dodge also contributed substantially to bringing our manuscript into print.

Family friends and colleagues also provided moral support and encouragement while we researched and wrote this history. These included Oscar Berland, Paulette Burnard, Robert Cherny, Lauren Coodley, Howard A. DeWitt, Vince DiGirolamo, Richard Kandel, Jane LaTour, Lou McKee, Rhoda McLaughlin, Tom McLaughlin, Thanh Nyan, Barbara O'Brien,

Bill Pieper, Jerry Reed, James B. Snyder, Christopher Wagstaff, and Sadie Williams. For anyone overlooked in any category, we offer our sincere apologies.

Schwartz notes also that he owes a tremendous debt to his immediate family members, David Schwartz and Kiley Brokaw, and to his wife, Marilyn M. Schwartz, former managing editor at the University of California Press, who volunteered extreme patience and editorial skill extraordinaire over many years.

INTERVIEWEES

The name of each interviewee is followed by a brief description. These short sketches should function as references for readers. Geographical information about people interviewed is added. Recording session dates and places follow. Interviews conducted for the ILWU Pacific Coast Pensioners Association Oral History Project are indicated by PCPA. Conor M. Casey, head of the Labor Archives of Washington, handled recording technicalities and asked questions during PCPA interviews. Initials identify the main interviewers: RM for Ronald Magden, HS for Harvey Schwartz. A few interviewees are listed who are not quoted directly in the text. They are included because they contributed useful background information.

All recordings except those marked PCPA are in digital format in the ILWU Oral History Collection at the ILWU library and archives in the ILWU International's Harry R. Bridges building in San Francisco. The PCPA recordings are in digital format at the Labor Archives of Washington at the University of Washington in Seattle. All of the interviews from both collections quoted in the text have been transcribed.

William (Willie) E. Adams, ILWU longshore worker, International secretary-treasurer, International president, Tacoma, Washington, interviewed August 8, 2011, May 15, 2018, San Francisco, California—HS

Richard (Rich) Austin Sr., ILWU longshore worker, union officer, San Francisco, California, interviewed September 12, 2016, Tacoma, Washington (PCPA)—HS

Donald (Don) Birrer, ILWU longshore worker, union officer, Vancouver, Washington, interviewed September 18, 2013, Portland, Oregon (PCPA)—RM

John Castanho, ILWU longshore worker, coast benefits specialist, San Francisco, California, interviewed January 25, 2017, San Francisco, California—HS

LaDonna Chamberlain, spouse of ILWU longshore worker, Longview, Washington, interviewed June 7, 2018, Portland, Oregon—HS

Bradley (Brad) Clark, ILWU longshore worker, union officer, Vancouver, Washington, interviewed April 8, 2018, Vancouver, Washington—RM, HS

George Cobbs, ILWU longshore worker, San Francisco, California, interviewed July 22, 2016, San Francisco, California—HS

Daniel (Dan) Coffman, ILWU longshore worker, union officer, Longview, Washington, interviewed June 3, 2018, Portland, Oregon—HS

Joseph (Joe) Cortez, ILWU longshore worker, union officer, Los Angeles, California, interviewed March 3, 2014, San Francisco, California—RM, HS

Padraig (Paddy) Crumlin, Maritime Union of Australia (MUA) maritime worker, national secretary, Sydney, New South Wales, Australia, interviewed June 4, 2018, Portland, Oregon—HS

Clayton W. Dela Cruz, ILWU organizer, union officer, Hawaii, interviewed September 18, 2018, Portland, Oregon (PCPA)—RM, HS

Jimmy Donovan, MUA maritime worker, union officer, Sydney, New South Wales, Australia, interviewed September 11, 13, 2016, Tacoma, Washington (PCPA)—RM, HS

Thomas (Tom) Dufresne, ILWU longshore worker, ILWU Canada president, Vancouver, British Columbia, Canada, interviewed September 16, 2013, Portland, Oregon (PCPA)—HS

Raymond (Ray) Familathe, ILWU maritime worker, International vice president (mainland), Los Angeles, California, interviewed December 2, 2016, San Francisco, California—HS

Edwin R. (Ed) Ferris, ILWU longshore worker, International secretary-treasurer, San Francisco California, interviewed January 6, 2017, San Francisco, California—HS

Joseph (Joe) Fleetwood, Maritime Union of New Zealand (MUNZ) maritime worker, general secretary, Wellington, New Zealand, interviewed June 6, 2018, Portland, Oregon—HS

Wesley Furtado, ILWU longshore worker, International vice president (Hawaii), Honolulu, Hawaii, interviewed February 28, 2014, March 2, 2014, San Francisco, California—RM, HS

Luisa Gratz, ILWU warehouse worker, union officer, Los Angeles, California, interviewed August 21, 2019, San Francisco, California—HS (access restricted)

Thomas (Tom) Hebert, ILWU longshore worker, Los Angeles, California, interviewed March 6, 2014, San Francisco, California—RM, HS

Michael (Mike) Jagielski, ILWU longshore worker, Tacoma, Washington, interviewed September 17, 2017, Long Beach, California (PCPA)—HS; June 4, 2018, Portland, Oregon—HS

Michael (Mike) Johnson, ILWU longshore worker, Vancouver, Washington, interviewed June 1, 2013, Vancouver, Washington—RM

Helena Jones, ILWU longshore worker, Los Angeles, California, interviewed September 16, 2014, Vancouver, British Columbia, Canada (PCPA)—HS

Linda Kuhn, ILWU International staff member, executive secretary, San Francisco, California, interviewed Mill Valley, California, July 12, 2016—HS

Eusebio (Bo) Lapenia Jr., ILWU agricultural worker, union officer, Honolulu, Hawaii, interviewed June 9, 2015, Honolulu, Hawaii—RM, HS

Melvin Mackay, ILWU longshore worker, union officer, San Francisco, California, interviewed February 1, 2017, Oakland, California—HS

Terri Mast, Inlandboatmen's Union of the Pacific (IBU)-ILWU cannery worker, secretary-treasurer, Seattle, Washington, interviewed June 4, 2018, Portland, Oregon—HS

Robert M. (Big Bob) McEllrath, ILWU longshore worker, International vice president (mainland), International president, Vancouver, Washington, interviewed July 29, 30, 31, 2013, May 15, 2018, November 13, 2019, San Francisco, California—RM, HS

Sally McEllrath, spouse of Bob McEllrath, Vancouver, Washington, interviewed September 13, 2016, Tacoma, Washington—RM, HS

Norman McLeod, ILWU longshore worker, San Francisco, California, interviewed September 17, 2019, Vancouver, British Columbia, Canada (PCPA)—HS

Daniel (Danny) Miranda, ILWU longshore worker, union officer, Los Angeles, California, interviewed March 3, 2014, San Francisco, California—RM, HS

Troy Olson, ILWU longshore worker, local dispatcher, Vancouver, Washington, interviewed April 8, 2018, Vancouver, Washington—RM, HS

Robert (Bobby) Olvera Jr., ILWU longshore worker, International vice president (mainland), Los Angeles, California, interviewed June 21, 2019, San Francisco, California—HS

George O'Neil, ILWU longshore worker, local dispatcher, Portland, Oregon, interviewed March 5, 2014, San Francisco, California—RM, HS

Norman (Norm) S. Parks, ILWU longshore worker, union officer, Portland, Oregon, interviewed April 5, 2016, Goodyear, Arizona (PCPA)—HS (telephone interview)

Fred Jonas Pecker, ILWU warehouse worker, union officer, San Francisco, California, interviewed July 6, 13, 2018, San Francisco, California—HS

Robert (Rob) S. Remar, ILWU attorney, San Francisco, California, interviewed December 15, 2016, January 12, 2017, February 2, 2017, San Francisco, California—HS

George Romero, ILWU longshore worker, coast benefits specialist, San Francisco, California, interviewed November 1, 2016, San Francisco, California—HS

Walter (Pee Wee) C. Smith, ILWU longshore worker, Ketchikan, Alaska, interviewed September 16, 2014, Vancouver, British Columbia, Canada (PCPA)—HS

Conrad Spell, ILWU longshore worker, union officer, Tacoma, Washington, interviewed March 7, 2014, San Francisco, California—RM, HS

Lawrence Thibeaux, ILWU longshore worker, union officer, San Francisco, California, interviewed September 23, 2016, San Francisco, California—HS

Thomas (Tom) Wallenborn, high school basketball coach, Vancouver, Washington, interviewed September 15, 2013, Vancouver, Washington—RM

NOTES

INTRODUCTION

1 Lincoln Fairley, *Facing Mechanization: The West Coast Longshore Plan* (Los Angeles: Institute of Industrial Relations, University of California, 1979), 69–70, 322.

2 Charles P. Larowe, *Harry Bridges: The Rise and Fall of Radical Labor in the U.S.* (New York: Lawrence Hill, 1972), 294.

3 Years later, the lifetime ban on rehiring former strikers was lifted and a new union, the National Air Traffic Controllers Association, emerged to replace PATCO. On the 1981 PATCO strike, see Joseph A. McCartin, *Collision Course: Ronald Reagan, the Air Controllers, and the Strike That Changed America* (New York: Oxford University Press, 2011); Erik Loomis, "Air Traffic Controllers and the New Assault on Unions," in *A History of America in Ten Strikes* (New York: New Press, 2018).

4 Kathleen Schalch, "1981 Strike Leaves Legacy for American Workers," National Public Radio, August 3, 2006. See also Timothy J. Minchin, *Labor under Fire: A History of the AFL-CIO since 1979* (Chapel Hill: University of North Carolina Press, 2017). Rosemary Feurer and Chad Pearson, eds., *Against Labor: How U.S. Employers Organized to Defeat Union Activism* (Chicago: University of Illinois Press, 2017).

5 Steve Greenhouse, "Union Membership in U.S. Fell to a 70-Year Low Last Year," *New York Times*, January 11, 2011; "Union Members Summary," Economic News Release, U.S. Bureau of Labor Statistics, Washington, DC, January 22, 2020; Jane Slaughter, "Concessions Didn't Work Then and They Won't Work Now," *Labor Notes*, August 2020, 4.

6 Ron Magden, "Bob McEllrath Chronology Chart," email to Harvey Schwartz, August 9, 2017.

7 Robert W. Cherny, William Issel, and Kieran Walsh Taylor, eds., *American Labor and the Cold War: Grassroots Politics and Postwar Political Culture* (New

Brunswick, NJ: Rutgers University Press, 2004), 14–15, 141–53. The CIO was separate from the American Federation of Labor (AFL) from its founding in 1935 to its merger with the AFL in 1955.

8 During 1934–37 the union was affiliated with the East Coast International Longshoremen's Association (ILA/AFL) as the Pacific Coast Branch. It left and became the ILWU/CIO in 1937. For an in-depth study of the ILWU's commitment to social justice and community solidarity, see John A. Ahlquist and Margaret Levi, *In the Interest of Others: Organizations and Social Activism* (Princeton, NJ: Princeton University Press, 2013).

9 Harvey Schwartz, *Solidarity Stories: An Oral History of the ILWU* (Seattle: University of Washington Press, 2009), 39, 206; Peter Cole, *Dockworker Power: Race and Activism in Durban and the San Francisco Bay Area* (Urbana: University of Illinois Press, 2018), 1. For historical precedents for Black and White waterfront unity, see Eric Arnesen, *Waterfront Workers of New Orleans: Race, Class, and Politics, 1863–1923* (Urbana: University of Illinois Press, 1994); Peter Cole, *Wobblies on the Waterfront: Interracial Unionism in Progressive-Era Philadelphia* (Urbana: University of Illinois Press, 2007) and *Ben Fletcher: The Life and Times of a Black Wobbly*, 2nd ed. (Oakland, CA: PM Press, 2021).

10 For widespread discrimination against women and Black workers generally in the construction trades in recent decades, see Jane Latour, *Sisters in the Brotherhoods: Working Women Organizing for Equality in New York City* (New York: Palgrave Macmillan, 2008).

11 Schwartz, *Solidarity Stories*, 72–80, 159–66, 186–98, 220–73.

12 Bridges quoted in Schwartz, *Solidarity Stories*, 6–7.

13 The Wagner Act initially benefitted many thousands of Americans, although agricultural and domestic workers were excluded from coverage to placate conservative southern Democrats. In 1940 even youthful Cleveland newsboys appealed to the NLRB for aid during a wage strike. See Vincent DiGirolamo, *Crying the News: A History of America's Newsboys* (New York: Oxford University Press, 2019), 535–36.

14 For a comprehensive investigation into the erosion of workers' rights under modern labor law, see David Brody, *Labor Embattled: History, Power, Rights* (Urbana: University of Illinois Press, 2005). Chapter 7 includes an incisive evaluation of the NLRA. See also David Montgomery, *Workers' Control in America: Studies in the History of Work, Technology, and Labor Struggles* (Cambridge: Cambridge University Press, 1979), 166–67; Nelson Lichtenstein, "Taft-Hartley: A Slave-Labor Law," *Catholic University Law Review* 47 (1997): 763–89, and *State of the Union: A Century of American Labor* (Princeton, NJ: Princeton University Press, 2002), 114–22, 165; James A. Gross, *Rights Not Interests: Resolving Value Clashes under the National Labor Relations Act* (Ithaca, NY: Cornell University Press, 2017). For a discussion of CIO politics and the

coming of Taft-Hartley, see Adam Dean and Jonathan Obert, "Rewarded by Friends and Punished by Enemies: The CIO and the Taft-Hartley Act," *Labor: Studies in Working-Class History* 18, no. 3 (2021): 78–143. See also the comments by Dorothy Sue Cobble, Devin Caughey, Eric Schickler, and Kristoffer Smemo, and Dean and Obert's response on pages 114–43.

15 Larrowe, *Harry Bridges*, 293–99.

16 *ILWU Dispatcher*, December 7, 1951, 1, January 8, 1952, 1, 5–6; Juneau Spruce Corporation, Records, 1947–1956, MS 191, "Guide to Collection," Historical Collections, Alaska State Library. See also Sanford Zalburg, *A Spark Is Struck! Jack Hall and the ILWU in Hawaii* (Honolulu: University of Hawaii Press, 1979; reprint Honolulu: Watermark Publishing 2007), 382–88.

17 McEllrath quoted in Eduardo Soriano-Castillo, "Longshore Union, Occupy Poised to Greet Grain Ship," *Labor Notes*, February 2012, 2.

18 For a detailed description of the ILWU Oral History Collection, see Harvey Schwartz and Robin Walker, "The ILWU History Project," Labor and Working-Class History Association Online, September 17, 2016. All of the collection's analog interviews except for a series of recordings of Harry Bridges were digitized in 2017 under the direction of Walker, the union's director of educational services, librarian, and archivist. The Bridges tapes, recorded by his wife, Nikki, around 1978, were digitized through Walker's agency in 2021.

19 Alessandro Portelli, *The Order Has Been Carried Out: History, Memory, and Meaning of a Nazi Massacre in Rome* (New York: Palgrave Macmillan, 2003), 15. See also Michael Frisch, *A Shared Authority: Essays on the Craft and Meaning of Oral and Public History* (Albany: State University of New York Press, 1990).

20 Alessandro Portelli, *They Say in Harlan County: An Oral History* (New York: Oxford University Press, 2011), 10.

21 Donald A. Ritchie, *Doing Oral History* (New York: Twayne Publishers, 1995), 102.

1. "ASSHOLES AND ELBOWS"

1 "Of History and Horizons: The Port of Vancouver, 1912–1982," *The Columbian* (Vancouver, WA), August 9, 1982, A1, A6; Rick Rubin, "Bulk and Break Bulk Cargoes Keep Vancouver Thriving," *Marine Digest*, July 9, 1988, 11–17, 29–30.

2 *Vancouver Evening Columbian* (Vancouver, WA), May 8–10, 1934; ILWU, *Proceedings of the First Annual Convention of the International Longshoremen's and Warehousemen's Union* (Aberdeen, WA, April 4–17, 1938), 140.

3 There were twenty-eight thousand Vancouver residents in 1950. But, growing up in the 1950s on the outskirts of town, Vancouver felt rural to Bob.

4 In basketball, a post player competes near the basket. An outside shooter takes shots from a distance.

5 Darby's Rangers was an elite US Army World War II commando unit led by Colonel William O. Darby. It served in the North African and Italian campaigns.

6 "Sgt. McEllrath Recovering from Combat Injuries," *Belvidere Daily Republican* (Belvidere, IL), October 23, 1944, 2.

7 According to the online *Urban Dictionary*, "assholes and elbows," referring to working hard, originated in farm work. US Army sergeants used the expression in the 1960s to motivate troops.

8 A news reporter estimated Local 4's membership as 150 in 1987. See Julie Anderson, "Change at the Port," *The Columbian* (Vancouver, WA), December 6, 1987, C1.

9 In the precontainer era, winch drivers operated ships' equipment to lift or lower slings of heavy cargo. Winch driving took skill and experience. The lift job reference is to forklift driving.

10 Handling tapioca sacks was hard work. The sacks were heavy and slick.

11 The strike lasted for 134 days.

12 It is ten miles from Vancouver, Washington, to Portland, Oregon, across the I–5 Bridge over the Columbia River.

13 Bridges was not happy about the union striking during 1971–72. He criticized the membership, which voted strongly for the walkout. This is probably why he was booed in Portland. Since the Portland local had also resisted integration until the 1960s, perhaps some White Local 8 members also resented his long-standing advocacy of Black equality.

14 ILWU Labor Relations Committees meet with employer representatives to deal with grievances.

15 Local 5 of the Association of Western Pulp and Paper Workers (AWPPW) struck the Camas Crown Zellerbach mill in 1964 and 1969.

16 Section 8.42 of the West Coast longshore contract has long stated, "Dispatching of men and gangs shall be under the principle of low-man, low-gang, first-to-be-dispatched, except where local dispatching rules provide otherwise for dispatching of special skilled men and gangs." See, for example, *Pacific Coast Longshore Contract Document between International Longshore and Warehouse Union and Pacific Maritime Association*, July 1, 1996–July 1, 1999, p. 49.

17 Coast committeemen are important ILWU officers who oversee the ILWU Longshore Division's West Coast master contract. They are based at the ILWU International office in San Francisco.

18 *ILWU Dispatcher*, June 7, 1985, 1.

19 The coast-level officers accompanying Herman from the ILWU International office in San Francisco were Robert Olvera Sr. and Dick Wise. *ILWU Dispatcher*, June 7, 1985, 3.

20 Election figures from Ron Magden, "Bob McEllrath chronology chart."

21 ILWU, *Proceedings of the Twenty-Eighth Convention of the International Longshoremen's and Warehousemen's Union* (Seattle, June 3–7, 1991), 497, 595.

22 O'Neil, who was interviewed in 2014, also told the dragon boat story at the ILWU International Convention in 2018. See ILWU, *Proceedings of the Thirty-Seventh Convention of the International Longshore and Warehouse Union* (Portland, OR, June 4–8, 2018), 416.

2. "COUNTRY BOY WITH PENCIL"

1 The Leonard Carder law firm of San Francisco is the current incarnation of the legendary Gladstein, Anderson, and Leonard firm that defended the ILWU and Harry Bridges, the union's founding president, during the middle decades of the twentieth century. See Colin Wark and John F. Galliher, *Progressive Lawyers under Siege: Moral Panic during the McCarthy Years* (Lanham, MD: Lexington Books, 2015); Estolv Ward, *Norman Leonard: Life of a Leftist Labor Lawyer* (Berkeley: Regional Oral History Office, Bancroft Library, University of California, 1986).

2 The reference is to the Joint Coast Labor Relations Committee (JCLRC), which consists of the ILWU Coast Committee members and representatives from the employers' Pacific Coast Maritime Association (PMA). It stands above a hierarchy of port and area committees. The JCLRC administers the Pacific Coast Longshore and Clerks Agreement. If the union and the employer members of the JCLRC fail to agree on a question, then, at the request of either party, that question is referred to a Coast Arbitrator for a hearing and a decision.

3 Local 8 had a long record going back to the 1930s of resisting acceptance of African Americans. It was close to unique in this compared to other ILWU locals. This stance probably reflected Oregon's history of predominantly White settlement from its Oregon Trail days in the nineteenth century, when many White people from the American South moved to the Northwest, through the early 1920s, when the Ku Klux Klan boasted a state membership of thirty-five thousand and was a major factor in state politics. Portland's Black population remained small until World War II. Local 8's policy of exclusion started changing in the 1960s following a major push from ILWU president Harry Bridges and ILWU secretary-treasurer Louis Goldblatt. See William W. Pilcher, *The Portland Longshoremen: A Dispersed Urban Community* (New York: Holt, Rinehart, and Winston, 1972), 67–76; Edward Balloch DeBra, "An Injury to One: The Politics of Racial Exclusion in the Portland Local of the International Longshoremen's and Warehousemen's Union," BA thesis, University of Oregon, 1992; Jerome Polk, Local 8, ILWU, interview by Harvey Schwartz, January 15, 2015, ILWU Oral History Collection, ILWU Library, San Francisco.

4 The fear was of a reverse discrimination lawsuit by White people. Rob Remar, telephone discussion with Schwartz, Oakland, California, April 7, 2021.

5 ILWU International Conventions have been held periodically since 1938. Initially held yearly and later every two years, they have been called every three years since 1988.

6 The job board refers to the job dispatch listing in a local's hiring hall. Often that listing will be on a big board on the wall.

7 A bucket loader is a machine-driven scoop.

8 The reference is to the heavy lines that hold a ship to a pier when moored in port. The lines board is the union hiring hall's job dispatch board for registered lines workers.

9 The Longshore Caucus is a representative body of longshore workers, marine clerks, and waterfront foremen elected by the union's Longshore Division membership. It meets at least annually. It meets before longshore contract negotiations and develops a list of contract demands. The caucus then elects a negotiating committee from its ranks. Included will be ILWU International officers and the two coast committeemen. The negotiating committee remains in San Francisco during contract negotiations with the employers' PMA. If an agreement is reached, the contract is sent back to the caucus for approval. If the caucus votes it up, it is sent to the Longshore Division membership for a ratification vote. If voted down, the caucus may call for a strike vote or send the negotiating committee back to the bargaining table. See ILWU, *How the Union Works* (trifold flyer), updated March 2017 (San Francisco: ILWU, 2017), 2. See also *How the Union Works*, accessed October 4, 2021, at https://www .ilwu.org/wp-content/uploads/2010/12/how-the-union-works.pdf.

10 Steady workers are waterfront employees who labor for one company on a permanent basis. They differ from other longshore workers because they do not have to circulate through the union-controlled hiring hall picking up a series of short-term jobs. All West Coast waterfront jobs went through the union hall from 1934 to 1966. The employers gained the right to hire steady workers in their 1966 contract with the union. Because of its potential to divide worker loyalty, the "steady man" provision in the contract has remained controversial.

11 Typically, there are executive boards in each local that meet periodically. There is also an ILWU International Executive Board (IEB), which is the union's highest governing body that meets between International Conventions. Its elected members meet at least three times a year. One of the IEB's main functions is to implement the decisions of the International Convention's delegates.

12 ILWU Local 142 in Hawaii is divided into divisions covering different islands, including Kauai, Oahu, Maui, and the "Big Island" of Hawaii. Company groupings of Local 142 workers, such as employees of a particular hotel, are called units.

13 Hawaiians call the continental North American (US) states "the mainland."

14 Nominations for coast committeemen are taken at the Longshore Caucus the week immediately following the ILWU International Convention. Then ballots

are distributed to the members of the Longshore Division, who vote to decide which two people among those nominated will be the coast committeemen for the Northwest and for California. *ILWU Dispatcher*, February 2018, 2; ILWU, *How the Union Works*, 2.

15 There are labor relations committees in each port. They include representatives from the union and the employers. These committees deal with grievances on a local level. For years, when there were disagreements, individual area arbitrators were called in to make decisions on the grievances. Their decisions were sometimes appealed to the coast arbitrator. In 2015, under changes made in the Pacific Coast Longshore and Clerks Agreement, the individual area arbitrators were replaced with three-member panels consisting of a union representative, an employer representative, and an "outside" (non-longshore industry) neutral person. Thanks to Cameron Williams, ILWU Northwest committeeman, for reviewing these issues with Schwartz in 2017.

16 A walking boss is a foreman who supervises longshore operations. Waterfront foremen are members of the ILWU.

17 Bob followed through on this scenario in early 2019, shortly after retiring from office in 2018. Robert McEllrath, telephone discussion with Schwartz, Vancouver, Washington, February 2019.

18 The historic record suggests the wisdom of McEllrath's perspective. The first unified Pacific Coast longshore strike occurred in 1916, two decades before there was an ILWU. It was broken with disastrous results for longshore workers coastwide when San Francisco's waterfront contingency broke ranks and took a separate peace with the ship owners. See Ronald E. Magden and A. D. Martinson, *The Working Waterfront: The Story of Tacoma's Ships and Men* (Tacoma, WA: ILWU Local 23 and the Washington Commission for the Humanities, 1982), 31–38; Ronald E. Magden, *The Working Longshoreman* (Tacoma, WA: ILWU Local 23, 1991), 70–84; Mary J. Renfro, "The Decline and Fall of the San Francisco Riggers' and Stevedores' Union: A History of the Years 1916–1919," senior thesis, San Francisco State University, 1995. For Harry Bridges's recollections of his insistence in 1934 on the need for a coastwide longshore contract, see Harvey Schwartz, *Solidarity Stories: An Oral History of the ILWU* (Seattle: University of Washington Press, 2009), 19–20.

19 The references here are to hand-working cargo in the holds of ships during the precontainer or "break-bulk" era on the waterfront and to lashing containers to the decks of ships in later years. Both jobs are physically demanding.

20 A gear man was a longshoreman who prepared waterfront equipment for use during the "break-bulk" era. He would repair cargo slings to ensure that longshore operations were safe. The issue referred to here was the local gear man supplement to the main coastwide longshore contract.

21 The Pacific Coast Pensioners Association, composed of Longshore Division retirees from the US West Coast and Canada, meets in convention each year.

22 Sadly, Williams passed away in 2016, three years after Bob's testimony here. For longer profiles of Williams, see Schwartz, *Solidarity Stories*, 45–51; *ILWU Dispatcher*, July/August 2016, 6.

23 Veteran longshore Local 8 member and later anthropology professor William W. Pilcher discusses the culture of drinking on the waterfront in *The Portland Longshoremen*, 93–94. See also Aaron Goings, *The Port of Missing Men: Billy Gohl, Labor, and Brutal Times in the Pacific Northwest* (Seattle: University of Washington Press, 2020), 129.

24 With backing from Los Angeles/Long Beach Harbor Local 13, the largest longshore local on the Pacific Coast, and Hawaii's Local 142, the largest local in the ILWU, anyone active in ILWU politics is likely to succeed.

25 Registration here refers to adding workers to the longshore workforce.

26 A stop-work meeting is a special local union assembly.

27 For example, members of longshore Local 10 in Northern California have been especially active in social justice causes. See Peter Cole, *Dockworker Power: Race and Activism in Durban and the San Francisco Bay Area* (Urbana: University of Illinois Press, 2018); Clarence Thomas, *Mobilizing in Our Own Name: Million Worker March* (Middletown, DE: DeClare Publishing, 2021).

28 *ILWU Dispatcher*, March 8, 1998, 8.

29 *ILWU Dispatcher*, January 2004, 3; October 2004, 4; Robert McEllrath, telephone discussion with Schwartz, Vancouver, Washington, March 10, 2021.

30 *ILWU Dispatcher*, March 2005, 9; February 2010, 6; January 2014, 1, 3; March 2014, 1; McEllrath, telephone discussion with Schwartz, March 10, 2021.

3. "GOING TO SHAKE HANDS"

1 ILWU, *Proceedings of the Thirty-First Convention of the International Longshore and Warehouse Union* (Portland, OR, May 1–5, 2000), 376–79.

2 Pile butt is a nickname for a pile driver.

3 The B or A would indicate an auxiliary group attached to the local.

4 Tommy Trask was a longtime organizer and union officer for the ILWU in Hawaii. See Rehabilitation Hospital of the Pacific, *Visions of a Man: Tommy Trask and the ILWU* (Aiea, HI: Island Heritage Publishing, 1991).

5 Jack Hall was a major figure in ILWU history. He played a key part in bringing the union to the Islands in the mid-1940s and was Hawaii's chief ILWU official from 1944 to 1969. He was elected International vice president for Hawaii in 1969, moved to San Francisco, and died in office there in 1971. See Sanford Zalburg, *A Spark Is Struck! Jack Hall and the ILWU in Hawaii* (Honolulu: University of Hawaii Press, 1979; reprint Honolulu: Watermark Publishing, 2007); Edward D. Beechert, *Working in Hawaii: A Labor History* (Honolulu: University of Hawaii Press, 1985); Michael T. Holmes, *The Specter of Communism in Hawaii* (Honolulu: University of Hawaii Press, 1994); Harvey Schwartz, "Jack Hall: Islands Organizer, 1934–1951," in *Solidarity Stories: An*

Oral History of the ILWU (Seattle: University of Washington Press, 2009), 226–33.

6 A winch man was an experienced longshore worker who operated steam-driven winches during the pre-container, break-bulk cargo era. The winches moved slings of products into and out of ships' holds.

7 A hammerhead crane is a heavy-duty crane with a horizontal counterbalanced arm.

8 That is, they had people sign cards in support of unionization.

9 Furtado was interviewed during a March 2014 ILWU Longshore Division Caucus in San Francisco. After breaking for lunch, the caucus was scheduled to reconvene at 2:00 p.m.

10 ILWU International Conventions set union policy goals between conventions. At the 1997 International Convention, it was resolved that "not less than thirty percent (30%) of the International's per capita income shall be used for organizing." ILWU, *Proceedings of the Thirtieth Convention of the International Longshore and Warehouse Union* (Honolulu, HI, April 7–11, 1997), 426.

11 See ILWU, *Proceedings of the Thirty-Second Convention of the International Longshore and Warehouse Union* (San Francisco, CA, April 28–May 2, 2003), 56; ILWU, *Proceedings of the Thirty-Third Convention of the International Longshore and Warehouse Union* (Vancouver, BC, Canada, May 15–19, 2006), 27. Organizing success in Hawaii continued over time under Furtado's lead. Five hundred new members were brought into Local 142 just between September and November 2013. See *ILWU Dispatcher*, February 2014, 3. In late 2018 Furtado listed categories in Hawaii the union had under contract. These included "supermarkets, graveyards, hotels, spas, golf courses, agricultural workers, coffee, candy, beer distribution and more." Although the ILWU's Hawaiian agricultural jurisdiction continued to decline as companies moved out of the Islands, much recent ILWU expansion into these other areas occurred because of Furtado's guidance with Bob's support. *ILWU Dispatcher*, December 2018, 7. Furtado also organized waterfront supervisors into a new ILWU group, Hawaii Local 100.

12 In the 2001 ILWU directory, John Bukoskey is identified as Local 200 regional director. This was an appointed position. There is no mention of Pete Danelski. Local 200 then had thirteen units. In the 2002 directory, Bukoskey is listed as Local 200 president and Danelski as the new Alaska Longshore Division secretary-treasurer and that group's Kodiak unit president. Local 200 then had six units and the Alaska Longshore Division six. The 2002 Local 200 units included one in seafood, one in public service, one in healthcare, and three in longshoring. The healthcare group, Unit 2201 in Juneau, contained nurses. It was the largest unit in Local 200. All of the units in the new Alaska Longshore Division were described as longshore or longshore and waterfront-related entities. See *ILWU Directory* (San Francisco, 2001), 15–16; *ILWU Directory* (San Francisco, 2002), 15–16.

13 Robert McEllrath, conversation with Schwartz, ILWU Coast Longshore, Clerk, and Walking Boss Caucus, San Francisco, December 6, 2018.

14 The literature comparing the ILA and the ILWU is extensive. Examples include Charles P. Larrowe, *Shape-Up and Hiring Hall: A Comparison of Hiring Methods and Labor Relations on the New York and Seattle Waterfronts* (Berkeley: University of California Press, 1955); Howard Kimeldorf, *Reds or Rackets? The Making of Radical and Conservative Unions on the Waterfront* (Berkeley: University of California Press, 1988).

15 The ILA held its International Convention in San Juan, Puerto Rico, in 2015.

16 Harold J. Daggett became ILA International president in 2011. He won reelection in 2015.

17 Suzan Erem and E. Paul Durrenberger, *On the Global Waterfront: The Fight to Free the Charleston 5* (New York: Monthly Review Press, 2008); Chris Kromm, "Flashback: The Charleston Five and the Black Struggle for Justice," *Facing South*, July 2, 2105.

18 John M. Bowers was ILA International president between 1987 and 2007.

19 Jim Spinosa became ILWU International president a few months after the arrest of the Charleston Five.

20 Ray Ortiz and Joe Wenzel were the ILWU coast committeemen in 2000–2001.

21 For much detail on the lockout, see Kathleen McGinn and Dina Witter, "Showdown on the Waterfront: The 2002 West Coast Port Dispute," Case N9-904-045, Harvard Business School, March 23, 2004. Thanks to Rob Remar for this document.

22 In his 2013 interview, McEllrath asserted that the union did win a good "framework for automation with the clerks" in 2002. But, he cautioned, over time the employers often failed to adhere in good faith to the intent of the clerk clause in the contract and that enforcement by the union could be very time-consuming and difficult.

23 George Raine, "Dock Group Recommends Contract OK," *San Francisco Chronicle*, December 13, 2002; *ILWU Dispatcher*, January 2003, 3.

24 Andrew Siff was counselor to the George W. Bush administration's secretary of labor, Elaine L. Chao, during 2001–2003. Siff has served as counselor to the US Senate Committee on Rules and Administration for conservative Senate Republican Party leader Mitch McConnell. He has also been on the executive committee of the Labor and Employment Practice Group of the conservative Federalist Society for Law and Public Policy Studies.

25 Miniace was fired by the PMA less than two years after the lockout. He sued the ship owners association for a million dollars in compensation and bonuses he claimed he was owed. *San Francisco Chronicle*, August 25, 2004.

26 Eugene Dennis Vrana, a former ILWU longshore Local 10 member, was the union's director of educational services, librarian, and archivist between 1987

and his retirement in 2010. His innovations included a series of educational retreats for union officers and active rank-and-file members. *ILWU Dispatcher*, January 2010, 7.

27 "Militarize you guys" meant replacing strikers with military personnel.

28 For Local 5's origins, see Schwartz, *Solidarity Stories*, 159–66; Kristin Russ, "Remembering Our Roots: Local 5 Marks 20-Year Anniversary," *ILWU Dispatcher*, September 2020, 4–5.

29 Local 5's second contract was negotiated with Powell's Books in fall 2003. See Sarah Mirk, *Portland Mercury*, April 12, 2010.

30 In 2019, Local 5 retained open bargaining. It also had one of the most active memberships in the union. While the local was more experienced by 2019, its bargaining style still encouraged transparency and "buy in" from the members.

31 Peter Olney was the ILWU director of organizing for many years. He retired in that post in 2013. Olney was crucial to the success of the 1998–2000 Local 5 organizing drive. During the Powell's Books second contract negotiations, though, he was away from the ILWU while serving as the associate director of the Institute for Labor and Employment at the University of California, Berkeley. He held that post between 2001 and 2004.

32 Thanks to Eugene Dennis Vrana for emphasizing the importance of Bob's focus on international solidarity when this project was being planned.

33 Robert Cherny, Bridges's biographer, telephone discussion with Schwartz, San Francisco, March 29, 2019. See also Margo Beasley, *Wharfies: The History of the Waterside Workers' Federation* (Rushcutters Bay, NSW, Australia: Halstead Press, 1996), 207.

34 Founded in 1896, the ITF is a federation of 670 seagoing, waterfront, railroad, and aviation unions in 140 countries. It functions on a global basis on behalf of workers' rights, equality, and justice. The ILWU and the MUA are committed ITF supporters. Crumlin has served as ITF president. The ILWU joined the ITF in 1986. ILWU, *Proceedings of the Thirty-First Convention* (2000), 42; Eugene Dennis Vrana, text, Harvey Schwartz, additional research, Steve Stallone and Marcy Rein, editing, *The ILWU Story: Six Decades of Militant Unionism* (San Francisco: International Longshoremen's and Warehousemen's Union, 1997), 75; Peter Cole, *Dockworker Power: Race and Activism in Durban and the San Francisco Bay Area* (Urbana: University of Illinois Press, 2018), 184–85.

35 Taffy Sweetensen passed away in 2017. Maritime Union of Australia, *Queensland Branch News*, September 5, 2017.

36 On the merger of the SUA and the WWF, see Beasley, *Wharfies*, 282–90; Tas Bull, *An Autobiography: Life on the Waterfront* (Sydney, NSW, Australia: HarperCollins, 1998), 247–48.

37 The First International Mining and Maritime Conference was held in Newcastle, Australia, in 2002. "Fourth International Mining and Maritime Conference," *The Maritimes: Magazine of the Maritime Union of New Zealand*, Summer 2011–12, 10.

38 For a wide-ranging essay on supply chain organizing and its implications for the ILWU and other workers' organizations, see Peter Olney, "Beyond the Waterfront: Maintaining and Expanding Worker Power in the Maritime Supply Chain," in *Choke Points: Logistics Workers Disrupting the Global Supply Chain*, ed. Jake Alimahomed-Wilson and Immanuel Ness (London: Pluto Press, 2018), 243–58. See also Edna Bonacich and Jake B. Wilson, *Getting the Goods: Ports, Labor, and the Logistics Revolution* (Ithaca, NY: Cornell University Press, 2008).

39 The reference is to popular Black History events Adams organized in Tacoma.

40 Robert McEllrath, telephone discussion with Schwartz, Vancouver, Washington, March 10, 2021.

41 Ultimately the PMA dropped its charges against Irminger, a member of the Inlandboatmen's Union (IBU), an ILWU affiliate.

42 Robert McEllrath, telephone discussion with Schwartz, Vancouver, Washington, March 10, 2021.

43 In 2018 Crumlin became international president of Australia's new Construction, Forestry, Maritime, Mining, and Energy Union (CFMEU). A recent union consolidation movement had created the CFMEU. Crumlin retained his post as MUA national secretary. See Paddy Crumlin, "Vote Yes for Amalgamation," *The Maritime Workers' Journal* (Australia), Spring 2017, 4; *ILWU Dispatcher*, May 2017, 3.

44 Fleetwood joined the New Zealand Seafarers' Union in 1980. See ILWU, *Proceedings of the Thirty-Fifth Convention of the International Longshore and Warehouse Union* (San Diego, CA, June 4–8, 2012), 196.

45 The 2002 merger that created the MUNZ joined the New Zealand Seafarers' Union and the New Zealand Waterside Workers' Union.

46 On the Domingo-Viernes tragedy, see Ron Chew, *Remembering Silme Domingo and Gene Viernes: The Legacy of Filipino American Labor Activism* (Seattle: University of Washington Press, 2012); Rene Ciria Cruz, Cindy Domingo, and Bruce Occena, eds., *A Time to Rise: Collective Memoirs of the Union of Democratic Filipinos (KDP)* (Seattle: University of Washington Press, 2017); Michael Withey, *Summary Execution: The Seattle Assassination of Silme Domingo and Gene Viernes* (Evergreen, CO: WildBlue Press, 2018).

47 Bob was acknowledging that non-longshore ILWU locals and workers invariably had less money than ILWU Longshore Division locals and members.

48 In 2018, Mast became the ITF's second vice chair of Inland Waterways. *ILWU Dispatcher*, December 2018, 6.

49 Section 27 of the US federal Merchant Marine Act of 1920 is known as the Jones Act. It deals with cabotage (coastal trade) and requires that waterborne cargo transported between US ports must be carried in US-flagged and

US-built vessels employing crews consisting of US citizens or US permanent residents. The law also provides for certain seamen's rights.

4. "I GOT A PLAN"

1 ILWU, *Proceedings of the Thirty-Third Convention of the International Longshore and Warehouse Union* (Vancouver, BC, Canada, May 15–19, 2006), 488–91.

2 ILWU, *Proceedings of the Thirty-Third Convention* (2006), 491.

3 For the 2006 election results by locals, see *ILWU Dispatcher*, September 2006, 7.

4 The tests were on a pass/fail basis. Later, in longshore Local 10 in the San Francisco Bay Area at least, they were administrated for evaluation only. Former ILWU longshore Local 10 president Mike Villeggiante, telephone discussion with Schwartz, San Francisco, September 28, 2020.

5 The headquarters office of the Pacific Maritime Association, the ship owners' bargaining representative, was at 555 Market Street in San Francisco.

6 To suppress May Day and its militant legacy, in 1894 US President Grover Cleveland signed legislation creating the neutral September "Labor Day" as a federal holiday.

7 Jack Heyman, then a member of the ILWU-affiliated Inlandboatmen's Union, helped lead the 1984 boycott. Later a Local 10 adherent, he was also an important figure in the 2008 protest. Other key 1984 boycott leaders included Local 10 members Leon Ingram, Charlie Jones, Howard Keylor, Bill Proctor, Leo Robinson, Dave Stewart, Larry Wright, and ILWU ship clerks Local 34 member Alex Bagwell. Peter Cole, *Dockworker Power: Race and Activism in Durban and the San Francisco Bay Area* (Urbana: University of Illinois Press, 2018), 181–200; Peter Cole and Peter Limb, "Hooks Down! Anti-Apartheid Activism and Solidarity among Maritime Unions in Australia and the United States," *Labor History* 58, no. 3 (2017): 303–26.

8 Mike Parker, "Longshore Workers Shut Ports to Protest War," *Labor Notes*, May 31, 2008; Peter Cole, "Don't Like War? Then Don't Work! Remembering When Dockworkers Shut Down the Ports on May Day," *In These Times*, April 26, 2018; *Pacific Coast Longshore Contract Document, July 1, 2002–July 1, 2008, between International Longshore and Warehouse Union and Pacific Maritime Association* (n.p.: ILWU-PMA, [2002]), Sections 12.31–12.32.

9 See *Los Angeles Times*, May 2, 2008; *The Internationalist*, May 2008.

10 In 2008 John Kagel was the coast arbitrator for the West Coast longshore industry. John Kagel is the son of Sam Kagel, a legendary West Coast waterfront figure who, as an employee of the Pacific Coast Labor Bureau, worked with Harry Bridges and the longshore union during 1934–42. He served as coast arbitrator between 1948 and 2002.

11 The ILWU has a long history of representing Crockett's California and Hawaii Sugar Corporation longshore and warehouse workers. See Harvey Schwartz,

The March Inland: Origins of the ILWU Warehouse Division, 1934–1938 (Los Angeles: Institute of Industrial Relations, University of California, 1978; reprint, San Francisco: ILWU, 2000), 7–9, 27, 39–56, 149–51.

12 Sadly, Cobbs passed away in 2017. *ILWU Dispatcher*, September 2017, 7.

13 Norman McLeod, a former ILWU Local 10 longshoreman and Northern California Area Alcohol and Drug Recovery Program representative, worked closely with Cobbs for years. In his 2019 oral history, McLeod concurred that Bob always supported the program. "Big Bob was receptive to anything and everything we did because he know he was helping people out," he said.

14 See Section 1.72, International Longshore and Warehouse Union and Pacific Maritime Association, *Pacific Coast Longshore Contract Document, July 1, 2008–July 1, 2014* (n.p.: ILWU-PMA, June 15, 2009), 9–10.

15 Paul Eliel, *The Waterfront and General Strikes, San Francisco, 1934* (San Francisco: Hooper Publishing, 1934), 243.

16 On the container revolution, see Marc Levinson, *The Box: How the Shipping Container Made the World Smaller and the World Economy Bigger* (Princeton, NJ: Princeton University Press, 2006).

17 For discussions of the coming of the M and M Agreements, see Otto Hagel and Louis Goldblatt, *A Photo Story of the Mechanization and Modernization Agreement between the International Longshoremen's and Warehousemen's Union and the Pacific Maritime Association Now in Operation in the Ports of California, Oregon and Washington* (San Francisco: ILWU and PMA, 1963); Charles Larrowe, *Harry Bridges: The Rise and Fall of Radical Labor in the United States*, 2nd ed. (New York: Lawrence Hill, 1977), 351–58, 382; Lincoln Fairley, *Facing Mechanization: The West Coast Longshore Plan* (Los Angeles: Institute of Industrial Relations, University of California, 1979); Levinson, *The Box*, 101–18, 274; Cole, *Dockworker Power*, 2, 118, 133–79, 213. Cole, an innovative comparative maritime labor historian, raises serious questions about the consequences of M and M.

18 Cole, *Dockworker Power*, 132.

19 Fairley, *Facing Mechanization*, 296–304, 339–41.

20 Quoted in Paul Rosenberg, "Uproar Greets Pier 400 Automation Plans," *Random Lengths*, February 7–20, 2019, 3.

21 *ILWU Dispatcher*, March 2019, 1, 7; *Random Lengths*, June 27–July 10, 2019, 2, 6; July 25–August 7, 2019, 1–3.

22 Thanks to Robin Walker, ILWU director of educational services, librarian, and archivist, for emphasizing that the union courted community support in trying to reduce the impact of automation in Los Angeles/Long Beach.

23 Canadian longshore workers are not covered by the US Pacific Coast ILWU-PMA master contract. ILWU Canada has its own contract with the shippers.

24 Before containerization, hatch covers were placed over the holds of traditional ships that carried break-bulk cargo. Longshoremen removed the hatch covers when ships were in port before working cargo.

25 A gear man repaired traditional longshore equipment like slings in the break-bulk cargo handling era.

26 The reference here is to the Port of Los Angeles/Long Beach mechanics' agreement that serves as a port supplement to the Pacific Coast Longshore Contract.

27 Around the time of the 2008 longshore contract, the employers seemed to break the spirit if not "the letter of the contract" when they sold off chassis they had owned for years that truckers relied on for the delivery of containers. These sales were to chassis-leasing companies. To ILWU adherents, this maneuver looked like an effort to cut the union out of M and R work because the chassis would no longer be in the M and R jurisdiction the union negotiated for in good faith. Robert McEllrath, discussion with Schwartz, ILWU Longshore, Clerk, and Walking Boss Caucus, San Francisco, April 10, 2019; Bill Mongelluzzo, *Journal of Commerce*, May 23, 2015.

28 Olney's ideas are fully developed in Peter Olney, "Beyond the Waterfront: Maintaining and Expanding Worker Power in the Maritime Supply Chain," in *Choke Points: Logistics Workers Disrupting the Global Supply Chain*, ed. Jake Alimahomed-Wilson and Immanuel Ness (London: Pluto Press, 2018), 243–58. For the union's 1930s warehouse organizing drive, see Schwartz, *The March Inland*.

29 This was in the 1990s.

30 ERISA is the Employee Retirement Income Security Act, passed by Congress in 1974. The law sets minimum standards for most voluntarily established pension and health plans in private industry. In 2019, the ILWU-PMA Pension Plan was funded at 99 percent. Coast Committee Report, ILWU Coast Longshore Division, *Longshore, Clerk, and Walking Boss Caucus*, San Francisco, April 8–12, 2019, 5.

31 Health coverage was soon expanded to include dependent children of workers who died with five vested years on the waterfront. See ILWU-PMA Memorandums of Understanding, July 15, 1999, 8, and November 23, 2002, 12. Thanks to ILWU benefits specialist John Castanho for bringing these documents to our attention.

32 Travel pay covered bridge tolls. With the Bay Bridge between the Local 10 dispatch hall in San Francisco and many jobs in Oakland, this was an important issue for Local 10 members.

33 The 2008 coast contract states, "All registrants dispatched from San Francisco to work in the East Bay shall receive the $4.00 Bay Bridge toll. This toll allowance shall be increased with any increase in the Bay Bridge toll." See International Longshore and Warehouse Union and Pacific Maritime Association, *Pacific Coast Longshore Contract Document, July 1, 2008–July 1, 2014*, 36.

34 On employer "captive audience" meetings as coercive but allowable under labor law during union organizing drives, see David Brody, *Labor Embattled: History, Power, Rights* (Urbana: University of Illinois Press, 2005), 105–6. In captive

meetings, workers must listen to employer or employer consultant anti-union arguments with no counterarguments allowed.

35 *ILWU Dispatcher*, May 2006, 3; ILWU, *Proceedings of the Thirty-Third Convention* (2006), 153–57; Celia Lamb, "Blue Diamond Workers Reject Union," *Sacramento Business Journal* 25, no. 38 (November 21, 2008): 6.

36 One exception was the successful organizing of the Pacific Beach Hotel in Hawaii into ILWU Local 142. That drive, concluded in 2012, took several years to complete. But, as noted earlier, organizing in the Islands under Vice President Wesley Furtado (Hawaii) differed from organizing on the US mainland.

37 The signing of authorization cards is a standard method for employees to organize into a union. If the majority of employees in a bargaining unit sign cards stating their wish to join a union, the National Labor Relations Board can require their employer to recognize that labor organization. If 30 percent sign cards, the board can order a secret ballot of the workers to determine if there will be a union. See National Labor Relations Board, *A Guide to Basic Law and Protections under the National Labor Relations Act* (Washington, DC: US Government Printing Office, 1991).

5. "SEEING WHERE PEOPLE ARE GOING"

1 ILWU, *Proceedings of the Thirty-Fourth Convention of the International Longshore and Warehouse Union* (Seattle, June 8–12, 2009), 418.

2 ILWU, *Proceedings of the Thirty-Fourth Convention* (2009), 419–21.

3 Peter Olney, "Battle in the Mojave: Lessons from the Rio Tinto Lockout," *New Labor Forum* 20, no. 2 (Spring 2011): 76; Mike Davis, "Labor War in the Mojave," *The Nation* 290, no. 12 (March 29, 2010): 12–15.

4 Local 30 affiliated with the ILWU in 1964. For Local 30's early history with the ILWU, see Harvey Schwartz, "Ray Panter: Desert Activist and Local 30 President," *ILWU Dispatcher*, January 2009, 4–8; Olney, "Battle in the Mojave," 76; Davis, "Labor War in the Mojave," 13.

5 Olney, "Battle in the Mojave," 76; Davis, "Labor War in the Mojave," 13; Jane Slaughter, "Victory in Miners' Lockout," *Labor Notes*, June 2010, 1; *ILWU Dispatcher*, February 2010, 3–4.

6 Davis, "Labor War in the Mojave," 13.

7 Olney, "Battle in the Mojave," 76.

8 Olney, "Battle in the Mojave," 76–78; Davis, "Labor War in the Mojave," 13; *ILWU Dispatcher*, February 2010, 1.

9 Davis, "Labor War in the Mojave," 16–18; Olney, "Battle in the Mojave," 78–80; *ILWU Dispatcher*, February 2010, 4; March 2010, 1, 4–5, 7; Slaughter, "Victory," 13.

10 Olney, "Battle in the Mojave," 80; Slaughter, "Victory," 1; *ILWU Dispatcher*, April/May 2010, 1–2.

11 Morton took over as lead attorney when Remar had conflicting demands. Christopher J. Robison was vice president and chief operating officer for Rio Tinto Metals from 2006 to 2012.

12 McEllrath visited Boron and addressed a Local 30 rally on November 4, 2009, the day the miners' old contract expired. There he said, "If you stay strong in Boron, you'll have support from your friends at home and around the world." Adams attended the Boron rally that day. *ILWU Dispatcher*, December 2009, 2.

13 *ILWU Dispatcher*, January 2016, 3.

14 On May 15, 2010, the miners voted 275 to 95 to accept the new agreement with Rio Tinto. Olney, "Battle in the Mojave," 80.

15 *ILWU Dispatcher*, November 2006, 5; April 2008, 1–3; September 2008, 4; February 2009, 3; March 2010, 6; September 2010, 6–7.

16 *ILWU Dispatcher*, February 2009, 3; March 2009, 1–3; May 2009, 4–5; July/August 2009, 6–8; September 2009, 6; December 2009, 3; February 2011, 4; Southern California Pensioners Group, Longshore Division, *Newsletter*, March 2011, 1; United Students against Sweatshops, "Rite Aid's High-Flying Execs Have Golden Parachutes," pamphlet, May 2011, 3; *ILWU Dispatcher*, May 2011, 1, 4–5; *Random Lengths*, August 26–September 8, 2011, 18.

17 In June 2012, Local 26 president Luisa Gratz reported that the union was still dealing with harassment at Rite Aid a year after the company signed a contract. The local had filed two hundred grievances and seen 128 cases go to arbitration. Rite Aid had fired twenty union members, including several rank-and-file leaders. *ILWU Dispatcher*, June 2012, 18; ILWU, *Proceedings of the Thirty-Fifth Convention of the International Longshore and Warehouse Union* (San Diego, CA, June 4–8, 2012), 246–47. Gratz, a persistent advocate for worker rights in grievance cases, ultimately got the twenty dismissed unionists reinstated.

18 Robert McEllrath, telephone discussion with Schwartz, Vancouver, Washington, July 15, 2019.

19 Toward the end of the union's first contract struggle with Rite Aid, Familathe urged the company's vice president to fly to California and participate in negotiations. She did and was there for the final round of talks that went on for several days before concluding on May 1, 2011. *ILWU Dispatcher*, May 2011, 5.

20 ILWU, *Proceedings of the Thirty-Fifth Convention* (2012), 93.

21 *ILWU Dispatcher*, January 2015, 4, 8.

22 At the ILWU International Convention in June 2012, Bob acknowledged Greg Mitre of Local 13 for his role as Latin American liaison in helping to bring the Panama Canal pilots into the ILWU. ILWU, *Proceedings of the Thirty-Fifth Convention* (2012), 120–21.

23 Unfortunately, six years after the affiliation, a controversy developed over Panama's ballots in the union's 2018 elections for International officers. In April 2019, the Department of Labor filed a complaint in the U.S. District Court in Northern California asking the judge to require a new election. That issue was still unresolved at this writing. The Panama Canal pilots disaffiliated

with the ILWU in 2020. The next year the ILWU International Executive
Board voted to disaffiliate the Panama dockworkers.

24 *ILWU Dispatcher*, January 2012, 3; February 2012, 1, 6; ILWU, *Proceedings of the Thirty-Fifth Convention* (2012), 196–97.

25 *ILWU Dispatcher*, February 2012, 1.

26 *ILWU Dispatcher*, February 2012, 1; March 2012, 1, 4–5; April 2012, 4; ILWU, *Proceedings of the Thirty-Fifth Convention* (2012), 92, 197–98.

27 "Maritime Union Settles Dispute with Ports of Auckland," *New Zealand Herald*, February 18, 2015.

28 The sixteen-person ILWU delegation that went to Auckland in March 2012 was a mixture of Longshore Division local presidents, other local officers, and active rank-and-file members. *ILWU Dispatcher*, March 2012, 4.

29 Fleetwood spoke at the ILWU Longshore Caucus that was held near San Diego, California, during June 2012. *ILWU Dispatcher*, June 2012, 4.

30 *ILWU Dispatcher*, January 2000, 17; February 2000, 11.

31 Robert McEllrath, telephone discussion with Schwartz, Vancouver, Washington, March 10, 2021.

32 ILWU, *Proceedings of the Thirty-Fifth Convention* (2012), 179.

33 ILWU, *Proceedings of the Thirty-First Convention of the International Longshore and Warehouse Union* (Portland, OR, May 1–5, 2000), 71–76.

34 "Unity Statement between the ILWU and the All-Japan Dockworkers' Union (Zenkowan)," certificate, June 6, 2012, Conference Room, ILWU International Headquarters, San Francisco, California.

35 ILWU, *Proceedings of the Thirty-Fifth Convention* (2012), 180. See also *ILWU Dispatcher*, June 2012, 10. By 2012, Zenkowan had already boycotted the Pacific Beach Hotel in solidarity with the ILWU for several years.

36 In sumo wrestling, both participants ceremonially throw rice in the air before their bout. The aim of this ritual is to purify the ring.

37 One of the most commonly used Japanese words for crazy is *kichigai*. *Bakatare* is generally considered insulting. But *bakatare* is the word Furtado knew to use.

38 Robert McEllrath, telephone discussion with Schwartz, Vancouver, Washington, July 15, 2019.

39 *ILWU Dispatcher*, January 2013, 1, 7. The Local 142 contract with the Pacific Beach Hotel was signed on December 29, 2012. The Zenkowan-ILWU friendship and solidarity agreement was formally renewed at the ILWU International Convention in 2018. *ILWU Dispatcher*, June 2018, 10.

6. "TRYING TO WIN A BATTLE"

1 ILWU, *Proceedings of the Thirty-Fifth Convention of the International Longshore and Warehouse Union* (San Diego, CA, June 4–8, 2012), 342.

2 ILWU, *Proceedings of the Thirty-Fifth Convention* (2012), 343–47.

3 ILWU, *Proceedings of the Thirty-Fifth Convention* (2012), 8; ILWU, *Proceedings of the First Annual Convention of the International Longshoremen's and Warehousemen's Union* (Aberdeen, WA, April 4–17, 1938), 142, 167; *ILWU Dispatcher*, July/August, 2011, 1, 7; October 2011, 4; Terelle Jerricks, "The Assault on Labor Continues," *Random Lengths*, September 23–October 6, 2011, 1. Thanks to former ILWU communications director and *Dispatcher* managing editor Craig Merrilees and ILWU Northwest Coast committeeman Cameron Williams for analyzing the Pacific Northwest grain industry for Schwartz on January 10, 2020.

4 *ILWU Dispatcher*, July/August 2011, 1, 7, September 2011, 3, December 2011, 4.

5 *ILWU Dispatcher*, July/August 2011, 1; ILWU, *Proceedings of the Thirty-Fifth Convention* (2012), 9; Erik Olson, "400 Union Workers Protest EGT-Bound Train, Clash with Police," *Longview Daily News*, September 21, 2011; *ILWU Dispatcher*, September 2011, 3; Evan Rohar, "Longshore Workers Block Trains, Shut Ports to Protect Good Jobs," *Labor Notes*, October 2011, 1, 14; Bill Mongelluzzo, "Labor's Long View," *Journal of Commerce*, September 19, 2011, 20–21.

6 Olson, "400 Union Workers Protest"; ILWU, *Proceedings of the Thirty-Fifth Convention* (2012), 9; Jerricks, "The Assault on Labor," 1; *ILWU Dispatcher*, September 2011, 3; Evan Rohar, "Longshore Workers Block Trains," 1; Mongelluzzo, "Labor's Long View," 21.

7 Jerricks, "The Assault on Labor," 17; Rohar, "Longshore Workers Block Trains," 14; *ILWU Dispatcher*, October 2011, 4.

8 Evan Rohar, "West Coast Terminals Close," Jane Slaughter, "Occupy Wake-up Call Caps Remarkable Year," and "Port Actions Spark Debate," *Labor Notes*, January 2012, 1, 8–11; Eduardo Soriano-Castillo, "Longshore Union, Occupy Poised to Greet Grain Ship," *Labor Notes*, February 2012, 2–3; *ILWU Dispatcher*, October 2011, 3; November 2011, 2, 4; December 2011, 2.

9 Soriano-Castillo, "Longshore Union, Occupy," February 2012, 1–2; Mischa Gaus, Jane Slaughter, and Eduardo Soriano-Castillo, "Longview: Union Takes Risks, Breaks Rules, Gets Deal with EGT," *Labor Notes*, March 2012, 1, 15; *ILWU Dispatcher*, January 2012, 1, 6; Jack Heyman and Jack Mulcahy, "Longview: Snatching Defeat from the Jaws of Victory," *Maritime Worker Monitor*, March 14, 2012, 3.

10 *ILWU Dispatcher*, January 2012, 1, 6.

11 *ILWU Dispatcher*, February 2012, 3, 7; April 2012, 3; Leslie Slape, "ILWU President Guilty of Obstruction for Role in Grain Terminal Protest," *Longview Daily News*, September 28, 2012; *ILWU Dispatcher*, October 2012, 2.

12 *ILWU Dispatcher*, April 2012, 3, 8; October 2013, 8.

13 *ILWU Dispatcher*, June 2012, 2, 3; October 2013, 2; ILWU, *Proceedings of the Thirty-Fifth Convention* (2012), 94–95, 181, 187; Mark Brenner, "Longshore Workers Leave over Turf Battles," *Labor Notes*, October 2013, 4.

14 Article 20 of the AFL-CIO Constitution outlines procedures for a member union to file a complaint about the jurisdictional infringements of another AFL-CIO member organization. The process can be time-consuming and political. *Constitution of the AFL-CIO, Amended at the AFL-CIO 28th Constitutional Convention*, Washington, DC, October 22–25, 2017.

15 Vancouver, Washington, is in Clark County. Longview is in Cowlitz County. So the warrant, issued for Cowlitz Country, was not valid in Clark County.

16 Early in the morning on September 8 grain was dumped out of seventy railcars at the EGT plant.

17 Tragically, Jacobs, a fifth-generation longshore worker, was killed in a waterfront accident on June 28, 2018. He was thirty-four. Some five hundred people attended a memorial service for him on July 6. Jack Heyman, "The Tragic Death of Byron Jacobs, Hero of the EGT Longshore Struggle," *Internationalist*, November 2018, 1.

18 Camas is fourteen miles east of Vancouver.

19 This reference is to the September 16, 2011, effort Local 21 made to surrender its entire membership of two hundred to the Cowlitz County Sheriff's Department. Terelle Jerricks, "The Assault on Labor Continues," 17; Evan Rohar, "Longshore Workers Block Trains," 14.

20 ILWU supporters accompanied Bob to the police station.

21 Jack Heyman and Jack Mulcahy, "Longview: Snatching Defeat from the Jaws of Victory," 1.

22 Norm Parks, telephone discussion with Schwartz, Goodyear, Arizona, April 5, 2016. Sadly, Parks passed away on January 8, 2017. *ILWU Dispatcher*, February 2018, 7.

23 The Coast Guard worked in tandem with law enforcement agencies to support EGT.

24 On the UBCJA, see Grace Palladino, *Skilled Hands, Strong Spirits: A Century of Building Trades History* (Ithaca, NY: Cornell University Press, 2005), especially the chapter entitled "'Sticking Apart': Work, Jurisdiction, and Solidarity." On Teamster raids on the ILWU in the 1930s and 1950s, see Harvey Schwartz, "Union Expansion and Labor Solidarity: Longshoremen, Warehousemen, and Teamsters, 1933–1937," *New Labor Review*, no. 2 (September 1978): 6–21; *The March Inland: Origins of the ILWU Warehouse Division, 1934–1938* (Los Angeles: Institute of Industrial Relations, University of California, 1978; reprint, San Francisco: ILWU, 2000); *Solidarity Stories: An Oral History of the ILWU* (Seattle: University of Washington Press, 2009).

25 Strikers John Knudsen and Dick Parker were fatally shot on May 15, 1934.

26 Occupy argued that the American economy was rigged to benefit the wealthy 1 percent of the population at the expense of the remaining 99 percent.

27 The trials were in June and September of 2012.

28 Sadly, Wesley Furtado passed away at sixty-four in 2020. *ILWU Dispatcher*, April 2020, 1, 4–5. His contribution to the ILWU was commemorated at the union's International Convention in June 2021.

29 *ILWU Dispatcher*, October 2013, 2, 8; Mark Brenner, "Longshore Workers Leave over Turf Battles," *Labor Notes*, October 2013, 4.

7. "UP AGAINST SOME DIFFICULT TIMES"

1 ILWU, *Proceedings of the Thirty-Sixth Convention of the International Longshore and Warehouse Union* (Honolulu, June 8–12, 2015), 355.

2 ILWU, *Proceedings of the Thirty-Sixth Convention* (2015), 363.

3 ILWU, *Proceedings of the Thirty-Sixth Convention* (2015), 355–64.

4 ILWU, *Proceedings of the First Annual Convention of the International Longshoremen's and Warehousemen's Union* (Aberdeen, WA, April 4–17, 1938), 142, 167; *ILWU Dispatcher*, September 2012, 6; May 2013, 4; October 2013, 1.

5 *ILWU Dispatcher*, September 2012, 6; May 2013, 4; Paul Bigman, "Grain Agreement Ends Lockouts in Northwest Ports," *Labor Notes*, September 10, 2014.

6 *ILWU Dispatcher*, May 2013, 4; July/August, 2; October 2013, 1, 3; November 2013, 3; ILWU, *Proceedings of the Thirty-Sixth Convention* (2015), 11.

7 ILWU, *Proceedings of the Thirty-Sixth Convention* (2015), 4, 11; Bigman, "Grain Agreement Ends Lockouts"; *ILWU Dispatcher*, September 2014, 3.

8 Thanks to Russell Miyashiro, ILWU ship clerks Local 34 relief dispatcher, for his help with this description of supercargo work.

9 ILWU, *Proceedings of the Thirty-Sixth Convention* (2015), 5; Bigman, "Grain Agreement Ends Lockouts"; *ILWU Dispatcher*, September 2014, 3.

10 Jack Heyman, "An Open Letter to Paul Bigman and *Labor Notes*," *Labor Notes*, October 23, 2014.

11 *ILWU Dispatcher*, September 2014, 3.

12 The mediator, Scot L. Beckenbaugh, was deputy director and national representative of the Federal Mediation and Conciliation Service. He served as the FMCS's "master mediator" for high-profile collective bargaining disputes.

13 The reference is to Kalama Export Company (KEX) of Kalama, Washington. In May 2018, when this statement from Bob was recorded, the ILWU was trying to improve KEX's health and pension benefits, which were inferior to ILWU Longshore Division contract standards. Marissa Luck, "Kalama Export Dockworkers Rally for Better Benefits," *Daily News* (Longview, WA), November 9, 2017, 1; *ILWU Dispatcher*, December 2017, 1.

14 ILWU, *Proceedings of the Thirty-Sixth Convention* (2015), 3–4, 11–12; *ILWU Dispatcher*, May 2014, 1; December 2014, 1; January 2015, 1; April 2015, 1; July–August 2015, 1; *Random Lengths*, January 22–February 4, 2015, 20; February 8–18, 2015, 1, 5; Mark Brenner, "Union Faces Fresh Questions in West Coast Longshore Standoff," *Labor Notes*, February 2015, 1, 3. Container chassis are

wheeled structures designed to carry marine containers. The chassis allow trucks to move containers between terminals and shipping facilities.

15 *ILWU Dispatcher*, April 2015, 1; Bill Mongelluzzo, "Tentative West Coast Contract Offers Union Perks, New Way to Settle Disputes," *Journal of Commerce*, March 16, 2015; Bill Mongelluzzo, "ILWU-PMA Contract No Game Changer for West Coast Productivity, *"Journal of Commerce*, May 23, 2015; Jack Heyman et al., "Which Way for the ILWU: Militant Unionism or Business Unionism," leaflet, San Francisco, March 23, 2015; ILWU bulletin, "ILWU Longshore Caucus Delegates Vote to Recommend Tentative Agreement to Membership for Ratification Vote," San Francisco, April 3, 2015.

16 The "big table" is where central contract issues that take first priority, like health and welfare, are negotiated. Other contract concerns are discussed separately.

17 When actively employed, workers with full ILWU Longshore Division membership are registered with the union and the PMA. Because he was already retired from the longshore industry, that was not a concern for Austin.

18 Perez joined the negotiations in San Francisco in February 2015. He gave notice that unless an agreement was reached soon the federal government would move bargaining to Washington, DC, and oversee it. *ILWU Dispatcher*, January 2015, 7.

19 A transtainer is a mobile gantry crane used for stacking intermodal containers.

20 The 1934 contract's exact wording is reproduced in Paul Eliel, *The Waterfront and General Strikes, San Francisco, 1934* (San Francisco: Hooper, 1934), 243.

21 Terelle Jerricks, "Pier 400 Automation Appealed: Public Meeting Set for March 21," *Random Lengths*, March 7–20, 2019, 9; Paul Rosenberg, "ILWU Faces Off with Automation," *Random Lengths*, April 4–17, 2019, 4–5; "Newest Automation Plan Hits a Nerve with LA Port Communities," *ILWU Dispatcher*, March 2019, 1, 7.

22 Employer-friendly publications took advantage of the long negotiations and the inconvenience of congestion on the West Coast waterfront to complain that the process of collective bargaining had to change so that it became more pleasing to business interests. See, for example, Mark Szakonyi and Joseph Bonney, "Dockworker Negotiating Process Must Change," *Journal of Commerce*, March 13, 2015.

23 Until near the end of negotiations, the ILWU Safety Committee met with employer representatives separately from the main, or "big table," discussions.

24 In May 2015, an article in the employer-friendly *Journal of Commerce* described the new arbitration system. See Mongelluzzo, "ILWU-PMA Contract No Game Changer," *Journal of Commerce*, May 23, 2015.

25 Sam Kagel was coast arbitrator for the longshore industry from 1948 to 2002. He was a legendary waterfront figure.

26 *The ILWU Story* is the union's official history. It is cited in the Further Reading section of this book.

27 ILWU, *Proceedings of the Thirty-Sixth Convention* (2015), 110–18.

28 This reference is to the legendary surfing mecca, the North Shore of the Hawaiian island of Oahu, which features thirty-foot waves during the winter, when it hosts world-class surfing competitions.

8. "LIVE TO FIGHT ANOTHER DAY"

1 See ILWU, *Proceedings of the Twenty-First Biennial Convention of the International Longshoremen's and Warehousemen's Union* (Vancouver, BC, Canada, April 7–12, 1975), 417.

2 ILWU, *Proceedings of the Thirty-Seventh Convention of the International Longshore and Warehouse Union* (Portland, OR, June 4–8, 2018), 394–95, 435.

3 ILWU, *Proceedings of the Thirty-Seventh Convention* (2018), 393–435.

4 ILWU, *Proceedings of the Twenty-Second Biennial Convention of the International Longshoremen's and Warehousemen's Union* (Seattle, April 18–23, 1977), 338–64.

5 ILWU, *Proceedings of the Twenty-Eighth Convention of the International Longshoremen's and Warehousemen's Union* (Seattle, June 3–7, 1991), 403–21.

6 ILWU, *Proceedings of the Thirty-Seventh Convention* (2018), 407–9, 420.

7 Bridges's outreach to the Black community in San Francisco during the 1934 strike is legendary. For Northern California Bay Area longshore Local 10's action in later years in opposing South African apartheid, see Peter Cole, *Dockworker Power: Race and Activism in Durban and the San Francisco Bay Area* (Urbana: University of Illinois Press, 2018).

8 *ILWU Dispatcher*, March 11, 1970, 5.

9 ILWU, *Proceedings of the Twentieth Biennial Convention of the International Longshoremen's and Warehousemen's Union* (San Francisco, April 30–May 5, 1973), 570–71. In 1973, Oglala Lakota members of the American Indian Movement (AIM) occupied Wounded Knee on the Pine Ridge Reservation in South Dakota to protest the failure of the US government to live up to its treaty promises and the 1890 US Army massacre at Wounded Knee of 150 Native Americans, half of them women and children.

10 ILWU, *Proceedings of the Thirty-Seventh Convention* (2018), 364–68, 539; Sam T. Levin, "Dakota Access Pipeline: The Who, What, and Why of the Standing Rock Protests," *The Guardian*, November 3, 2016; Nick Estes, *Our History Is the Future: Standing Rock versus the South Dakota Pipeline, and the Long Tradition of Indigenous Resistance* (London: Verso, 2019).

11 *ILWU Dispatcher*, January 2017, 1.

12 ILWU, *Proceedings of the Thirty-Seventh Convention* (2018), 303–5, 513.

13 ILWU, *Proceedings of the Thirty-Seventh Convention* (2018), 304–5.

14 Tax-supported US Army Corps of Engineers and National Guard troops were at Standing Rock.

15 Lisa Friedman, "Standing Rock Sioux Tribe Wins a Victory in Dakota Access Pipeline Case," *New York Times*, March 25, 2020.

16 Rob Gillies, "Keystone XL Pipeline Halted as Biden Revokes Permit," *AP News*, January 20, 2021.

17 *ILWU Dispatcher*, September 2016, 6; May 2017, 1; ILWU, *Proceedings of the Thirty-Seventh Convention* (2018), 15, 73.

18 The biggest longshore local on the coast, Los Angeles Local 13, passed the resolution by a 68 percent vote. ILWU Coast Longshore Division, "Memorandum, Ratification of Coast Contract Proposal," August 4, 2017.

19 The reference here is to the San Francisco Bay Area gatemen, watchmen, and security workers Local 75, ILWU.

20 There would be an election for International president in 2021.

21 That was the exact vote. ILWU, "Memorandum," August 4, 2017.

22 In May 2018 there were Republican majorities in both houses of Congress.

23 The union had recently been found guilty of a secondary boycott violation against ICTSI in Portland.

24 Mark Friedman, "$94 Million Judgment Threatens ILWU: Court Sides with Billionaire Cargo Operator Who Flaunts Labor Rights Abroad," *Random Lengths*, February 6–9, 2020, 3; "President Duterte Inaugurates First Container Barge Port in PH," News Release, Presidential Communications Operations Office, Republic of the Philippines, November 13, 2019; *ILWU Dispatcher*, March 2014, 4. For more on Razon and ICTSI's background, see Ari Paul, "The Multinational Trying to Bankrupt the Dock Workers Union Has a Sordid Past," *In These Times*, January 16, 2020; *ILWU Dispatcher*, March 2014, 1, 5.

25 *ILWU Dispatcher*, June 2012, 5; September 2012, 6; Friedman, "$94 Million Judgment," 14; Maxine Bernstein, "Oregon Jury's $93.6 Million in Damages Verdict against Longshore Union Reduced to $19 Million," *The Oregonian*, March 5, 2020; Fisher Phillips, "Jury Shocker: 93 Million Reasons Why the ILWU May Soon Cease to Exist," *Lexology*, November 7, 2019; Schwartz, personal notes, ICTSI v. ILWU, US District Court for the District of Oregon, Portland, October 28–30, 2019.

26 Mike Baker, "A $93.6 Million Verdict Threatens to Bankrupt the ILWU and Chill Unions," *Seattle Times*, November 22, 2019.

27 Friedman, "$94 Million Judgment," 3, 14; Phillips, "Jury Shocker"; Conrad Wilson, "Judge Delays $93 Million Payout in Longshore Union Case," Oregon Public Broadcasting, November 8, 2019; Schwartz, personal notes. In 2018, the ICTSI also sued the Maritime Union of Australia for $100 million. Sean Robertson, "Australian Unions Face $100 Million Suit after Docks Struggle," *Left Voice*, January 25, 2018.

28 Lichtenstein quoted in Mike Baker, "A $93.6 Million Verdict."

29 Gregory quoted in Paul, "The Multinational."

30 Simon quoted in Wilson, "Judge Delays."

31 Simon quoted in Meerah Powell, "Federal Judge Reduces Lawsuit Payout to Former Portland Terminal 6 Operator," Oregon Public Broadcasting, March 7, 2020.

32 Bill Mongelluzzo, "Portland Judge Slashes Award against ILWU," *Journal of Commerce*, March 7, 2020.

33 Bill Mongelluzzo, "ICTSI Portland Rejects $19 Million Award against ILWU," *Journal of Commerce*, March 21, 2020.

34 Recall that the case went through ILWU-PMA arbitration proceedings before it went to the National Labor Relations Board. The arbitration decision said the reefer jobs belonged to ILWU longshore Local 8 of Portland. *ILWU Dispatcher*, June 2012, 5.

35 Sundet was president of longshore Local 8 of Portland before becoming the Northwest Coast committeeman.

36 Lester Balog, Jack Olsen, Al Addy, and Bill Batchan, *Local 6 in Action: One Year in the Life of Our Union* (San Francisco: Warehouse Union 6, ILWU-CIO, March 1947), 1; Harvey Schwartz, *The March Inland: Origins of the ILWU Warehouse Division, 1934–1938* (Los Angeles: Institute of Industrial Relations, University of California, 1978; reprint, San Francisco: ILWU, 2000), ix; reprint, xvii.

37 Schwartz, *Solidarity Stories: An Oral History of the ILWU* (Seattle: University of Washington Press, 2009), 194, 279, 286–87; Schwartz, *The March Inland*, 171; ILWU, *Proceedings of the Thirty-Sixth Convention of the International Longshore and Warehouse Union* (Honolulu, June 8–12, 2015), 45.

38 ILWU, *Proceedings of the Twenty-Fourth Biennial Convention of the International Longshore and Warehouse Union* (Honolulu, April 27–May 2, 1981), 21.

39 ILWU, *Proceedings of the Thirty-Fifth Convention of the International Longshore and Warehouse Union* (San Diego, CA, June 4–8, 2012), 33.

40 Schwartz, *Solidarity Stories*, 235, 240–41; Edward D. Beechert, *Working in Hawaii: A Labor History* (Honolulu: University of Hawaii Press, 1985), 291; Sanford Zalburg, *A Spark Is Struck! Jack Hall and the ILWU in Hawaii* (Honolulu: University of Hawaii Press, 1979; reprint, Honolulu: Watermark Publishing, 2007), 110–11.

41 McEllrath quoted in ILWU, *Proceedings of the Thirty-Fifth Convention* (2012), 91.

42 ILWU, *Proceedings of the Thirty-Sixth Convention* (2015), 16–21, 40–41, 293–95; *ILWU Dispatcher*, February 2019, 4–5.

43 *ILWU Dispatcher*, February 2019, 5; ILWU, *Proceedings of the Thirty-Seventh Convention* (2018), 43.

44 Sadly, Fred Pecker passed away in December 2018. For more on his biography see *ILWU Dispatcher*, February 2019, 4–8; ILWU, *Proceedings of the Thirty-Seventh Convention* (2018), 197–204, 530–31.

45 *ILWU Dispatcher*, April 2018, 3, 8; February 2019, 1, 3.

46 Schwartz, *The March Inland*, 156–61, 164, 171; Schwartz, *Solidarity Stories*, 279, 286–87.

47 Another effort at labor law reform, the Protecting the Right to Organize Act, which would curb employer ability to intimidate workers, passed the House in March 2021. But as of this writing it still faced a difficult path in the Senate. *Labor Notes*, April 2021, 11.

FURTHER READING

Most of the books on the ILWU deal with events that predate Robert McEllrath's tenure as a coastwide officer. But the literature on the ILWU is rich and extensive. For the convenience of readers, here is a highly selective list of those books.

Afrasiabi, Peter. *Burning Bridges: America's 20-Year Crusade to Deport Labor Leader Harry Bridges*. Brooklyn: Thirlmere Books, 2016.

Beechert, Edward D. *Working in Hawaii: A Labor History*. Honolulu: University of Hawaii Press, 1985.

Carson, Robert, ed. *The Waterfront Writers: The Literature of Work*. San Francisco: Harper and Row, 1979.

Cherny, Robert W. *Harry Bridges: Labor Radical, Labor Legend*. Urbana: University of Illinois Press, 2022.

Chew, Ron. *Remembering Silme Domingo and Gene Viernes: The Legacy of Filipino American Labor Activism*. Seattle: University of Washington Press, 2012.

Cole, Peter. *Dockworker Power: Race and Activism in Durban and the San Francisco Bay Area*. Urbana: University of Illinois Press, 2018.

Fairley, Lincoln. *Facing Mechanization: The West Coast Longshore Plan*. Los Angeles: Institute of Industrial Relations, University of California, 1979.

Findlay, William. *Work on the Waterfront: Worker Power and Technological Change in a West Coast Port*. Philadelphia: Temple University Press, 1988.

Holmes, T. Michael. *The Specter of Communism in Hawaii*. Honolulu: University of Hawaii Press, 1994.

The ILWU Story: Six Decades of Militant Unionism. Text and research by Eugene Dennis Vrana. Additional research by Harvey Schwartz. Edited by Steve Stallone and Marcy Rein. San Francisco: ILWU, 1997.

Johnson, Victoria. *How Many Machine Guns Does It Take to Cook One Meal? The Seattle and San Francisco General Strikes*. Seattle: University of Washington Press, 2008.

Jung, Moon-Kie. *Reworking Race: The Making of Hawaii's Interracial Labor Movement*. New York: Columbia University Press, 2006.

Kimeldorf, Howard. *Reds or Rackets? The Making of Radical and Conservative Unions on the Waterfront*. Berkeley: University of California Press, 1988.

Larrowe, Charles P. *Harry Bridges: The Rise and Fall of Radical Labor in the United States*. 2nd ed. New York: Lawrence Hill, 1977.

Levinson, Marc. *The Box: How the Shipping Container Made the World Smaller and the World Economy Bigger*. Princeton, NJ: Princeton University Press, 2006.

Magden, Ronald E. *A History of Seattle Waterfront Workers, 1884–1934*. Seattle: ILWU Local 19 and the Washington Commission for the Humanities, 1991.

———. *The Working Longshoreman*. Tacoma, WA: ILWU Local 23, 1991.

Magden, Ronald E., and A. D. Martinson. *The Working Waterfront: The Story of Tacoma's Ships and Men*. Tacoma, WA: ILWU Local 23 and the Washington Commission for the Humanities, 1982.

Nelson, Bruce. *Workers on the Waterfront: Seamen, Longshoremen, and Unionism in the 1930s*. Urbana: University of Illinois Press, 1988.

Puette, William J. *The Hilo Massacre: Hawaii's Bloody Monday*. Honolulu: University of Hawaii Press, 1988.

Quin, Mike. *The Big Strike*. Olema, CA: Olema Publishing, 1949. Reprint. New York: International Publishers, 1979.

Schwartz, Harvey. *The March Inland: Origins of the ILWU Warehouse Division, 1934–1938*. Los Angeles: Institute of Industrial Relations, University of California, 1978. Reprint. San Francisco: ILWU, 2000.

———. *Solidarity Stories: An Oral History of the ILWU*. Seattle: University of Washington Press, 2009.

Selvin, David F. *A Terrible Anger: The 1934 Waterfront and General Strikes in San Francisco*. Detroit: Wayne State University Press, 1996.

Wellman, David. *The Union Makes Us Strong: Radical Unionism on the San Francisco Waterfront*. Cambridge: Cambridge University Press, 1995.

Zalburg, Sanford. *A Spark Is Struck! Jack Hall and the ILWU in Hawaii*. Honolulu: University of Hawaii Press, 1979. Reprint. Honolulu: Watermark Publishing, 2007.

INDEX

Page numbers in *italic* refer to illustrations.

Gettier Security, 203–4
Goldblatt, Louis, 225, 226, 269n3
Gordienko, Mark, 160
Gordon, Christine, 183–84
grain handlers, 160–96
Gregoire, Christine, 163–64, 183, 202
Gregory, James, 244–45

Hall, Jack, 61, 272n5
hand-work. *See* break-bulk cargo
  handling
Hansen, Richard, 148
Hawaii, 39–41, 60–66, 221–23; diversity
  of ILWU members, xiii; hotel
  boycotts, 155, 156. *See also* ILWU
  Local 142 (Hawaii)
healthcare, 112–13, 147, 188, 220
Healy, Jim, 87
Hebert, Tom, 25, 121–24
Herman, Jimmy, 23–25, 26, 63, 64,
  93, 225
Heyman, Jack, 181, 200, 277n7
Hitchcock, Sally. *See* McEllrath, Sally
Holiday, Sonny, 190
Honduras, 53
hotel boycotts, 155, 156
hotel workers, 53, *54*
Hunt, Steve, *233*

IAM. *See* International Association of
  Machinists (IAM)
IBU. *See* Inlandboatmen's Union of the
  Pacific (IBU)
ICTSI. *See* International Container
  Terminal Services, Inc. (ICTSI)
ILA. *See* International Longshoremen's
  Association (ILA)
ILWU (International Longshore and
  Warehouse Union): Alaska
  Longshore Division, 68, 225, 273n12;
  early history of, ix–xv; International
  Executive Board (IEB), 231, 270n11;
  International Organizing

Department, 59, 61–62, 66, 148, 249;
  Longshore Caucus, 72, 100, 109, 219,
  270n9, 270n14; Oral History
  Collection, xvi–xvii. *See also* ILWU
  International conventions; Joint
  Coast Labor Relations Committee
  (JCLRC)
ILWU Canada, 95, 120, 229
ILWU International conventions:
  Hawaii (1997), 39, 50, 273n10;
  Honolulu (2015), 197–98, 221–23; Los
  Angeles (1994), 33–34; Portland
  (2018), 224–26, *225*; San Diego (2012),
  154–55, 159–60, 165, 217; Seattle
  (2009), 131–32, 134–35; Vancouver,
  BC (2006), *85*, 95
ILWU Local 4 (Vancouver, WA), xi, 2,
  7–11, 34, 48; Birrer, 25; Clark, 173;
  Olson, 236; PNGHA lockout,
  199–200, 203–5; port mechanics, 60;
  security guards, 60; Standing Rock
  solidarity, 229
ILWU Local 5 (Portland, OR, Powell's
  Books employees), 81–83,
  275nn30–31
ILWU Local 6 (Oakland warehouse
  workers), 109, 246, 248–50
ILWU Local 8 (Portland, OR), 14–15,
  18–19, 33, 48, 51, 99; Jeff Smith, 160;
  PNGHA lockout, 199, 201, 203;
  resistance to racial integration,
  268n13, 269n3
ILWU Local 10 (San Francisco and
  Oakland), 43, 46, 47, 235; Castanho,
  109–10; Cobb, 114–15; Ferris, 216;
  inter-local solidarity, 72, 190;
  Mackay, 107, 126, 211; May Day
  waterfront shutdown, 2008, 101–8;
  Native American occupation of
  Alcatraz, 226; pensions, 128;
  Robinson, 253; Romero, 128; Rooker,
  128; Standing Rock solidarity, 229;
  Thibeaux, 124; travel pay, 128–29

Waterside Workers' Federation (WWF) (Australia), 87, 88, 90

Wechsler, Michael, 112–13

Wenzel, Joe, 72

West Coast lockout of 2002, 73–80

West Coast waterfront strike of 1934, 2, 118, 216; Knudsen and Parker, 184, 284n25

West Coast waterfront strike of 1971–72, xv, 14, 74, 119, 268n13

Whiteside, Jacob, 162, 190

Wilken, Claudia, 105

Williams, Cameron, 206

Williams, Cleophas, 46, 47

Willis, Amy, 249

Winzig, Mary, 82, 83

workday, twelve-hour, 181, 208, 254

Wyatt, Bill, 245

Young, Dennis, 225

Zenkowan (All-Japan Dock Workers' Union), 154–56